Biró

Sautéed White Asparagus in Parmesan
Tuile with Summer Greens & Lemon Aïoli

Biró

European-Inspired Cuisine

Marcel Biró and Shannon Kring Biró

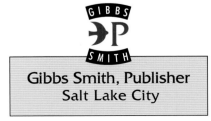

Gibbs Smith, Publisher
Salt Lake City

First Edition
09 08 07 06 05   10 9 8 7 6 5 4 3 2 1

Portions of Marcel's introduction appeared in the Fall 2002 issue of
Gastronomica, "Beyond the Berlin Wall" by Marcel Biró and Shannon Kring Biró.

Published by
Gibbs Smith, Publisher
PO Box 667
Layton, Utah 84041

Orders: 1.800.748.5439
www.gibbs-smith.com

Printed in Hong Kong

Library of Congress Cataloging-in-Publication Data

Biró, Marcel.
  Biró : European-inspired cuisine / Marcel Biró and Shannon Kring Biró.— 1st ed.
     p. cm.
  ISBN 1-58685-740-1
  1. Cookery, American. 2. Cookery, European. 3. Biró Restaurant. 4. Marcel Biró
Culinary School. I. Biró, Shannon Kring. II. Title.
TX715.B49925 2005
641.594—dc22
                              2004023353

To the loyal guests of Biró Restaurant and Wine Bar. Thank you for supporting our restaurant in an unlikely city. Also to the courageous chefs and restaurateurs who dare tread uncharted waters, thank you for inspiring and challenging us.

AMUSE-BOUCHES

Fennel Salad with Orange Vinaigrette, Crème Fraîche & Parmesan Crisp 24

Lemon-Mint Sorbet with Red Peppercorns* 27

Double-Melon Ball with Balsamic Glaze 28

Ahi Tuna with Spiced Balsamic Glaze 29

Smoked, Cured-Pork Roulade with Sun-Dried Tomatoes, Baby Spinach & Feta 30

Striped Beets with Caraway Vinaigrette & Hawaiian Black Lava Salt 32

Fruit Shots with Grand Marnier 33

Potato-Crusted Oyster Purse with Herb Aïoli* 35

Three-Pepper Mousse* 36

Fiddlehead, Morel, Tomato & Celery Root Napoleon with Aïoli* 39

Purple-Potato Gnocchi with Mint Pesto 40

Gougères with Roasted Ratatouille Nest* 41

Gruyère-Carrot Quenelles 42

Sautéed Ramps with Orange Oil* 43

Fig Chips with Chive–Goat Cheese Mousse 45

Champagne-Herb Kraut* 46

Citrus Soup with Orange-Blossom Honey & Pickled Ginger 47

Herb Crêpe with Wasabi Tobiko Crème Fraîche 48

Crostini with Exotic Mushroom Ragoût & Rosemary 49

Wild Mushroom Custard with Herb Broth 50

APPETIZERS

Half-Dozen Alsatian Escargots with Garlic-Herb Butter 54

Razor Clams in Parsley Jus 55

Baked Brie with Lingonberry Sauce 56

Prosciutto-Wrapped Shrimp with Basil, Mozzarella, Extra Vecchio Balsamico & Aïoli* 59

Smoked Lachs on Rösti with Crème Fraîche & Beluga Caviar* 60

Baked Feta & Heirloom Tomatoes in Garlic-Herb Butter* 63

Bouquet Prawn Skewer with Olive Oil, Basil, Rosemary & Dill* 64

Tarte Flambée with Crème Fraîche, Onion & Smoked Bacon* 66

Peekytoe Crab Cakes on Grilled Chicory with Roasted-Red-Pepper Coulis 67

Herb-Quark Soufflé with Glazed Carrots 68

Pine Nut–Crusted Soft-Shell Crab with Tomato-Cumin Vinaigrette 69

White Asparagus Pizzetti with Gravad Lachs, Baby Spinach & Crème Fraîche 70

Wild Scottish Salmon with Seven Salts on Mâche* 71

Napa Cabbage Rolls with Sweetbreads, Prawns & Spicy Mustard Seed Vinaigrette 72

Spinach Torte with Parmesan, Thyme & Roasted-Red-Pepper Coulis 73

Decorative "Apple" & "Watermelon" Sushi* 75

Fennel Gratinée with Pears 76

Marinated Sea Bass with Avocado–Pearl Onion Ragoût 77

Gorgonzola-Risotto Quenelles with Tomato Glaze 78

Roasted Artichokes with Garlic, Sun-Dried Tomatoes & Goat Cheese 79

* Presented on **The Kitchens of Biró**, Season One

contents

ENTRÉES

Black Pheasant with Thyme Demi-Glace
on Creamed Salsify with Lemon-Parsley
Glazed Potatoes 140

Prosciutto-Wrapped Veal Cutlet with
Port Wine–Morel Sauce & Spinach Pasta 141

Medallions of Pork in Black Cherry–Pepper
Sauce with Spätzle & Braised Fennel* 142

Herb-&-Mustard-Crusted Milk Rabbit Loin
with Bordelaise Sauce & Sautéed Fingerling
Potatoes 144

Wild Mushroom Ravioli with Sautéed Baby Spinach
& Chive-Garlic Velouté 145

Lamb Loin à la Provençale with Escargot
Ragoût, Smoked Bacon–Wrapped
Haricots Verts & Schupfnudeln* 146

Filet Mignon Madagascar Flambé in
Cognac Crème & Crushed Red Pepper
with Garlic Potato Rosettes* 148

Sole en Papillote on Sautéed Baby Spinach
with Tomato Fettuccini* 149

Tender Milk Rabbit Loin in Lingonberry Sauce with
Poached Williams' Bon Pear & Sage Spätzle* 150

Glazed Moulard Duck Breast Filet
with Vichy Carrots & Duchesse Potatoes 152

Summer Vegetable Tower with Montrachet Cheese
Medallion, Spätzle & Tomato Glaze* 153

Lime-Grilled Mahi Mahi with Morel Sauce
& Chanterelle-Stuffed Ravioli* 155

Black Pepper–Seared Salmon Filet with
Egg Pasta, Sautéed Green Asparagus &
Champagne-Lemon Crème 156

Zucchini-Wrapped Fettuccini with
Sun-Dried Tomatoes, Mushrooms, Baby
Spinach & Roasted-Red-Pepper Coulis* 157

Ahi Tuna Filet with Lobster-Veal Roulade on
Glass Noodle Salad with Sauce Américaine* 158

Portabella Schnitzel with Brie
& Garlic Mashed Potato Rosettes* 160

Horseradish-Encrusted Sirloin with
Roasted Beets & Lyonnaise Potatoes 163

Ahi Tuna with Wilted Greens, Borlotti Beans,
Cumin Toast & Orange-Sherry Vinaigrette 164

Maltese Baked Swordfish with
Lemon-Parsley Glazed Potatoes* 165

Venison Ragoût with Juniper Crème,
Napa Cabbage & Garlic Mashed Potatoes* 166

Hanger Steak with Herb-Sautéed Fettuccini,
Grilled Blue Prawns, Spinach & Roquefort-Infused
Demi-Glace 167

Rainbow Trout with Sautéed Grapes & Almonds,
Summer Vegetables & Garlic-Parsley Potatoes 168

Capon with Sherry-Chanterelle Sauce
on Sautéed Napa Cabbage with
Lemon-Parsley Glazed Potatoes 169

Seared Sea Scallops with Pumpkin-Sage Crème,
Wild Mushroom Risotto & Prosciutto Frivolity 170

Spring Spätzle Gratinée with Sautéed Vegetables
& Montrachet Cheese Medallions 172

* Presented on **The Kitchens of Biró** Season One

acknowledgements

Our heartfelt appreciation to Heather Blamey, Shannon's fantastic assistant. It was Heather who, equipped with a microcasette recorder, captured Marcel's attention and words so that she could transcribe a number of the recipes contained in this book. Anyone who has seen Marcel in action knows this is no easy feat.

Thank you to the McCallum family who lent their cottage to Shannon to write this book and then three generations of expert eyes to help edit it at the eleventh hour. Your gracious hospitality and boundless encouragement makes us feel as if we are family.

Thank you to Cathy Fowler, our diligent literary agent, who has guided this project through several incarnations and has offered guidance, candor, and assistance long after her duties were complete. You have shared in the responsibilities of what we're building and we now look forward to sharing in the successes.

Thank you to Suzanne Taylor and the entire Gibbs Smith team for believing in us. We appreciate the freedom you gave us to create and the care you took to preserve and promote our vision. Marty Snortum and Harriett Granthen, thank you for capturing our food so beautifully and for being so patient with our perfectionism. Sherry Smies and the entire ZDO team, thank you for giving our words and Marty's photography such a beautiful backdrop. Megan Dyer, Scott Pansky, and the entire Allison & Partners team, thank you for spreading the word about this collaboration.

Thank you to Robert Rauh, Michael Taus, Rob Seideman, and especially Rob Sinskey for taking the time to lend your support to this book. Thank you also to those of you who tested these recipes in home kitchens, especially Karen Sullivan and her students.

To our friends, family, guests, and students—far too many to name personally—thank you for the encouragement you gave us every step of the way. A special thanks to Shawn and Liesl for your unwavering support. Jeff, you were one of the first believers and we're forever grateful.

In the revolving door of the restaurant world, the talented staff of Biró Restaurant and Wine Bar has been with us from the beginning. It's more than great food and service that keeps people coming back; your obvious love for what you do—whether that be create the evening's features, wait tables, peel potatoes, or wash dishes—has created a feel-good atmosphere beyond compare. A special thanks to Lawrence Turcotte, our sommelier, for creating the wine pairings for this book and for imparting his wisdom to our front-of-house staff, and to Craig Wolf, our executive sous chef, for eating, drinking, thinking, and living all things Biró at all times.

join the revolution

"You want me to go where?" I exclaimed to my Wisconsin wine distributor.

"It's a restaurant called Biró in the town of Sheboygan, and they want you to host a wine dinner," answered the voice on the other end of the line.

Needing some time to do my homework, I muttered, "I'll get back to you," and hung up the line.

I slipped my atlas out from under a stack of long neglected paper and looked up Sheboygan, Wisconsin. I found a little dot on the coast of Lake Michigan, not too far from Milwaukee. It looked pleasant enough . . . at least as far as one could ascertain by reflecting on a little dot. Out came the laptop. I typed "Biró" into the query line of my favorite search engine, not expecting to find much. I mean, I was looking up a restaurant I'd never heard of in a town far off my radar. Before you write me off as a snob, consider that in addition to my duties at my winery, I spend an inordinate amount of time sniffing out restaurants throughout the USA and beyond. Along with all the calories consumed on the road, I have earned the right to make some assumptions—chief among them that ambitious American chefs gravitate toward major cities where they pursue their fortunes in a high profile setting. I quickly learned I was guilty of culinary profiling.

My research revealed that Biró was well documented in the etherland of the web, discovering that young Marcel Biró held the title of Master Chef. I raised an eyebrow and read his philosophy of working with seasonal ingredients. I was intrigued. A "small world" moment surfaced as I learned that Marcel worked for the great chef Emile Jung of Au Crocodile in Strasbourg. My wife Maria, in her early career as a chef, also worked in Monsieur Jung's influential kitchen and, on a later wine junket, the two of us experienced several memorable evenings dining in his restaurant. The possibility occurred to me that Marcel might well have been in that Strasbourg kitchen on those evenings. I became more intrigued. Then I viewed photos of the quaint storefront restaurant in Sheboygan. It looked as though it had been lifted from a European village. It was decorated in a way that was sparse yet elegant, there was no clutter, no false pretense. The restaurant beckoned me and I answered the call.

I arrived at the restaurant expecting chaos. Forewarned that the Birós were in the midst of filming a television series, I envisioned a screaming director surrounded by scurrying production assistants with a nervous producer berating a harried cameraman who in turn hassled the frazzled soundman while huddled around an anxious chef who would rather be prepping a wine dinner than repeating his lines in front of a camera. Instead, I entered a calm room of gracious people who took time to ensure my comfort. The calm emanated from one Marcel Biró, a gracious professional who through mastery of his craft is able to be a truly whole person. In contrast to many frazzled chefs who become self-absorbed while executing their art, Chef Biró focuses his energies outward, creating an inclusive environment, drawing the guest into the experience instead of forcing him to merely be an outside observer.

The dinner that evening was a resounding success. The food was impeccable, not only delicious, but perfectly paired with the wines. However, it wasn't the food that impressed me most, it was the guests. They were like extended family. They were not only on a first name basis with the chef, they were on a first name basis with each other. Then it dawned on me: Marcel had replicated the European model of the village restaurant. He successfully created a community of the table. The guests at Biró were more than passive diners, they were crusaders on the front line of the new revolution in American cuisine.

I see a parallel between Marcel's upbringing in East Germany and the culinary history of the USA. Behind the Iron Curtain, the lack of culinary choice was imposed on the people by their government. In the USA, the lack of culinary choice was self-imposed as people opted for the convenience and low price of industrial agriculture, corporate grocery stores and chain restaurants. In East Germany, the revolutionaries tore down the wall. The wall may not be as visible in the USA, but needs to be torn down nonetheless.

Marcel has the insight and the skill to help lead this American culinary revolution. Having lived without, he can appreciate the simple pleasure of a well-grown vegetable or an animal properly raised. In the DDR, Marcel did not have a choice. He was forced to cook with whatever he could find. In the USA, we have choice, but the options are dwindling. Quality food should be a right, not a privilege. However, if we continue to choose price over quality, our farmers will no longer be able to provide artisanal products, instead they will be pushed aside by factory farms and the soulless and nutritionally degraded produce they churn out.

Marcel is a quiet revolutionary. He is an elegant craftsman who has much to offer an eager student of cuisine. The recipes in this book merge his old-world upbringing with the promise of his new home. Marcel recognizes that it will be the consumer that drives the revolution in American cuisine and recruits footsoldiers in that battle by arming his audience with an appetite for quality ingredients. He has built a culinary community around his restaurant in his small town home of Sheboygan and now, through this book, is expanding his community to include the reader. The revolution has begun.

—Rob Sinskey
Robert Sinskey Vineyards
Napa, California

Meeting Marcel Biró
by Shannon Kring Biró

On the evening of December 8, 1998, I was invited by a German business acquaintance to a private dinner party at the upscale Midwestern condominium resort where I worked as marketing director, and where he and a dozen colleagues were attending a ten-day cultural event that I had coordinated. I arrived late, and when I entered the dining room of his condo, I had no idea of the significance of the meal that I was about to be served.

I sat at a large oak table adorned with tapers and a towering bouquet of red roses, and before me was placed the feature of the evening's meal. I did not know who had prepared this dish, and until I tasted it, I did not care. But that changed once I took a bite of the perfectly al dente fettuccini topped with freshly grated Parmesan-Reggiano and a delicate crème sauce infused with chanterelles, sun-dried tomatoes, onions, and garlic. The day's stresses left me, and at once I felt both ecstasy and disbelief. How could something so flawless in taste, texture, and appearance have been created by human hands? I needed to know who made this dish.

At first, I did not ask. Each of the ingredients within the silky crème maintained its clarity, yet no one flavor dominated, and I dared not even chew for fear of disturbing the harmony of tastes on my tongue. When I had at last fully savored this fateful bite, I looked around the table for the source of this seemingly divine creation.

The red-haired woman to my left chewed with her eyes closed, her torso swaying rhythmically toward her plate, and then back to her chair. Wolfgang, the man who extended me the dinner invitation, sat to her left. His usually hollow cheeks were plump with pasta as his jaw moved up and down in triple time—one two three, one two three. As if on cue, the two gentlemen to my right lifted their forks to their mouths in unison, their shared moan of pleasure a crescendo. I was not alone in hearing this meal's perfect melody. Each of us was obviously appreciating the symphony of flavors.

"Who prepared the pasta?" I asked. Everyone continued eating in silence as if I had not spoken. Knowing that the other diners did not understand my English and assuming that either my host was too mesmerized by his dinner to hear me or that my question was not clear to his German-trained ear, I asked again, this time drawing from my limited German vocabulary. "Who . . . machen . . . pasta?"

Wolfgang looked up from his plate and began laughing heartily, shaking his head as if my question had been asked in jest.

"Was ist?" the redhead asked, obviously pleading with Wolfgang to share the joke. He answered her, his hands moving animatedly, his voice stretching to rise above the others' roar. When the laughter began to subside, Wolfgang took his napkin from his lap and dabbed at his eyes. Not until his laughter ended with a contented sigh did he seem to notice that I had not shared in the humor. He studied me a moment, and then his brow furrowed as he replied in broken English, "Marcel Biró make it. Of course, you know this, no?"

"Who?" I asked. Wolfgang's expression suggested that my ignorance was an insult, though I was unsure of how or to whom. His attention, as well as the attention of the other guests, moved down the table, coming to rest on the person sitting opposite me, the one I hadn't yet noticed beyond the floral arrangement between us. I searched for a gap in the tangle of rose stems and found a pair of dark eyes watching me intently. The guests grew silent. Watching. Waiting.

I leaned over, seeking the face to whom the eyes belonged. There he sat, the charismatic, mysterious, and proud man I couldn't help but notice the previous four days. He sat back from the table, the plate before him untouched. He leaned against his chair with ease, his arms folded, his head tilted slightly as he watched me.

"You're kidding?" I blurted, unable to hide my surprise that a man so young could have possibly been the maestro of this meal.

Marcel glanced at Wolfgang, his dark brow lifting. Wolfgang rose from the table and knelt beside him. As Wolfgang translated my words, Marcel continued to watch me, his expression indiscernible. The other diners fidgeted as they waited for Marcel's response. When he spoke to Wolfgang in German, his voice conveyed the same calm as his posture.

Wolfgang returned to his seat. "Shannon, Marcel wishes to know why you not believe he make this food?"

My reply was immediate and directed to Marcel. "Because to my palate, this is perfection, and I find it hard to believe that perfection could be achieved by someone so young. It is as if you made this pasta for me."

As Wolfgang translated my response, the right side of Marcel's mouth curled into a grin. Wolfgang smiled also. "That's because he did."

I later came to understand through Wolfgang how wrong I had been to make my assumption about culinary expertise and age. Less than one year before his meal that brought us together, Marcel had, at age 24, become one of the youngest European chefs in history to achieve the title Master. He had worked at internationally acclaimed restaurants throughout Europe, toured Europe with Olympia Master Chef François Geiger, and was personal chef to German Chancellor Helmut Kohl. He had won several coveted culinary titles while still in his teens and by the age of 21 was a European Certified Chef Instructor, teaching aspiring chefs by day and cooking in Europe's premier *Michelin*-starred restaurants by night.

While some may believe that it was Marcel's acclaim that wowed those of us around the dinner table that evening and has drawn to him millions of restaurant guests, thousands of home and professional chef students, and hundreds of culinary clients in nine countries and thirty-four U.S. states, I know otherwise. I did not taste my first Marcel Biró meal with the knowledge of his rising culinary fame, but my palate told me that it was, indeed, a great honor to be given the opportunity to eat his food. In this meal, and every one he has prepared for me since, I tasted his passion. Marcel Biró has a love affair with food.

" . . . when asked by his future wife what he did for a living, replied simply, 'I am a cook.' "

Just as great food transcends any language barrier, so too does love. Following a whirlwind romance, Marcel and I were wed in Germany in June 1999. When we returned to the United States to create a life together, that life inevitably revolved around our shared passion for cuisine and for inspiring others to discover this passion within themselves. We founded Biró Internationale Consultants, our international restaurant and marketing consultancy, in October 2000; opened Biró, our flagship restaurant, in December 2002; the Marcel Biró Culinary School, our first cooking school, in April 2003; launched Biró OmniMedia, the production company for our national PBS reality cooking series, in November 2003; and opened Ó, the SpanAsian companion restaurant to Biró, in July 2004. These businesses are located two hours north of Chicago on the shores of Lake Michigan in Sheboygan, Wisconsin—a quaint city that provides us the opportunity to feed those hungry for fine dining and professional culinary instruction. Our mission in these endeavors, as in this book, is to articulate the great enthusiasm Marcel has for his art to lead those around us to personal fulfillment. I do so with great pride, for if asked what has meant most to him in his culinary career, my husband will not cite becoming a Master Chef, cooking with Emile Jung at the renowned *Michelin* three-starred Au Crocodile, or winning first place in the prestigious Rhein-Pfalz Meisterschaften competition for *Michelin*-starred restaurants. He says, "What meant most to me is the letter I received from a nineteen-year-old girl who wrote to me from culinary school, saying that I had inspired her to become a chef." He means it. After all, this is the man who, when asked by his future wife what he did for a living, replied simply, "I am a cook."

This—the ability to share his passion with humility and to inspire others proudly to discover the passion within themselves—is truly Marcel Biró's greatest accomplishment and will undoubtedly be the foundation of all his future endeavors.

In the Beginning
By Marcel Biró

I was sixteen years old when I first experienced the undeniable link between food and power. A chef's apprentice in the kitchens of Ratshaus—the Mayor's Office and Town Hall in Plauen, East Germany—I was, on October 7, 1989, charged with prepping for the most elaborate meal of my young career: the feast commemorating the 40th anniversary of the Deutsche Demokratische Republik (DDR), or the Communist East German Party.

That morning, as on several others at Ratshaus, I was summoned to accompany the executive chef to the specialty dry storage room to gather the day's ingredients. Though we were trusted to use his keys to open the vegetable and dry storage rooms, fish tanks, freezers, coolers, and liquor storage, it was only in the presence of the executive chef with his master checklist that we were permitted entry to the specialty storage room.

" 'Exotic' products long absent from East German pantries crowded the shelves . . . "

The bounty locked behind the wooden door at the end of the hallway never failed to impress me. "Exotic" products long absent from East German pantries crowded the shelves: canned pineapples and figs, raisins, Couverture, ripe bananas and oranges, olives, dried morels, fine cognacs and whiskeys, specialty spices such as saffron and cumin, reserve Rhein wines. When I held the shiny, robust oranges that would be turned into parfait or orange crème, I remembered the shriveled, pulpy, seed-packed Cuban "14 Day Fruits" that were handed out as a special treat in elementary school at Advent, two weeks before Christmas. When I chose the rich, sweet chocolate that would become mousse, I

was reminded of the bitter East German chocolate rumored to contain steer blood to make up for its scant cocoa.

The other apprentices and I assembled to cook the standard East German dinner fare for the regular restaurant guests: cold cheese, salami, and egg-salad sandwiches. Meanwhile, in the front of the kitchen, the chefs prepared for the evening's expected gathering of four hundred Plauen DDR officials.

The birthplace of the Hitlerjungend, the group of German children who were from the age of ten immersed in Hitler's Nazi dogma, my hometown of Plauen had long been a hotbed for politics. Few, however, expected that events there would be a catalyst for the collapse of the East German state.

Only the most highly decorated Master Chefs were assigned to create the special meal's savory offerings, which included Trout with Dill Sauce and Salmon Caviar; Smoked Beef Tongue with White Asparagus Heads; Consommé of Turkey with Pistachio Dumplings and Tomato Royale; Baked Hen; Corn Purée; Filet Ensemble Trianon of Veal, Beef, and Chicken Medallions; and Dessert Surprise of Éclairs and Biscuits with Marzipan and Ice Cream. Ironically, as chefs and apprentices alike worked diligently in the belief that the DDR gala would be the climax of the day, just outside our kitchen's windowless stone walls East Germany's first mass anti-DDR demonstration had begun.

By five p.m., the first of the canapés for the evening's white-glove cocktail and hors d'oeuvre reception were taken upstairs, and my ten-hour shift was over. Though I had been warned to stay within the safety of Ratshaus by servers who watched the escalating protest from the second-story windows, I pushed through the front door, past the Kampfgruppen soldiers, and walked into what was to become a pivotal event in my country's history and in my life.

Protesters—later said to number over 20,000, Plaueners of every socioeconomic background and age—stood in the rain holding anti-DDR signs, filling the Ratshaus grounds, the streets, the Lutheran church lawn, and lining the Straßenbahn tracks as far as I could see. The chop of the helicopters hovering just above the rooftops joined the protesters' chant—"Freiheit! Freiheit!" ("Freedom! Freedom!")—while Stasi agents delivered blows and made arrests.

As water cannons fired around me, my parents' sentiments about the inequality between the masses and those who controlled the masses struck me. I thought of the connection between food and power, of how effortlessly precious foods were attained by the people for whom we had just prepared the feast, while common citizens could acquire them only through connections.

When I was a child, my mother was administrator to the man responsible for the distribution of food rations to the restaurants and grocery stores taken over by the DDR after the divide of Germany. This connection allowed us to obtain gifts of mandarin oranges and bananas presented by business owners on holidays. My father's connections enabled him to purchase grapes and watermelons for his restaurant on the black market and to acquire tomatoes and peppers directly from trains passing through Plauen from Hungary, Bulgaria, and Czechoslovakia.

I hurried to join my fellow citizens, so many of them less fortunate than I, in their courageous demand to end oppression. Risking injury and arrest by the Polizei, Stasi, and Kampfgruppen, we dared hope that our actions would one day yield freedom.

Only fifty of the four hundred invited guests braved the crowds to attend the DDR feast, the last ever held in Plauen. Four weeks and two days later, the way was paved for German reunification when the Berlin Wall crumbled. As the wall collapsed, East German protesters who had for so long been without fresh fruit chanted, "Nim unsere Hand, führe uns ins Bananenland!" ("Take our hand, lead us into Bananaland"). When East Germans drove across the border for the first time in twenty-eight years, bananas and Coca-Colas were ceremoniously placed on the hoods of their cars by West German well-wishers. Shortly thereafter, we learned that while we had waited in block-long lines to purchase overripe bananas on the rare occasions when they were available, Erich Honecker, the former East German leader, and nearly two dozen of his family members, ministers, and their families, spent 62,405,738 Deutsche Mark and 13 Pfennige (equal to approximately $33 million U.S. dollars at the time) between 1980 and 1989 on food and incidentals while in private residence with their 650 bodyguards at "Wandlitz," the compound referred to by the people as "The Island of Nightmares" because of its malevolent inhabitants.

In January 1990, I took the 100 Deutsch marks given to me by my new government as a reunification gift and rode 167 kilometers on the overcrowded Eisenbahn, standing up, to Nürnberg, where I bought three Bosc pears, a fresh pineapple, four kiwis, some Milka chocolate bars, and a smoked eel as a gift for my grandmother. I bought these items because they looked and smelled exotic. For so long I had dreamt of being able to touch them, to create with them, and to at last taste freedom.

My East German roots left an indelible mark on my career, for it was in the challenges of creating unique dishes with limited products and equipment that my creativity was born. It was in working with only the produce we could grow ourselves that I developed an appreciation for seasonal cooking. It was in experiencing food as a precious commodity that I learned to respect and conserve it, and why today, nearly fifteen years after the reunification of my homeland, I still find great pleasure in experimenting with a wealth of exotic ingredients.

I have lived and cooked in two different worlds, one of deprivation and oppression, the other of abundance and choice. This is evident in my cuisine, which simultaneously blends classic European culinary technique and flavor with ingredients that were unavailable to me as a young East German chef. Take, for instance, the Poularde à la Bressane from Biró's winter menu. Poularde à la Bressane is a fat hen from the Bressane region of France. Only two French farmers raise these prized corn-fed hens, which are therefore quite rare and expensive. I serve this delicacy with a sherry-boletus sauce and Potatoes Rustica, simple turned potatoes sautéed in clarified butter and seasoned with sea salt, freshly ground black pepper, and coarsely chopped parsley. I also take great pleasure in introducing a bit of luxury to simple foundations, such as with our appetizer House-Smoked Lachs on Rösti with Crème Fraîche & Beluga Caviar, which you'll find in this book. Rösti is a Swiss specialty of potatoes parboiled in their skins, peeled, and then coarsely grated and fried until it becomes a golden potato cake. On its own, rösti is traditionally a peasant dish, but with the addition of our House-Smoked Lachs, or Scottish salmon, that we cold-smoke over a slow-burning fire for forty-eight hours; Beluga Caviar, the most precious and expensive variety; and rich Crème Fraîche, this dish becomes the perfect balance of elegance and simplicity.

This balance has become Biró's trademark, for while I believe that upscale dining should be a lavish experience, it should never be stuffy or overly formal. This is apparent from the moment one enters our restaurant. Housed in an 1887 Cream City Brick building that Shannon and I lovingly restored to its original splendor, our 36-seat restaurant features the space's original hardwood floors and exposed brick walls. We decorated not only with period furniture that proudly bears its age but also with platinum-framed art by famed German artist Manfred Feiler. Our servers treat each guest like a VIP and provide full French service, but they do so with midwestern warmth and graciousness. In our lower-level wine and tapas bar, we left the original stone, brick, and hand-hewn one-by-one-foot timber beams exposed yet serve our drinks in the finest German crystal.

The simply elegant recipes contained within this book are adapted for the home chef from Biró, the Marcel Biró Culinary School, and from our national PBS reality-cooking series, *The Kitchens of Biró*. They reflect the favorite regions in which I worked—Alsace, southern Germany, Tuscany, and Andalusia—and are meticulously handcrafted from the finest free-range and organic ingredients. Should you have difficulty locating the recommended ingredients, I have made suggestions for appropriate substitutions. If the

level of difficulty of a particular dish exceeds your ability to make it, feel free to make only a part of it. If you don't have time to make each recipe component by hand, feel free to purchase high-quality substitutions.

Whether you prepare the recipes as outlined or put your own unique spin on them—which I encourage—I hope that you take a moment to really touch the ingredients, to inhale their wondrous scent, and to appreciate their beauty. In my life and career, I have come to fully comprehend the value of freedom and the great privilege I have to work with food. For me, it is an honor never to be taken for granted.

It is with great pride that I share my passion with you.

What you need to know

INGREDIENTS

High-quality ingredients yield high-quality results. Read past the calorie and fat content on labels to see if what you're putting in your dishes is good for the preparation and, more importantly, for you. When possible, purchase organic and free-range items. Make certain that your dairy products are not laden with fillers. Cream should contain at least 40 percent milkfat. Butter should be unsalted. Olive oil, which is called for throughout this book, should be from the first cold press and contain olives from only one country of origin.

TOOLS, COOKWARE & APPLIANCES

Though some of the recipes within this book call for special tools such as a chinoise or tamis, the tools most important for all home and professional chefs to invest in are a good knife or two and some high-quality cookware. A knife should fit comfortably in your hand. It should not be too big for your fingers to completely wrap around, but also not so small that it gets lost in your palm and prevents you from keeping a firm grip at all times. It should be well balanced and have a full tang. All cookware should be heavy. Clad and copper cookware are best. Home appliances are becoming more and more like those found in professional kitchens, which is great. These recipes were tested on home gas ranges.

TABLEWARE & TABLETOP DÉCOR

All tableware and tabletop décor should reflect your own personal style but also play a supporting role to the star: your food. We use simple white dishes, as they best show off our creations. Flowers should be beautiful but not overpowering in fragrance. Candles should be unscented.

SPECIFICS

Unless otherwise noted, all herbs are fresh. All eggs are large. All flour is all-purpose. All sugar is granulated. All pepper is freshly ground. All items that would normally be peeled—such as garlic and onions—are. You'll notice that quite often our recipes call for sautéing in both olive oil and butter. This is done for flavor and also because the olive oil increases the burning point of the butter. We use only unsalted butter, as the chef is the only person to add seasoning to a dish.

For more information on recommended ingredients, tools, and equipment, see the Sources section at the back of this book.

Lemon-Mint Sorbet with Red Peppercorns

amuse-bouches

Fennel Salad with Orange Vinaigrette,
Crème Fraîche & Parmesan Crisp

Lemon-Mint Sorbet with Red Peppercorns

Double-Melon Ball with Balsamic Glaze

Ahi Tuna with Spiced Balsamic Glaze

Smoked, Cured-Pork Roulade with
Sun-Dried Tomatoes, Baby Spinach & Feta

Striped Beets with Caraway Vinaigrette
& Hawaiian Black Lava Salt

Fruit Shots with Grand Marnier

Potato-Crusted Oyster Purse with Herb Aïoli

Three-Pepper Mousse

Fiddlehead, Morel, Tomato
& Celery Root Napoleon with Aïoli

Purple-Potato Gnocchi with Mint Pesto

Gougères with Roasted Ratatouille Nest

Gruyère-Carrot Quenelles

Sautéed Ramps with Orange Oil

Fig Chips with Chive Goat Cheese Mousse

Champagne-Herb Kraut

Citrus Soup with Orange-Blossom Honey
& Pickled Ginger

Herb Crêpe with Wasabi Tobiko Crème Fraîche

Crostini with Exotic Mushroom Ragoût
& Rosemary

Wild Mushroom Custard with Herb Broth

Fennel Salad with Orange Vinaigrette, Crème Fraîche & Parmesan Crisp

This salad is simple, yet its ingredients yield profound flavor and unexpected texture. You may wish to increase the recipe and serve it as a main-course salad, placing it in a form-giving mold or ramekin for unique presentation. For variation, add $1/4$ cup chopped raisins.

WINE PAIRING *2002 Zind-Humbrecht, Muscat d'Alsace, Alsace, France*
2002 Eyrie Vineyard, Pinot Gris, Willamette Valley, Oregon

PARMESAN CRISP

$2^1/_2$ cups flour

$3/_4$ cup water

$1/_4$ cup extra virgin olive oil

$1/_8$ cup sea salt

$1/_2$ cup grated Parmesan cheese

FENNEL SALAD

1 teaspoon orange juice

1 teaspoon extra virgin olive oil

$1/_2$ fennel bulb, grated

$1/_2$ carrot, peeled and grated

$1/_3$ cup crème fraîche

Sea salt

Freshly ground black pepper

SERVES 6

FOR THE PARMESAN CRISP

1. Preheat oven to 400 degrees.

2. In a stand mixer fitted with the paddle attachment, mix one-half the flour with the water, oil, and salt. Add enough additional flour until the dough comes together in a ball. Switch to the dough hook and knead on low for 5 minutes, adding flour as necessary to make a smooth dough that is not sticky, nor overly stiff. Allow to rest for 30 minutes.

3. Turn dough out onto a lightly floured counter and roll with a rolling pin until the dough is thin enough to see through. Sprinkle with the Parmesan and bake until golden brown, about 5 to 7 minutes. Break or cut into six pieces when cool.

FOR THE FENNEL SALAD

In a small mixing bowl, pour in the juice and oil. Whisk until emulsified, about 30 seconds. Add the fennel, carrot, and crème fraîche and toss. Season to taste with salt and pepper.

PRESENTATION

Using two tablespoons, shape the fennel salad into a quenelle, or egg shape, by scooping the salad in one spoon and smoothing it with another. Place a quenelle in the center of each small plate and prop a Parmesan Crisp against it. You could also serve this dish as a fork amuse—placing the quenelle directly on a fork and then resting it on the plate. Serve immediately.

Fennel Salad with Orange Vinaigrette,
Crème Fraîche & Parmesan Crisp

Lemon-Mint Sorbet with Red Peppercorns

Lemon-Mint Sorbet with Red Peppercorns

This was the very first item I prepared on The Kitchens of Biró, *and as with every recipe on the series, we shot the dish preparation three times to make certain we'd get every possible camera angle. When we wrapped on the recipe, within minutes the camera crew ate all three gallons I'd prepared, saying they couldn't believe that lemon, mint, and pepper worked so well together.*

Though you could use it as a warm-weather dessert, I serve Lemon-Mint Sorbet with Red Peppercorns as an amuse-bouche. It has the qualities I'm looking for in a meal prelude: it's refreshing and light, it cleans the palate, and, most importantly, it leaves my guests wanting more.

WINE PAIRING *NV Veuve Clicquot Ponsardin, Brut, Reims, France*
NV Gruet, Blanc de Noir, New Mexico

1. If using an ice cream machine for this recipe, prepare the bowl inserts as per your machine manufacturer's instructions. If you do not have an ice cream machine, place a medium-sized stainless steel bowl in the freezer to chill.

2. Place the cold water in a small saucepan. Add the sugar. Bring to a boil, and then remove from heat. Allow to cool.

3. Add the juice and zest to the cooled sugar syrup mixture.

4. Place the peppercorns in a food processor and pulse until cracked, about 10 seconds. Add the peppercorns and mint to the sugar syrup mixture and stir.

5. Pour the mixture into your ice cream machine or chilled bowl. If using an ice cream machine, process according to your machine's specifications. If using the stainless steel bowl method, remove from freezer every half hour and stir. This process can take up to 2 hours, depending on your freezer and the climate in which you live.

1 cup cold water

1 cup sugar

Juice of 4 lemons

Zest of 3 lemons

1 ounce red peppercorns

$1/2$ ounce mint leaves, *en chiffonade*

Mint leaves, for garnish

Peppercorns, for garnish

SERVES 4

PRESENTATION

I like to use a clear, chilled 2-ounce shot glass for this dish, as it looks modern and shows off the vibrant green and red colors. We pipe the sorbet into the glass with a pastry bag fitted with a round tip. Garnish with mint leaves and whole red peppercorns. Serve immediately.

QUICK TIP: WHAT IS EN CHIFFONADE?

The French term *en chiffonade* translates literally to "made of rags" and simply means to cut herbs or greens into thin strips.

Double-Melon Ball with Balsamic Glaze

The light, sweet crunch of melon and the dark, acidic bite of balsamic vinegar has been presented together in Mediterranean countries for centuries, and this is an extremely simple but pretty take on the union. You'll need a large Parisian scoop, or melon baller, to form the balls for this recipe. We'll then slice the melon balls in half and join a watermelon and honeydew melon ball together with Balsamic Glaze. You could substitute the melon of your choice, but make certain the two varieties have contrasting colors to create a more stunning presentation.

WINE PAIRING *NV Bodegas Hidalgo, Manzanilla La Gitana, Sanlúcar de Barrameda, Spain*
2002 Cloudy Bay, Sauvignon Blanc, Marlborough, New Zealand

$^1/_4$ **pound seedless red watermelon, cut into balls**

$^1/_4$ **pound honeydew melon, cut into balls**

Balsamic Glaze (see page 213)

8 large mint leaves, for garnish

SERVES 8

1. Carefully slice the watermelon and honeydew melon balls in half, making certain that the halves are as even in size as possible.

2. Dip the tip of a knife or spoon into the Balsamic Glaze and place a pea-sized or smaller drop of the glaze onto the center of the cut edge of a watermelon ball half. Place the cut side of a half ball of honeydew melon on the watermelon half and carefully press the two halves together. Practice until the Balsamic Glaze doesn't ooze out from between the two halves. Repeat the process until you have eight completed balls; refrigerate for 10 minutes.

PRESENTATION

Place a mint leaf on the center of each small serving plate. Place a melon ball on the center of the mint leaf and serve immediately.

Ahi Tuna with Spiced Balsamic Glaze

This is an extremely quick and elegant dish that showcases the rich flavor and firm, tender flesh of the ahi tuna. It's important when working with tuna to use high-quality fish, preferably Grade A, and to leave the center rare when cooking. The beauty and flavor is in this rareness, and tuna cooked beyond this temperature will be dry and chewy and will fall apart.

WINE PAIRING *2001 Wild Hog Estate, Pinot Noir, Russian River, California*
2001 De Loach Vineyards, Chardonnay O.F.S., Russian River Valley, Sonoma, California

FOR THE AHI TUNA

1. Rub the tuna filet on all sides with the cayenne pepper and season with the salt and pepper.

2. Heat the olive oil in a sauté pan over high heat. Sear the tuna until lightly golden, about 1 to 2 minutes on each side. Reserving the pan and drippings, remove the tuna from the pan and loosely tent with aluminum foil.

FOR THE SPICED BALSAMIC GLAZE

1. Using the same pan in which you seared the tuna, sauté the shallot until translucent, about 1 minute.

2. Pour in the juice, sherry vinegar, balsamic vinegar, and cumin and reduce the mixture over high heat until it has a syrup consistency, about 5 to 10 minutes.

PRESENTATION

Slice the tuna into four equal pieces. Place one slice of the tuna, cut side up, onto the center of each serving plate. Drizzle the Spiced Balsamic Glaze around the tuna and place a small mound of micro greens next to the fish. Sprinkle a few toasted sesame seeds around the plate.

AHI TUNA

1 (4-ounce) ahi tuna filet

1 tablespoon cayenne pepper

Sea salt

Freshly ground white pepper

1 tablespoon extra virgin olive oil

SPICED BALSAMIC GLAZE

1 shallot, finely diced

1 tablespoon orange juice

1 tablespoon sherry vinegar

1 cup balsamic vinegar

1 teaspoon cumin

DISH

Micro greens, for garnish

Toasted black and white sesame seeds, for garnish

SERVES 4

Smoked, Cured-Pork Roulade with Sun-Dried Tomatoes, Baby Spinach & Feta

This beautiful amuse-bouche, which is best made on a charcoal grill, has a robust, multidimensional flavor of smoke, earth, and spice. I suggest doubling the spice-blend recipe and storing it in a cool, dry location for later use on steak, poultry, fish, or vegetables.

WINE PAIRING *1999 Domaine de Gachon, St. Joseph, Rhône, France*
2001 Joseph Phelps, Vin du Mistral Syrah, Napa, California

PORK ROULADE

1 (1^1/$_4$-pound) pork tenderloin, silver skin removed and roll filleted

1 cup tightly packed baby spinach, stems removed

^{1}/$_2$ cup sun-dried tomato halves

2 ounces Feta cheese, crumbled

1 tablespoon extra virgin olive oil

1 tablespoon unsalted butter

SPICE BLEND

1 teaspoon herbes de Provence

^{1}/$_4$ teaspoon cinnamon

^{1}/$_2$ teaspoon paprika

1 teaspoon garlic powder

^{1}/$_4$ teaspoon oregano

^{1}/$_2$ teaspoon dried chives

^{1}/$_8$ teaspoon freshly ground nutmeg

^{1}/$_8$ teaspoon allspice

^{1}/$_8$ teaspoon freshly ground black pepper

^{1}/$_8$ teaspoon freshly ground white pepper

DRY CURE

1 cup kosher salt

1^1/$_4$ cups sugar

1 yellow onion, coarsely chopped

4 Turkish bay leaves, crushed

10 black peppercorns

2 cloves garlic, minced

DISH

Hickory wood chips, soaked in water per package instructions

Tomato Glaze, for garnish (see page 218)

Baby spinach leaves, stems removed, for garnish

4 cherry tomatoes, halved, for garnish

SERVES 8

1. To ensure even cooking, pound the pork tenderloin with a meat mallet until it is even in thickness.

2. In a small mixing bowl, combine all spices for the spice blend. Sprinkle the spice blend on one side of pork tenderloin and gently rub it into the meat.

3. Layer the spinach evenly over the seasoned side of pork, covering all but one-quarter of one end of the meat. Layer sun-dried tomatoes evenly over the spinach. Top sun-dried tomatoes with the Feta.

4. Turn the pork so that the end with no seasoning or vegetables is closest to you. Starting at the far end, begin rolling toward yourself to create the roulade. Seal well with your fingertips at each turn. Using butcher's twine, truss the pork (see Quick Tip on page 31).

5. In a small mixing bowl, combine the ingredients for the dry cure.

6. Line a pan double the size of the roulade with plastic wrap. Place the roulade on top of the plastic wrap and pack in the dry cure. Loosely cover the packed roulade with plastic wrap. Place a large pan or weights on top of the plastic wrap so that the dry cure presses into the meat. Allow to cure in the refrigerator for 18 to 24 hours. The longer the cure time, the saltier the roulade will be.

7. Remove the roulade from the refrigerator and remove the top layer of plastic wrap. Place the roulade in a fine-mesh strainer and rinse thoroughly with cold water to remove excess cure. Allow to air dry.

8. In a sauté pan over high heat, melt the olive oil with the butter. Sear the roulade on each side until golden brown, about 2 to 3 minutes.

9. In a charcoal grill, make a small bed of hot coals. When the coals become white hot, add one-quarter of the soaked wood chips. Place the cooking grate over the coals and chips.

10. Place the roulade on the cooking grate and cover with the lid. Periodically check to see that the flames are not coming into contact with the meat. If the flames are too high, add more soaked chips or spray the coals with water.

11. Rotating the roulade every 15 minutes, cook the meat until it is medium, or until its internal temperature reaches 145 degrees. This will take approximately 45 minutes.

12. Remove from heat and allow to cool completely. Remove the twine and slice the roulade thinly, about ^{3}/$_8$-inch thick, and serve at room temperature.

PRESENTATION

Place two slices of pork roulade on each serving plate. Spread a semicircle of chilled Tomato Glaze around them with a teaspoon and garnish with a leaf of baby spinach and half a cherry tomato.

Smoked, Cured-Pork Roulade with
Sun-Dried Tomatoes, Baby Spinach & Feta

Tie butcher's twine around one end of the meat. Leaving one end uncut, tie a knot in the string. Hold one hand over the roulade with your fingers outstretched. Pass the string around your fingers and thumb so that the string comes from behind the fingers, and then around the thumb and back behind itself. Twist the loop so that the base of the loop twists back on itself. Spread out your hand so that the loop becomes wide enough to be slid around the meat. Pull the string's loose end so that the loop is tightened around the meat. Continue until the entire piece of meat has been trussed. Turn the meat over and pass the loose end of the string through the loop, and then pass it back through the bottom side of the loop. Pull the string taut and continue down the side of the meat. Turn the meat over and tie the loose end of the string securely to the first loop.

Striped Beets with Caraway Vinaigrette & Hawaiian Black Lava Salt

This is an extremely simple dish that Shannon came up with on camera while taping our backyard barbeque episode. You may wish to do as our guests did on the episode and eat the sliced raw beets atop lightly toasted pieces of cocktail rye spread with plain chèvre or aïoli.

You can easily find Hawaiian black lava salt online (see page 219) or simply substitute fleur de sel, which will yield a milder flavor. It's important not to oversalt the vinaigrette itself, as the Hawaiian black lava salt has such a pronounced flavor.

WINE PAIRING *2001 Reisling "Le Kottabe," Josmeyer, Alsace, France*
1999 Château Haut-Brion (Blanc), Graves, Bordeaux, France

1 tablespoon toasted caraway seeds

2¹/₂ tablespoons sherry vinegar

¹/₂ cup extra virgin olive oil

Sea salt

Freshly ground black pepper

4 striped beets, peeled and thinly sliced

Hawaiian black lava salt

1 tablespoon chopped parsley, for garnish

SERVES 4

1. Place the caraway seeds and vinegar in a small bowl and slowly whisk in the olive oil. Season to taste with salt and pepper.

2. Add the beets to the vinaigrette and allow to infuse for at least 15 minutes.

PRESENTATION

Place a few slices of beet onto each serving plate. Drizzle some vinaigrette around the plate's perimeter and garnish the beets with just a bit of Hawaiian black lava salt. Sprinkle parsley over the dish.

Fruit Shots with Grand Marnier

This is a fun little presentation that your guests may eat as a shot by tipping their heads back and "drinking" the sweet fruit. My guests think this is fun, but if yours are less adventurous, you may wish to serve your Fruit Shots with a demitasse spoon.

Though they work perfectly as an amuse-bouche, Fruit Shots with Grand Marnier are also perfect as an hors d'oeuvre at a casual party, where guests can easily eat them with one hand while standing and not fumble with utensils. If your berries are large, you may need to cut them in half so that they fit into your shot glasses and can be easily eaten. You could also keep the fruits separate, rather than mixing them, to create layers of colors and flavors.

WINE PAIRING *None, as it contains Grand Marnier*

Place the orange, strawberries, raspberries, blackberries, blueberries, and mint in a mixing bowl. Gently toss to combine. Pour in the sugar, juice, 1 tablespoon of the Grand Marnier and gently combine again. Allow to infuse for at least 20 minutes.

PRESENTATION

Place the marinated fruit salad into slender two- or three-ounce clear shot glasses. Drizzle the remaining Grand Marnier atop each serving and garnish with a mint leaf.

1 orange, peeled, filleted, and diced

4 ounces strawberries, quartered

4 ounces raspberries

4 ounces blackberrries

4 ounces blueberries

1 tablespoon mint, en chiffonade

1 tablespoon sugar

$1/4$ cup orange juice

2 tablespoons Grand Marnier, divided

Mint leaves, for garnish

SERVES 8–10

Potato-Crusted Oyster Purse with Herb Aïoli

Potato-Crusted Oyster Purse with Herb Aïoli

This recipe is quick and easy to make, but your guests will never know it. You may substitute clams or smoked salmon for the oysters.

WINE PAIRING *Domaine Bessin, Chablis Fourchaume, Burgundy, France*
NV Taittinger La Française, Brut, Reims, France

1. Grate the potatoes into a large bowl. Season with salt and pepper, and then drizzle with the lemon juice to prevent the potatoes from oxidizing.

2. On a flat surface, lay a 6-inch-long sheet of plastic wrap. Place shredded potatoes on the center of the plastic wrap, making a 4-x 4-inch square. Place one oyster in the center of the potato square. Gather the top and sides of the plastic wrap, creating a purse shape. Twist the top of the plastic until the potato packet becomes compact. Depending on the amount of moisture in the potatoes you're using, you may squeeze out water as you twist the packet. If you're frying the oyster purse right away, allow it to rest in the plastic wrap for at least 10 minutes so it retains its shape. If you're frying the oyster purses later, place the packet in a ramekin or in the cup of a muffin tin, pressing firmly into the cup so that the potato packet takes on the cup's shape. Repeat the process for the other oysters. If frying later, refrigerate purses up to 12 hours before using.

3. Remove the purses from the plastic wrap.

4. In a deep fryer or deep sauté pan, heat the vegetable oil to 350 degrees. Drop three Potato-Crusted Oyster Purses into the oil and cook until golden, about 3 to 4 minutes.

5. Remove from oil and drain on white paper towels. Wait for the oil to come back up to heat and then repeat the process with the three remaining purses.

2 large Russet potatoes, peeled

Sea salt

Freshly ground white pepper

1 teaspoon lemon juice

6 Bluepoint oysters, shucked

Vegetable oil

$1/2$ cup Herb Aïoli (see page 205)

6 baby spinach leaves, for garnish

6 cherry tomatoes, for garnish

SERVES 6

PRESENTATION

Place one Potato-Crusted Oyster Purse on each serving plate and garnish with a drizzle of Herb Aïoli, a baby spinach leaf, and a cherry tomato. You may also wish to slice the purses in half so the beautiful oysters show.

QUICK TIP: THE TAP-AND-PEEK TEST FOR OYSTERS

For decades oysters were eaten only during the months containing the letter "r," as warm water from May through August, coupled with the lack of proper refrigeration, resulted in an increased risk of illness from waterborne bacteria. But today, these tasty saltwater bivalve molluscs are cultivated and shipped using technology that enables them to be eaten safely throughout the year. You simply need to know how to select fresh, live oysters, and this is where the tap-and-peek test comes in.

Take a peek at the oyster you're considering purchasing. Is it closed or open? If it's tightly closed, take it with you. If the shell is wide open, it's bad. If it's open just a bit, you must lightly tap on it. If it quickly snaps shut when tapped, the oyster is still alive and is therefore safe to purchase. If not, don't buy it. The oysters you select should contain salt water and will therefore feel quite heavy.

To keep your oysters fresh for later use, place them with the small shell up in a shallow dish. You do this so that the oyster remains in the salt water contained in the deeper shell. Cover the oysters with a damp paper towel and refrigerate for up to 36 hours.

Three-Pepper Mousse

Originally created as an amuse-bouche for a special wine dinner, this mousse was an instant hit. Guests loved the frothy texture, stunning appearance, and surprisingly mild taste. On television I prepared this recipe with sautéed peppers; using roasted peppers, which is usually how we prepare the mousse at Biró, creates a more complex flavor profile.

If you prefer a milder flavor and faster preparation method, simply dice the peppers, rather than roasting them, and sauté them in 2 tablespoons vegetable oil before proceeding with the recipe as outlined. Experiment with both techniques and find the one that works best for you.

When served in a clear glass vessel, this mousse is as beautiful as it is delicious. We serve it in a two- or three-ounce shot glass. It's the perfect portion size and allows guests to see the vibrant strata of mousse.

You'll need to gather three times the amount of ingredients in the list for Red Pepper Mousse.

WINE PAIRING *2003 Corral Creek Vineyards, Chehalem Dry Riesling, Willamette Valley, Oregon*
2002 Willa Kenzie Estate, Pinot Blanc, Willamette Valley, Oregon

RED PEPPER MOUSSE

$^3/_4$ cup minced onion

1 garlic clove, finely minced

1 tablespoon extra virgin olive oil

3 red bell peppers, roasted, cleaned, and julienned

1 cup Chicken Stock (see p. 14)

2 tablespoons tomato paste

Sea salt

Freshly ground white pepper

2 leaves gelatin

$^1/_4$ cup white wine

$^3/_4$ cup heavy cream, whipped

YELLOW PEPPER MOUSSE

Same ingredients as for Red Pepper Mousse, except use yellow peppers

2 saffron threads, crushed

GREEN PEPPER MOUSSE

Same ingredients as for Red Pepper Mousse, except use green peppers

DISH

Minced red pepper, for garnish

SERVES 10–20

FOR THE RED PEPPER MOUSSE

1. Sauté the onion and garlic in oil over high heat until golden. Add the peppers, stock, tomato paste, and salt and pepper to taste; cook until the liquid is reduced by one-half. Bloom the gelatin in the wine.

2. Purée the pepper mixture in a food processor or blender. Add the bloomed gelatin and wine while the pepper mixture is still hot and blend to combine all ingredients well. Cool the mixture over an ice bath until it mounds when dropped from a spoon.

3. Fold the whipped cream into the mixture. Transfer the mousse to a pastry bag fitted with a round tip. Pipe mousse into the bottom of each shot glass.

FOR THE YELLOW PEPPER MOUSSE

Follow steps 1–3 above. Add saffron in step 1.

FOR THE GREEN PEPPER MOUSSE

Follow steps 1–3 above.

PRESENTATION

Garnish the top of each Three-Pepper Mousse with red pepper dices. You may wish to present the mousse to your guests as we do ours, on a small square plate with a demitasse spoon.

Three-Pepper Mousse

QUICK TIP: ROASTING BELL PEPPERS

Depending on the application, leaving the skin on bell peppers may yield a slightly bitter flavor and unpleasant texture. The way to peel a bell pepper is to roast it, and there are two methods by which this can best be achieved:

Open-flame method for gas ranges:
Using a long-handled fork or skewer, char the whole pepper over an open flame by placing it directly on the burner. When the skin becomes blackened and blistered, turn the pepper so that each side becomes completely charred. Allow the pepper to cool slightly then simply rinse the skins off under cool running water and pat dry. You can also use this method on a grill.

Oven-roasting method:
Preheat the oven to 450 degrees. Place the whole pepper, or peppers, in a shallow stainless steel baking pan and drizzle with olive oil. Cover the pan with aluminum foil and bake until the skin of the peppers blisters, about 30 to 45 minutes. Immediately place the peppers in a plastic bag and seal, being careful not to burn yourself. Allow the peppers to steam inside the bag until they are cool enough to handle. Remove them from the bag and rub the skins off under cool running water. Pat dry. This method takes longer, but you can reuse the olive oil that remained in the baking dish; it will be infused with a nice pepper aroma and works wonderfully for sautéing, for drizzling on meats or fish, or for dressing salads.

Fiddlehead, Morel, Tomato &
Celery Root Napoleon with Aïoli

Fiddlehead, Morel, Tomato & Celery Root Napoleon with Aïoli

It's in the springtime that our sommelier, Lawrence, my dog, Joop, and I retreat to the deep vegetation of the Lake Michigan shoreline to forage for morels and fiddleheads. We usually do quite well with fiddleheads, but when it comes to morels, we sometimes come back with little more than dirty hands and tall tales. But on those occasions when we discover these coveted relatives of the truffle, we rush back to the restaurant to indulge in their smoky, nutty earth flavor. My guests like it when we save some for them, especially if it's part of this gorgeous dish.

WINE PAIRING *2000 Sanford & Benedict Vineyards, Foxen Pinot Noir , Santa Barbara, California*
2002 Eberle, Remo Belli Vineyard Zinfandel, Paso Robles, California

1. Preheat oven to 400 degrees.

2. Pour the milk into a medium bowl. Peel celery root and place it in the milk. Allow it to soak for 2 minutes. Remove the root from the milk and thinly slice into twelve pieces.

3. Line a sheet pan with Silpat or parchment paper and place the celery root slices on it. Place in the oven and cook until the celery root slices are dried out and resemble potato chips, about 5 minutes.

4. In a large sauté pan, sauté shallots in olive oil until softened. Add the heavy cream and tomatoes and cook over medium-low heat until reduced by one-half. Remove from heat and add the basil.

5. In a large sauté pan, sauté morels in butter until softened, about 1 minute. Add fiddleheads and cook for another 2 minutes. Add the tomato-cream mixture and cook over low heat until it reduces by one-third and becomes a ragoût. Season to taste with salt and pepper. Remove from heat.

PRESENTATION

Place one celery root chip in the center of each plate. Spoon a bit of the ragoût onto the chip. Stack a second chip atop the ragoût and top with more ragoût. Place a third chip atop the ragoût and cover with another spoonful of ragoût. Garnish the plate with a drizzle of Aïoli.

2 cups milk

1 celery root

1 tablespoon extra virgin olive oil

2 shallots, minced

$1/2$ cup heavy cream

2 vine-ripened tomatoes, chopped

2 tablespoons chopped basil

1 cup diced fresh morels

1 tablespoon unsalted butter

6 ounces fiddleheads, diced

Sea salt

Freshly ground black pepper

Aïoli, for garnish (see page 205)

SERVES 4

QUICK TIP: PURCHASING MORELS

If you're unable to find wild morels, which are available from about April through June, you may be able to find cultivated ones, which are available year round. Canned and frozen morels yield a decent flavor, and dried morels, which are generally the most widely available form, have a more intense, smoky flavor than fresh. When using dried morels in a recipe, it's important to first reconstitute them by soaking them in cool water, stock, or wine until they are softened, about 30 minutes. After soaking, carefully squeeze the excess liquid out of each morel. As much of the flavor from the mushrooms is left in the liquid, you may wish to strain it through dampened cheesecloth and use the morel-infused liquid in a dish preparation.

Purple-Potato Gnocchi with Mint Pesto

While purple potatoes are a relatively new addition to the U.S. marketplace, they have been growing in the South American Andes highlands for centuries. I use an heirloom Purple Peruvian potato for this dish. It has a medium-high starch content, gorgeous color, and a mild, creamy flavor that is perfect for gnocchi.

WINE PAIRING *2002 Murphy-Goode, Fumé Blanc, Alexander Valley, California*
2003 Preston Vineyards, Sauvignon Blanc, Napa, California

MINT PESTO

$1/2$ cup pine nuts, toasted

3 garlic cloves, peeled

$1/4$ cup grated Parmesan cheese

$1/2$ teaspoon crushed red pepper

$1/2$ teaspoon sea salt

$1/2$ teaspoon freshly ground black pepper

2 cups packed mint leaves

2 tablespoons lemon juice

$1/3$ cup extra virgin olive oil

PURPLE-POTATO GNOCCHI

2 pounds Purple Peruvian potatoes, peeled and diced

$1^1/4$ to $1^1/2$ cups flour

3 large egg yolks

2 tablespoons sea salt

2 tablespoons freshly ground black pepper

1 tablespoon unsalted butter

DISH

8 mint leaves, for garnish

SERVES 8

FOR THE MINT PESTO

Place all ingredients except olive oil in a food processor or blender. Begin puréeing and add the olive oil in a slow, steady stream until the ingredients are well combined.

FOR THE GNOCCHI

1. Boil the potatoes until tender, about 10 to 15 minutes. Drain and pass the potatoes through a potato ricer.

2. Place the hot riced potatoes on a board or counter. Make a well in the center of the potatoes and place $1/2$ cup flour into the well. Add the yolks and then $1/2$ cup more flour. Add the salt and pepper.

3. With a dough scraper, wooden spoon, or your hands, bring the mixture together, adding more flour as necessary to create a firm, barely sticky dough.

4. Roll the dough into $1/2$-inch-thick "sausages." Cut the sausages into 1-inch-long pieces and then indent each piece by rolling it over a gnocchi paddle or the back of a fork to create a grooved oval shape.

5. Bring a stockpot of salted water to a boil. Carefully add the gnocchis and cook them until they rise to the surface, about 1 to 2 minutes. Remove them from the water with a slotted spoon and allow to drain briefly on white paper towels or a kitchen towel.

6. In a large sauté pan, heat the butter over high heat. Add the gnocchi and sauté until lightly golden, about 1 minute. Turn off heat and add the pesto. Gently toss to coat.

PRESENTATION

Place a few gnocchi on the center of each serving plate and garnish with a mint leaf.

Gougères with Roasted Ratatouille Nest

These classical French pastries are ideal as a warm or cold amuse-bouche or hors d'oeuvre. The pastry dough used to make them is called a choux pastry and is also used to create éclairs and profiteroles. While baking, the eggs in the mixture puff and create a hollow, airy pastry. For color and added flavor, we have added a roasted ratatouille that can be shredded with a simple box grater. Encourage your guests to tear open the Gougères and use the pieces to scoop up the ratatouille.

WINE PAIRING *2002 Eberle, Syrah Rosé, Paso Robles, California*
2002 Georges Duboeuf, Beaujolais, Bergundy, France

FOR THE GOUGÈRES

1. Preheat oven to 425 degrees.

2. In a medium saucepan over medium-high heat, heat the milk, butter, salt, pepper, and sugar to a simmer. Add the flour and stir. Reduce heat to medium and stir until the mixture dries out, about 1 to 2 minutes. The dough will be sticky. Turn off heat and stir to cool.

3. Add the eggs to the cooled milk mixture one at a time, beating well to incorporate each egg before adding the next. Stir in 1 cup of the Gruyère, the mustard and mustard powder, and the cayenne and mix until smooth. Transfer the mixture to a pastry bag fitted with a large star tip. Pipe the batter into 1-inch mounds onto a sheet pan lined with Silpat or parchment paper.

4. Sprinkle the top of each gougères with the remaining $1/4$ cup Gruyère and bake for 10 minutes. Reduce the heat to 375 degrees and continue baking until golden brown, about 8 to 10 additional minutes.

FOR THE RATATOUILLE

1. Preheat oven to 450 degrees. In a small bowl, toss the eggplant and squash with one-half of the olive oil. Sprinkle with salt and pepper. Arrange on a large sheet pan.

2. Place the bell pepper and tomatoes in a bowl and toss with remaining half of the oil. Sprinkle with salt and pepper and place on the sheet pan with the other vegetables. Sprinkle the vegetables with basil, garlic, and onion. Roast until browned and tender, about 10 to 15 minutes.

PRESENTATION

Using a fork, wind the ratatouille into a nest shape. Place it on the middle of a small plate and top with a Gougère. Drizzle Balsamic Glaze on the plate. If using this recipe as an hors d'oeuvre, you may wish to slice the gougères open and place Roasted Ratatouille inside for easier handling.

GOUGÈRES
1 cup whole milk

$1/2$ cup unsalted butter, cut into $1/2$-inch pieces

$1/4$ teaspoon sea salt

$1/4$ teaspoon freshly ground white pepper

$1/4$ teaspoon sugar

1 cup flour

5 large eggs

$1 1/4$ cup grated Gruyère cheese, divided

1 teaspoon Dijon mustard

$1/2$ teaspoon mustard powder

$1/4$ teaspoon cayenne pepper

ROASTED RATATOUILLE NEST
2 Japanese eggplants, unpeeled and julienned

1 yellow squash, unpeeled and julienned

$1/4$ cup extra virgin olive oil, divided

Sea salt

Freshly ground black pepper

1 red bell pepper, stem and seeds removed, julienned

2 plum tomatoes, julienned

1 tablespoon basil, chopped

1 clove garlic, minced

1 small yellow onion, chopped

DISH
Balsamic Glaze (see page 213)

MAKES 48 GOUGÈRES

Gruyère-Carrot Quenelles

A quenelle *is a French egg-shaped dumpling based on the German* knödel. *It is made with a spiced meat or fish forcemeat—finely ground meat mixed with breadcrumbs and seasoning—bound with fat and eggs, as in our Beef Consommé with Thyme & Quenelles (see page 97). In this case, the quenelles are not dumplings, but rather quenelle-shaped portions of salad. The crisp sweetness of the carrot brightens up the rich, creamy nuttiness of the Gruyère in this delightful offering.*

The shreds of Gruyère and carrot should be equal in size, and this can best be achieved by grating both on a simple box grater.

WINE PAIRING *1999 Erbacher Marcobrunn Kabinett, Baron Von Knyphausen, Rheingau, Germany*
2002 Caymus Vineyards, Sauvignon Blanc, Napa, California

¹/₂ cup shredded Gruyère cheese

2 large carrots, peeled and shredded

3 orange filets, diced

1 tablespoon crushed walnuts

1 tablespoon chopped parsley

2 tablespoons orange juice

1 tablespoon heavy cream

1 teaspoon lemon juice

1 teaspoon Hungarian paprika

Sea salt

Freshly ground white pepper

Mâche, for garnish

SERVES 6

Place the Gruyère, carrots, orange dices, walnuts, and parsley in a small mixing bowl. Pour in the orange juice, heavy cream, and lemon juice and mix well to combine. Add the paprika and season to taste with salt and pepper. Allow to infuse for about 15 minutes and then mix again, adjusting the seasoning as necessary.

PRESENTATION

Using two tablespoons, form the salad into quenelles and place them on individual serving plates. Garnish each with two or three leaves of mâche.

Sautéed Ramps with Orange Oil

Proof that complex flavors needn't come from complex preparation methods, this amuse-bouche is a springtime favorite that was featured on a fun episode of The Kitchens of Biró *in which Lawrence, my dog, Joop, and I went on a ramp-picking expedition.*

I've left the ramps (wild onions) whole here, but I've also prepared them sliced on an angle. See what you like best. Store leftover orange oil in an airtight container for up to one week.

WINE PAIRING *1997 Rocca delle Macie, Chianti Classico Riserva, Italy*
1997 Marqués de Cáceres, Reserva, Rioja, Spain

1. Place all orange peels in a medium bowl. Top with the oil. Cover with plastic wrap and allow to rest at room temperature for 24 hours.

2. Fillet the oranges. Reserve the inner structure of the oranges and press the juice from the remaining membranes onto the ramps. Dice one-half of the orange segments and keep the rest whole.

3. Heat 1 tablespoon of the orange oil in a sauté pan over high heat. Add the shallot and garlic and cook until glossy, about 30 seconds. Add ramps and sauté until softened, about 10 to 15 seconds. You just want to release the oils and flavors of the ramps, not cook them through, as they would become bitter. Add the orange dices and season to taste with salt and pepper. Remove from heat and add mint.

PRESENTATION

Place two ramps in the center of each serving plate. I use small square plates for this recipe. Garnish with drizzles of orange oil and whole orange segments.

1 navel orange, washed and peeled (reserve peels)

1 blood orange, washed and peeled (reserve peels)

1 cup extra virgin olive oil

1 shallot, diced

1 clove garlic, sliced

1 pound freshly picked ramps, leaves trimmed and root ends removed

Sea salt

Freshly ground black pepper

1 teaspoon mint, en chiffonade

SERVES 6

Fig Chips with Chive Goat Cheese Mousse

Fig Chips with Chive Goat Cheese Mousse

Figs contain a lot of water, so when the moisture evaporates during the drying process in this recipe, their flavor becomes much more concentrated. To balance the sweet crisp of the fig chips in this recipe, we've added a creamy-sharp sensation with a goat cheese mousse containing crème fraîche and chives. The result is a new and delicious spin on the familiar combination of fig and goat cheese.

Mission or Dauphine Violette Figs work best for this recipe. Montrachet or Bûcheron goat cheese is preferred.

WINE PAIRING *2003 WillaKenzie Estate, Pinot Blanc, Willamette Valley, Oregon*
2002 Eberle, Syrah Rosé, Paso Robles, California

FOR THE FIG CHIPS

1. Preheat oven to 425 degrees.

2. Using a mandoline or a chef's knife, thinly slice figs into rounds about $1/8$ inch thick. You will need a total of 24 slices for this recipe.

3. Place figs on a Silpat- or parchment-lined sheet pan and sprinkle with the sugar. Bake until the figs are dry, about 5 to 10 minutes.

FOR THE CHIVE–GOAT CHEESE MOUSSE

Place the goat cheese and crème fraîche in the bowl of a food processor and combine until smooth but not runny. Add the chives and pulse to combine. Season to taste with salt and pepper.

PRESENTATION

I like to use square plates for this recipe to balance the fig rounds. Place three rounds on each serving plate. Pipe the mousse onto the center of each fig chip using a pastry bag fitted with a star tip, or simply spoon it on with a teaspoon. Cut six of the fig chips into thirds and prop a piece atop each mousse. Using a fine-nozzled squeeze bottle, make Balsamic Glaze circles on the plate.

FIG CHIPS

4 medium figs

2 teaspoons sugar

CHIVE–GOAT CHEESE MOUSSE

6 ounces goat cheese

5 tablespoons crème fraîche

1 tablespoon chopped chives

Sea salt

Freshly ground white pepper

DISH

Balsamic Glaze, for garnish (see page 213)

SERVES 6

Champagne-Herb Kraut

This creamy, sweet, and tangy Champagne-Herb Kraut is very versatile. Here we're using it as an amuse-bouche, but on The Kitchens of Biró, *I presented it as a side dish at an elegant backyard barbecue. It is great paired with pork, beef, lamb, poultry, or grilled sausages.*

WINE PAIRING *NV Taittinger, La Française Brut Champagne, Reims, France*
2001 Bryon, Estate Chardonnay, Santa Barbara, California

1 small yellow onion, diced

1 tablespoon extra virgin olive oil

1 tablespoon unsalted butter

1 cup heavy cream

1 pound sauerkraut

1 tablespoon honey

$1/2$ teaspoon freshly ground nutmeg

$1/2$ fresh pineapple, peeled and diced

1 split bottle (187 ml) Champagne or sparkling wine

1 tablespoon chopped parsley

Cayenne pepper

Parsley sprigs, for garnish

SERVES 8–10

1. Sauté onion in the oil and butter in a large stockpot over high heat until glossy. Add the cream and reduce by one-half.

2. Drain and wash the sauerkraut; add it to the creamed onion. Add the honey and nutmeg and simmer, stirring occasionally, for 15 minutes.

3. Add pineapple and cook for 3 additional minutes. Reduce heat to medium-low and allow to simmer for 20 minutes, stirring occasionally. Add Champagne and parsley and stir gently to combine. Simmer for an additional 15 minutes. Season to taste with cayenne pepper.

PRESENTATION

Place a small mound of Champagne-Herb Kraut on the center of each serving plate. I use small square plates for this amuse. Garnish with a sprig of parsley and serve immediately.

Citrus Soup with Orange-Blossom Honey & Pickled Ginger

This soup is light, refreshing, and tangy sweet, with just a bit of kick from the pickled ginger. If you're unable to find orange-blossom honey, substitute another very light amber honey with a delicate flavor and aroma.

WINE PAIRING *2002 Caymus Vineyards, Sauvignon Blanc, Napa, California*
2003 Domaine Trimbach, Gewürztraminer Reserve, Alsace, France

1. Wash and zest the fruits, reserving the zest.

2. Peel all the white membrane from the zested fruits. Working over a bowl to catch the juice, use a paring knife to fillet the fruits into segments. Cut the filets into small dices and reserve the juice. Squeeze the juice from the membranes into the bowl.

3. Place the honey, sugar, and water in a medium saucepan and bring to a boil over medium heat. Stir in the zest and reserved juice and simmer for 3 additional minutes. Remove from heat and add the diced citrus. Allow the soup to come to room temperature and then refrigerate for at least 2 hours.

PRESENTATION

Ladle the soup into chilled two- or three-ounce shot glasses or demitasse cups. Top each serving with the ginger and serve immediately.

2 navel oranges

1 blood orange

2 pink grapefruits

2 limes

$^3/_8$ cup orange-blossom honey

$^1/_4$ cup sugar

3 tablespoons water

2 tablespoons pickled ginger, julienned

SERVES 6–8

Herb Crêpe with Wasabi Tobiko Crème Fraîche

Crêpes, with their light, airy texture and subdued flavor, are the perfect backdrop for a wide array of sweet and savory garnishes. Here, the crêpes are given a bit more prominence through the addition of some aromatic herbs. The addition of silky crème fraîche flavored with spicy wasabi tobiko gives your mouth a literal and figurative pop.

I use an 8¹/₂-inch crêpe pan for this recipe.

WINE PAIRING *NV Bodegas Hidalgo, Manzanilla La Gitana, Sanlúcar de Barrameda, Spain*
NV Hakutsuru Sake, "Junmai Dai Ginjo," Kobe, Japan

HERB CRÊPE

1 cup all-purpose flour

¹/₄ teaspoon sea salt

3 large eggs, lightly beaten

1¹/₄ cups whole milk

4 tablespoons unsalted butter, melted, plus more for the pan

1 teaspoon minced chives

1 teaspoon minced rosemary

1 teaspoon minced thyme

1 teaspoon minced sage

WASABI TOBIKO CRÈME FRAÎCHE

¹/₂ cup crème fraîche

2 tablespoons heavy cream

2 tablespoons vodka

6 tablespoons wasabi tobiko

SERVES 8

FOR THE HERB CRÊPE

1. Place the flour and salt into a bowl and create a well in the center of the flour. Whisk the eggs and milk together and pour into the well. Whisk to combine and then whisk in the butter. Add the chives, rosemary, thyme, and sage and stir to combine.

2. Heat a crêpe pan over medium heat until hot. Add a bit of melted butter to the pan and then pour about 2 tablespoons of batter into the center of the pan. Rotate the pan in a circular motion so that the batter distributes evenly throughout the bottom of the pan. Cook until the bottom of the crêpe is lightly browned and spotted, about 30 to 45 seconds. Flip and cook for an additional 10 to 15 seconds. Transfer the prepared crêpe, nice side down, to a plate. Repeat this process, adding more melted butter to the pan as necessary, until you have a pile of eight crêpes.

FOR THE WASABI TOBIKO CRÈME FRAÎCHE

Place the crème fraîche, cream, and vodka in a mixing bowl and whisk until smooth. Fold in the wasabi tobiko.

PRESENTATION

Spread about 2 tablespoons of the Wasabi Tobiko Crème Fraîche on the center of the top crêpe and fold the crêpe over itself jelly-roll style. Slice the crêpes in half on a diagonal, trimming the ends, and place one half of the crêpe, seam side down, on the center of a serving plate; prop the other half against it. Serve immediately.

Crostini with Exotic Mushroom Ragoût & Rosemary

Mushrooms are the perfect topping for crostini, and this rich, meaty blend of earthy exotics is positively decadent. For an even more luxurious ragoût, add 1 tablespoon heavy cream when you add the red wine vinegar. Feel free to substitute whatever mixture of mushrooms are available, but I urge you to experiment with varieties unfamiliar to you. Try serving the ragoût over pasta, gnocchi, schupfnudeln, or spätzle for a special treat.

WINE PAIRING *2000 J. Rochioli, Pinot Noir Reserve, Russian River, Sonoma, California*
2003 Domaine Drouhin, Pinot Noir, Willamette, Oregon

1. Preheat oven to 375 degrees. Place the baguette slices on a sheet pan and toast in the oven until golden, about 8 to 10 minutes. Allow to cool at room temperature.

2. Heat the olive oil and butter in a large sauté pan over medium-high heat. Add the shallot and sauté until translucent, about 3 minutes. Add the mushrooms and sauté for an additional 3 minutes. Add the vinegar and rosemary and continue to cook until the mushrooms are tender, about 5 minutes. Season to taste with salt and pepper.

PRESENTATION

Spoon the mushroom ragoût onto the center of each toasted baguette slice. The amount of ragoût you have depends on the amount of water in the mushrooms you used, but you should have enough for about $1\frac{1}{2}$ to 2 tablespoons per crostini. Place one crostini on the center of each serving plate and prop a second crostini against it. Drizzle Balsamic Glaze around the perimeter of the plate and garnish each plate with a sprig of rosemary.

20 slices ($\frac{1}{3}$ inch thick) baguette

1 tablespoon extra virgin olive oil

1 tablespoon unsalted butter

1 shallot, minced

$\frac{1}{2}$ cup diced porcini mushrooms

$\frac{1}{2}$ cup diced Black Trumpet mushrooms

$\frac{1}{2}$ cup diced morels

$\frac{1}{2}$ cup diced Hedgehog mushrooms

$\frac{1}{2}$ cup diced Cinnamon Cap mushrooms

1 tablespoon red wine vinegar

1 teaspoon chopped rosemary

Sea salt

Freshly ground black pepper

Balsamic Glaze, for garnish (see page 213)

Rosemary sprigs, for garnish

SERVES 10

Wild Mushroom Custard with Herb Broth

Savory custards work wonderfully as an amuse-bouche, and this is one of my favorites. We use two-ounce ramekins for this recipe, but you may use larger ramekins and simply slice the custard into your desired portion size when cooled.

For variation, try serving this custard as a salad by placing it atop mesclun greens coated in our Light Champagne Vinaigrette (see page 123).

WINE PAIRING *2003 Beaujolais Brouilly, Georges Duboeuf, Burgundy, France*
1997 Marqués de Cáceres, Reserva, Rioja, Spain

WILD MUSHROOM CUSTARD

1 tablespoon extra virgin olive oil

$1/2$ tablespoon minced garlic

$1/2$ cup sliced shiitake mushrooms

$1/2$ cup sliced chanterelle mushrooms

$1/2$ cup sliced oyster mushrooms

$1/2$ cup sliced porcini mushrooms

$1/4$ cup white wine, preferably Chablis

4 large eggs, lightly beaten

1 cup heavy cream

1 tablespoon chopped chives

Sea salt

Freshly ground white pepper

Unsalted butter

HERB BROTH

$1/2$ cup Chicken Stock (see page 214)

$1/2$ teaspoon chopped rosemary

$1/2$ teaspoon chopped thyme

Sea salt

Freshly ground white pepper

1 Roma tomato, peeled, seeded, and julienned

1 teaspoon extra virgin olive oil

DISH

Whole chives, for garnish

SERVES 8–10

FOR THE WILD MUSHROOM CUSTARD

1. Preheat oven to 300 degrees.

2. Heat the oil in a large sauté pan over high heat. Add the garlic and sweat for 10 seconds. Add the mushrooms and sauté for an additional 1 minute. Deglaze with the wine and reduce, stirring occasionally, until nearly dry. Season to taste with salt and pepper, and then place the mushrooms in a single layer on a sheet pan and allow to cool completely.

3. In a large bowl, whisk together the eggs and cream. Mix in the cooled mushrooms and chives and lightly season with salt and pepper.

4. Butter ramekins and fill them three-quarters full with the custard. Bake the custards in a bain-marie (see Quick Tip page 185) until set, about 25 minutes. Remove from the bain-marie and allow to cool at room temperature.

FOR THE HERB BROTH

Warm the stock in a small saucepan over medium-high heat. Add the rosemary and thyme and season to taste with salt and pepper. Finish by adding the tomato juliennes and drizzling with the oil.

PRESENTATION

Invert an individual custard onto the center of each serving plate. Spoon Herb Broth around the custard and garnish each plate with two chives crossed into an X shape.

QUICK TIP: IS MY CUSTARD SET?

To test the doneness of custard, insert a wooden skewer into the custard's center. If it's clean when you remove it, the custard is set. If not, bake it a bit longer.

White Asparagus Pizzetti with Gravad Lachs,
Baby Spinach & Crème Fraîche

appetizers

Half-Dozen Alsatian Escargots with
Garlic-Herb Butter

Razor Clams in Parsley Jus

Baked Brie with Lingonberry Sauce

Prosciutto-Wrapped Shrimp with Basil,
Mozzarella, Extra Vecchio Balsamico & Aïoli

Smoked Lachs on Rösti with
Crème Fraîche & Beluga Caviar

Baked Feta & Heirloom Tomatoes
in Garlic-Herb Butter

Bouquet Prawn Skewer with Olive Oil,
Basil, Rosemary & Dill

Tarte Flambée with Crème Fraîche, Onion
& Smoked Bacon

Peekytoe Crab Cakes on Grilled Chicory
with Roasted-Red-Pepper Coulis

Herb-Quark Soufflé with Glazed Carrots

Pine Nut–Crusted Soft-Shell Crab with
Tomato-Cumin Vinaigrette

White Asparagus Pizzetti with Gravad Lachs,
Baby Spinach & Crème Fraîche

Wild Scottish Salmon with Seven Salts on Mâche

Napa Cabbage Rolls with Sweetbreads, Prawns
& Spicy Mustard Seed Vinaigrette

Spinach Torte with Parmesan, Thyme
& Roasted-Red-Pepper Coulis

Decorative "Apple" & "Watermelon" Sushi

Fennel Gratinée with Pears

Marinated Sea Bass with
Avocado–Pearl Onion Ragoût

Gorgonzola-Risotto Quenelles with Tomato Glaze

Roasted Artichokes with Garlic,
Sun-Dried Tomatoes & Goat Cheese

Half-Dozen Alsatian Escargots with Garlic-Herb Butter

Escargots, or snails, have been eaten since prehistoric times and have been considered a delicacy since the Roman era. This uncomplicated recipe—inspired by one of my favorite regions, Alsace, where escargots are eaten with liberal amounts of garlic butter—has been very well received by both connoisseurs and first-time escargot eaters at Biró.

When preparing escargots, it's important to sauté them for no more than a minute or two, as they quickly dry out and become rubbery. We serve our escargots in escargot dishes, which are convenient for holding the escargots during broiling and also make a nice presentation. Though elaborate escargot dishes can definitely be a splurge item, you can find simple and inexpensive versions at restaurant or kitchen supply stores. I happen to favor simple white escargot dishes for this dish, as they provide the perfect backdrop for the escargots and the allure of their accompanying bubbly, Garlic-Herb Butter. Serve with crusty bread.

WINE PAIRING *1999 Au Bon Climat, Benedict Vineyard Pinot Noir, Santa Ynez, California*
2001 Domaine de l'Oratoire, Côtes du Rhône, Rhône, France

1 tablespoon extra virgin olive oil

1 tablespoon unsalted butter

1 shallot, minced

1 clove garlic, minced

24 escargots

8 tablespoons Garlic-Herb Butter (see page 205)

SERVES 4

1. Preheat broiler.

2. In a medium sauté pan, melt the olive oil and butter together over high heat. Add the shallot and garlic and cook until softened, about 1 minute. Add the escargots and sauté until hot, about 1 additional minute. Transfer the escargots to escargot dishes and top with 2 tablespoons Garlic-Herb Butter per dish.

3. Broil until the butter becomes brown and crusty, about 2 to 3 minutes.

PRESENTATION

Carefully place the escargot dishes onto individual serving plates. Serve immediately.

QUICK TIP: PURCHASING AND WORKING WITH FRESH ESCARGOT

In the United States, escargots are generally sold in two forms: canned and fresh in the shell. Canned escargots simply need to be rinsed under cold running water before use. Fresh escargots in the shell will require just a bit more work.

Fresh escargots in the shell will need to be placed in cold water when you get home. Allow them to soak for 2 to 3 hours, stirring the water from time to time to extract any debris they may contain. Then place the escargots in a strainer and rinse them under cold running water to remove all their mucus. Finally, place them in fresh water and begin to remove the escargots from their shells. Have a second bowl of cold water handy in which to place the shelled escargots.

Using the tip of a paring knife, gently pry the head of the escargot from its shell. Using your fingers, carefully twist the rest of the body from the shell. Gently remove the black part at the end of the tail with the tip of your knife and place the cleaned escargots in water. It's best to use the escargots the same day they are cleaned.

Razor Clams in Parsley Jus

The best-known West Coast soft-shell clam, the razor clam, gets its name from its shape, which resembles a folded straight razor. This simple dish may be so popular that you'll want to begin serving it as an entrée.

WINE PAIRING *2001 Au Bon Climat, Sanford & Benedict Chardonnay, Santa Ynez, California*
2002 Catena, Chardonnay, Mendoza, Argentina

1. In a sauté pan with lid, heat the olive oil over medium heat. Sauté the carrot, leek, and onion until softened. Add the fennel greens and clams.

2. Pour in the stock and reduce heat to medium-low. Cover the pan and bring to a simmer. When the clams open, remove from heat. This will take about 1 to 2 minutes.

3. Remove the razor clams and reduce the remaining liquid over high heat. Add the cream and white wine and reduce by one-half. Add the parsley and juice. Remove the reduction from heat and pour into a blender. Blend to a purée, and then pass the jus through a fine-mesh sieve. Season to taste with salt and pepper.

PRESENTATION

Place four razor clams on each plate. Pour a ribbon of jus around the clams. Garnish with a sprig of fried parsley.

1 teaspoon extra virgin olive oil

1 carrot, peeled and julienned

1 leek, white part only, julienned

1 medium yellow onion, diced

1 tablespoon chopped fennel greens

16 razor clams

1 cup Fish Stock (see page 214)

1 cup heavy cream

1 tablespoon white wine, preferably Chablis

1 bunch parsley, chopped

1 teaspoon lemon juice

Sea salt

Freshly ground white pepper

Fried Herbs and Greens, for garnish (see page 218)

SERVES 4

QUICK TIP: SELECTING RAZOR CLAMS
When purchasing razor clams in the shell, look for shells that are tightly closed. If a shell is open slightly, gently tap it. If it doesn't snap shut, the clam is dead and should be discarded. Shucked clams should be plump and possess a clear, lightly scented liquid.

Baked Brie with Lingonberry Sauce

Brie, a cow's-milk cheese originating in the Île-de-France, has been considered a delicacy since the time of Charlemagne (a.d. 814–742). In 1814 it was proclaimed "King of Cheeses" at a Congress of Vienna dinner, and ever since, nearly every European dinner party includes the soft, mild cheese as either a canapé or conclusion to a meal.

This offering appears on the appetizer menu at Biró, and it's delightful enjoyed with a glass of wine as a light meal in itself. It is also appropriate as a dessert. We use high-quality canned lingonberries for this dish, but if you find fresh berries, heat them on the stovetop with sugar to taste before proceeding with the recipe. You may either purchase one wheel of Brie and slice it into four wedges, or purchase four wedges that are between 5 and 6 ounces each. It is important that the Brie is kept refrigerated until the moment you are ready to use it, as it is much more difficult to work with when soft.

WINE PAIRING *NV Codorníu, Brut Cava, Penedès, Spain*
NV Freixenet, Brut Cava, Penedès, Spain

2 cups flour

2 large eggs

$1/2$ cup whole milk

$1^1/_2$ pounds Brie

2 cups plain breadcrumbs

2 tablespoons extra virgin olive oil

2 tablespoons unsalted butter

8 ounces lingonberries

Fried Herbs and Greens, for garnish (see page 218)

SERVES 4

1. Preheat oven to 450 degrees.

2. Place the flour in a shallow dish. In a second shallow dish, whip the eggs and milk together to create an eggwash. Place the breadcrumbs in a third shallow dish.

3. Dredge the first wedge of Brie in the flour and make certain it's completely coated. Remove the Brie and tap off all excess flour. Place the floured wedge into the eggwash and cover it completely with egg. Remove the Brie from the eggwash, gently shaking it to remove any excess, and place it in the bowl containing the breadcrumbs. Completely cover the wedge in breadcrumbs and then remove it from the dish, tapping the cheese to remove all excess breadcrumbs. Repeat the process with the wedge so that it is double breaded, and then repeat the entire process with the remaining wedges of Brie. Place the breaded wedges in the refrigerator while you prepare the pan for sautéing. It's important to work quickly, as you do not want the breadcrumbs to get soggy.

4. Melt the olive oil and butter in a medium sauté pan over high heat. Remove the first wedge of Brie from the refrigerator and place it in the hot sauté pan. Sauté it until light golden brown, about 1 minute on each side. Repeat the process with the remaining cheese wedges.

5. Place the wedges into a preheated oven and cook until the Brie softens, about 5 to 7 minutes.

6. Meanwhile, place the lingonberries in a medium sauté pan and warm over high heat.

PRESENTATION

Stand each wedge up on an individual serving plate. Spoon lingonberry sauce onto the plate next to the baked Brie. Garnish the top of each wedge with fried parsley and serve immediately.

QUICK TIP: WHY DOUBLE BREAD?

Delicate items are coated with breadcrumbs prior to sautéing or baking so that they maintain their shape and appearance during the cooking process. With items that melt during cooking, such as Brie, double breading is crucial. Why? Any uncoated surface area provides a "door" through which the item could escape into the pan or baking dish. Many people are therefore tempted to load on the flour, eggwash, and breadcrumbs in one step, which results in uneven breading, an unpleasant appearance, and a floury, scrambled-eggs flavor that detracts from the flavor of the breaded item.

Double breading is a much better alternative, as you build up two layers of light breading that will properly seal the item without masking its flavor. While double breading, it's important to keep your fingers as clean as possible, as eggwash left on your fingers pulls off the breadcrumbs during handling. It may take a bit of practice to master double breading, but trust me, it's worth it. You don't want to lose even one drop of Brie in this recipe.

Baked Brie with Lingonberry Sauce

Prosciutto-Wrapped Shrimp with Basil,
Mozzarella, Extra Vecchio Balsamico & Aïoli

Prosciutto-Wrapped Shrimp with Basil, Mozzarella, Extra Vecchio Balsamico & Aïoli

This Italian-inspired dish is deceptively easy to prepare and is an excellent prelude to most any meal. It is one of only a few items that appears on our menu season after season and is so popular that any time I even hint that I may take it off the menu, the staff and guests rally to its defense. It's one of the very first dishes I prepared in the U.S. and I suspect I will be making it daily for the rest of my career.

I use red or pink Mediterranean prawns for this recipe, such as the Italian gambero rosso, as they yield the best flavor and have a beautiful color. You may also use tiger or banana prawns, but I don't suggest using common, or brown, shrimp. They're awkward to work with due to their small size, they aren't substantial enough for the dish, and they yield a brown color that will get lost against the Prosciutto.

WINE PAIRING *2003 Leeuwin Estate, Chardonnay, Margaret River, Australia*
NV Bodegas Hidalgo, Manzanilla La Gitana, Sanlúcar de Barrameda, Spain

1. Melt 1 tablespoon of the olive oil and 1 tablespoon of the butter in a large sauté pan over high heat. Add the shrimp and sauté until red, about 3 minutes. Remove from heat and allow to cool slightly.

2. Wrap each shrimp in one basil leaf and then in one slice of the prosciutto ham.

3. In sauté pan, heat the remaining 1 tablespoon olive oil and 1 tablespoon butter, saffron seeds, and garlic over high heat until the garlic is softened but not browned, about 30 seconds. Add the shrimp and sauté until the prosciutto is golden brown, about 1 additional minute.

PRESENTATION

Place spring greens in the center of each serving plate. Place a slice of mozzarella at the 12:00, 4:00, and 8:00 positions of each serving plate. Place one Prosciutto-Wrapped Shrimp, tail side standing up and facing inward, on each slice of mozzarella. Place a vine-ripe tomato slice at the 2:00, 6:00, and 10:00 positions and cover with a dollop of Aïoli. Drizzle Extra Vecchio Balsamico over the dish.

2 tablespoons extra virgin olive oil, divided

2 tablespoons unsalted butter, divided

12 gambero rosso shrimp, peeled and cleaned

12 large basil leaves

12 slices prosciutto ham

1 tablespoon saffron seeds

2 cloves garlic, sliced

2 cups loosely packed spring greens

12 slices fresh mozzarella

2 vine-ripened tomatoes, cut into 12 slices

Aïoli (see page 205)

Extra Vecchio Balsamico

SERVES 4

QUICK TIP: WHAT IS EXTRA VECCHIO BALSAMICO?

True balsamic vinegar is made from concentrated juice from the Trebbiano white grape. When shopping, you'll know if a bottle of balsamic vinegar is authentic if it is marked Aceto Balsamico Tradizionale on the bottle. If not, the bottle most likely contains red wine vinegar fortified with grape juice, caramelized sugar, and sometimes even artificial flavoring and coloring. Most true balsamic vinegars widely available in the United States are aged four to twelve years.

Extra Vecchio Balsamico is true balsamic vinegar that has matured in wooden casks for at least thirty and as many as a hundred plus years . It has a much richer flavor and fuller body than even true balsamic vinegar and can command prices into the thousands per small flask. If you don't have access to the real thing, or don't wish to spend the money to get it, you can do a fair job of mimicking the sweet tang and thicker consistency of true Extra Vecchio Balsamico by creating a Balsamic Glaze. See page 213.

Smoked Lachs on Rösti with Crème Fraîche & Beluga Caviar

I take great pleasure in introducing a bit of luxury to simple foundations, and this dish is a prime example. Rösti is a Swiss specialty of potatoes parboiled in their skins, peeled and coarsely grated, and then fried until they become a golden potato cake. On its own, rösti is traditionally a peasant dish, but this dish becomes the perfect balance of elegance and simplicity with the addition of our house-smoked lachs, or Scottish salmon, that we cold-smoke over a slow-burning fire for 48 hours; beluga caviar, the most precious and expensive variety; and rich crème fraîche. Though rösti is typically created by first parboiling the potatoes, this version saves time and produces equally satisfying results.

WINE PAIRING *2002 Lucien Albrecht, Gewürtztraminer, Alsace, France*
1999 Selbach-Oster, Bernkasteler Badstube Riesling Spätlese, Mosel, Germany

6 large Russet potatoes

2 yellow onions

Sea salt

Freshly ground black pepper

1 tablespoon extra virgin olive oil

3 tablespoons unsalted butter

18 ounces smoked salmon, thinly sliced

2 tablespoons crème fraîche

1 teaspoon beluga caviar

Chopped chives, for garnish

SERVES 6

1. Peel the potatoes and coarsely grate them into a nonreactive bowl. Repeat with the onions. Combine the potatoes and onions; salt and pepper to taste.

2. Heat a nonstick sauté pan over high heat. Melt the oil and butter and then add one-sixth the amount of potato-onion mixture to the pan. Cook on both sides until golden brown. Repeat this process until all the röstis are complete.

PRESENTATION

Place one rösti onto the center of each plate. Layer the salmon atop the rösti. Garnish with a dollop of crème fraîche and top with caviar. Sprinkle with chives.

QUICK TIP: CAVIAR SUBSTITUTIONS

Caviar is roe, or eggs, from the sturgeon that have been salted and matured. For this dish, I like beluga, which is the most expensive of the three types of caviar (ossetra and sevruga being the other two). Regardless of the type of caviar you select, it's pretty pricey, and you may wish to leave the caviar off altogether or substitute a more inexpensive roe. Tobiko is my first choice; in fact, it works so well that I used it on this dish for television. Tobiko is the roe of the flying fish and is widely used in Japanese cooking. It has a great flavor and stunning red color in its natural state. If flavored with wasabi, it has a vibrant green color and spicy flavor.

Smoked Lachs on Rösti with
Crème Fraîche & Beluga Caviar

Baked Feta & Heirloom Tomatoes
in Garlic-Herb Butter

Baked Feta & Heirloom Tomatoes in Garlic-Herb Butter

This simple and extremely popular appetizer has humble roots.

When I was eighteen, I moved to Bellheim, Germany, and began working as a Chef de Entremitier at Braustübel, a Michelin-starred restaurant. I was poor and lonely at first, and when I'd finish my sixteen-hour shift, I'd retreat to my closet-sized, nineteenth-century room above the kitchen with little energy—or food—to make myself something to eat. As tomatoes grew plentifully on the property, whatever I made myself invariably contained them. On one particularly lonely night this dish was born, and it's held a special place in my heart—and stomach—ever since.

We serve Baked Feta & Heirloom Tomatoes in Garlic-Herb Butter with crusty bread, but you could serve it over greens for a salad or on a toasted baguette for a sandwich. For a flavorful variation, sauté shrimp in a teaspoon of Garlic-Herb Butter and place it atop the cheese. You may substitute vine-ripe tomatoes for the heirloom tomatoes in this recipe.

WINE PAIRING *2001 Pojer & Sandri, Müller-Thurgau, Trentino, Italy*
2000 Fontodi, Chianti Classico, Tuscany, Italy

1. Preheat oven to 350 degrees.

2. Place tomato slices in a long, single layer on a sheet pan brushed with the oil. Season with pepper to taste. Layer the basil, Feta, shallots, and garlic on top of the tomato slices. Add the Garlic-Herb Butter and cherry tomato halves and bake, uncovered, until the cheese is softened, about 15 minutes. Remove from oven and heat broiler.

3. Placed the Baked Feta under the broiler and cook until bubbly and browned around the edges, about 1 minute.

PRESENTATION

Remove the Baked Feta from the sheet pan with a spatula and carefully slide equal portions onto the center of each serving plate. Garnish with basil and drizzles of Chive Oil and Balsamic Glaze.

1 large heirloom tomato, sliced

2 tablespoons extra virgin olive oil

Freshly ground black pepper

4 large basil leaves

1 (8-ounce) brick Feta cheese, sliced lengthwise into $1/2$-inch-thick slices

1 shallot, finely diced

4 cloves garlic, shaved

$1/2$ cup Garlic-Herb Butter (see page 205)

2 cherry tomatoes, halved

Basil leaves, for garnish

Chive Oil, for garnish (see page 218)

Balsamic Glaze, for garnish (see page 213)

SERVES 4

QUICK TIP: HEIRLOOM TOMATOES
Heirloom tomatoes are open-pollinated, non-hybrid, stabilized varieties over fifty years old. They yield the best possible flavor. Common varieties are the Amana Orange, Green Grape, Green Zebra, Brandywine, Mortgage Lifter, Red Pear, Yellow Pear, Soldacki, San Marzano, Pruden's Purple, White Wonder, Persimmon, Stupice, Cherokee Purple, and Costoluto Genovese varieties. If you can't find them, you may substitute vine-ripened tomatoes in most dishes.

Bouquet Prawn Skewer with Olive Oil, Basil, Rosemary & Dill

As I mentioned on the episode of The Kitchens of Biró *that featured this appetizer, skewers can be fashioned from metal, wood, plastic, and even porcelain. I most often use bamboo or edible skewers, such as in this recipe, where I use rosemary sprigs as skewers. The rosemary sprigs not only hold the prawns perfectly during the cooking process but, more importantly, they infuse the shellfish with flavor from the inside, which when combined with the aromatic herbs brushed on their surface, yields an incredible flavor.*

WINE PAIRING *1999 Domaine de la Bongrand (Jean Thevenet), Macon Clesse, Burgundy, France*
2002 Château Gaudrelle, Vouvray, Loire, France

16 blue or tiger prawns

8 sprigs rosemary

8 tablespoons extra virgin olive oil, divided

2 shallots, diced

1 ounce chopped basil

1 tablespoon chopped dill

2 tablespoons white wine

2 cups mesclun greens

SERVES 4

1. Clean the prawns, keeping the tails on.

2. Remove all but the top quarter of blooms from the rosemary sprigs. Reserve the blooms. Skewer the bare end of the stalks through the prawns, placing two prawns on each skewer.

3. Heat 4 tablespoons of the olive oil in a large sauté pan and sauté the shallots until glossy. Add the prawn skewers and sauté on both sides until the prawns become reddish, about 1 to 2 minutes. Remove the prawn skewers from the pan and reserve the pan and drippings. Add the remaining 4 tablespoons olive oil, basil, dill, and the reserved rosemary blooms to the pan and cook for 1 minute. Pour in the white wine and remove from heat.

PRESENTATION

Place mesclun greens in the center of each serving plate. Top with two prawn skewers each and drizzle with the herb-wine mixture.

QUICK TIP: CLEANING SHRIMP OR PRAWNS

Most home and aspiring professional chefs I teach know how to remove the shell from a shrimp or prawn but stop before it's truly clean. Here's how to do it right. Begin at the shrimp's legs, as it's the weakest point of the shell, and pull the shell off. It will usually come off in segments rather than one or two pieces, so repeat this process until all the shell is removed. At the restaurant, we never discard the shells, as we use them to make stocks and soups and even to infuse oils.

Now is your time to make a decision. Will you leave the tail on or remove it? For a dish like this one, or for a finger food, I like to leave the tail on so the guest can hold onto it during eating. If you're going to remove the tail, do so now by simply pulling it off. We're not done yet, as the intestinal vein must now be removed, and this is a step that's often overlooked. The intestinal vein is the dark grey or black thread that can be found on the shrimp's spine. Using a knife, score the shrimp's spine and pull the vein out, removing any other dark spots you may find near the vein. Now rinse the shrimp under cold running water to remove any remaining dirt, and you're ready to go.

Bouquet Prawn Skewer with
Olive Oil, Basil, Rosemary & Dill

Tarte Flambée with Crème Fraîche, Onion & Smoked Bacon

Tarte Flambée, also called Flammenküche, is an Alsatian specialty that resembles an extremely thin-crust pizza and translates to "flame cake" because of the high heat at which it's cooked. It can be topped with a variety of sweet or savory items. This is the most traditional tarte flambée in Alsace and one of the most popular at Biró.

WINE PAIRING *2001 Domaine Marcel Deiss, Pinot Blanc, Alsace, France*
2001 Trimbach, Riesling "Cuvée Frédéric-Emile," Alsace, France

1 Tarte Flambée Crust
(see page 208)

$1/4$ cup crème fraîche

$1/2$ cup quark

$1/2$ teaspoon Hungarian paprika

Sea salt

$1/2$ cup diced yellow onion

4 slices smoked bacon, diced

Chopped parsley, for garnish

MAKES 1 TARTE

1. Preheat oven to 450 degrees.

2. Place the Tarte Flambée Crust on a sheet pan lined with parchment paper.

3. In a small mixing bowl, combine the crème fraîche, quark, paprika, and salt to taste. Using a rubber spatula or large spoon, spread the mixture over the crust.

4. Cover evenly with the onion and bacon and place in oven.

5. Bake until the edges of the tarte are golden brown, about 5 minutes. Cut and serve immediately.

PRESENTATION

At Biró Wine Bar, in the restaurant's lower level, we serve this dish traditionally, which is on a wooden board. You could use a cutting board, carefully sliding the tarte from the parchment paper onto the board and then slicing into pieces. Garnish with a sprinkle of parsley. This is a rustic dish, so your guests should feel free to roll and eat it with their hands.

QUICK TIP: ALTERNATE SAVORY TARTE TOPPINGS
We serve several dozen different types of Tarte Flambées, and you may wish to experiment with these popular savory toppings: Gruyère, Baby Spinach & Heirloom Tomato; Manchego, Parmesan, Cabrales Blue & Quark Cheeses; Chicken, Pesto & Manchego.

QUICK TIP: WHAT'S QUARK?
Quark is a smooth, soft German cheese with a light, tangy flavor. It's popping up in more and more specialty groceries in the U.S., but if you have trouble locating it, you can substitute cream cheese for it in this recipe. You would need to thin the cream cheese with 2 tablespoons heavy cream and eliminate the crème fraîche. Or you can simply use the crème fraîche on its own.

Peekytoe Crab Cakes on Grilled Chicory with Roasted-Red-Pepper Coulis

Peekytoe crabs are blue Maine rock crabs, also called bay crabs. They have exceptional pink meat with a delicate sweet flavor. You could use any sweet, succulent crab for this dish.

We use a two-ounce ladle to portion the crab cakes and freeze the cakes before frying so they maintain their shape better during the cooking process.

WINE PAIRING *2001 Vine Cliff, Chardonnay, Napa Valley, California*
2001 Domaine de la Bongrand (Jean Thevenet), Mâcon Cleese, Burgundy, France

FOR THE PEEKYTOE CRAB CAKES

1. Remove excess water from the crabmeat by pressing it between paper towels. Dice the meat and then place it in a medium mixing bowl. Add the mayonnaise, mustard, lemon juice, shallots, parsley, dill, cayenne pepper, and paprika and combine. Season to taste with salt and pepper. Allow to rest at room temperature for 10 minutes to let the flavors infuse. Adjust seasoning, if necessary.

2. Using a two-ounce ladle, scoop out the crab cake mixture. Drop the mixture onto a Silpat-lined sheet pan and flatten into uniform cakes. Repeat the process to create eight crab cakes. Place the cakes in the freezer for 20 to 30 minutes.

3. Preheat oven to 400 degrees. Place the flour in a shallow dish. In a second shallow dish, whip the eggs and milk together to create an eggwash. Place the breadcrumbs in a third shallow dish.

7. Remove the crab cakes from the freezer and dredge the first cake in the flour. Tap off all excess flour, and then place the cake into the eggwash; cover completely. Remove the cake from the eggwash, gently shaking off any excess, and place it in the breadcrumbs. Completely coat the cake in breadcrumbs and then remove it from the dish, tapping the cake to remove all excess. Repeat the process with the remaining cakes.

8. Melt the oil and butter in a large ovenproof sauté pan over high heat. Place the crab cakes in the pan, making certain there's room between cakes to allow air to circulate, and sauté until golden brown, about 1 minute on each side. Place the pan in the oven and bake until cooked through, about 4 to 5 minutes.

FOR THE GRILLED CHICORY

1. Cut the end off the chicory. Remove the leaves and place them in a bowl of lukewarm water. Add the lemon juice and allow the leaves to soak for 2 minutes. Remove from water and pat dry with a paper towel.

2. Heat a grill or grill pan on high heat. Place the chicory leaves on the grill to wilt slightly and create grill marks. Remove from heat.

PRESENTATION

Place four chicory leaves in the center of each serving plate to create a star shape. Place two crab cakes in the center of each star and spoon Roasted-Red-Pepper Coulis around the plate's perimeter.

PEEKYTOE CRAB CAKES

1 pound peekytoe crabmeat

2 tablespoons mayonnaise

2 teaspoons Dijon mustard

1 teaspoon lemon juice

2 shallots, minced

$1/2$ tablespoon chopped parsley

1 teaspoon chopped dill

1 teaspoon cayenne pepper

1 teaspoon Hungarian paprika

Sea salt

Freshly ground black pepper

2 cups flour

2 large eggs

$1/2$ cup whole milk

2 cups plain breadcrumbs

2 tablespoons extra virgin olive oil

2 tablespoons unsalted butter

GRILLED CHICORY

1 chicory

2 tablespoons lemon juice

DISH

Roasted-Red-Pepper Coulis (see page 217)

SERVES 4

QUICK TIP: PREPARING THE CHICORY WITHOUT A GRILL PAN

If you don't have a grill pan with ridges or a stovetop grill, no problem. Simply heat 1 tablespoon olive oil over high heat and sauté the leaves until they wilt slightly and become crispy around the edges, about 1 to 2 minutes.

Herb-Quark Soufflé with Glazed Carrots

This easy-to-create soufflé is so versatile. Served in individual soufflé dishes as an appetizer, it's a light and delicious prelude to any meal. Prepared in a large soufflé dish, it makes a glorious addition to a brunch. Or served with a piece of fish, it becomes an elegant entrée. If you can't find quark, substitute whole-milk ricotta cheese. Light ricotta contains too much water and would cause the soufflé to fall. Before using, place the ricotta in cheesecloth and squeeze the water from it.

WINE PAIRING *2003 Robert Sinskey Vineyards, Los Carneros Pinot Blanc, Napa, California*
2002 Cape Mentelle, Semillon Sauvignon Blanc, Margaret River, Australia

Unsalted butter

Flour

1 pound quark

6 eggs, separated

$^1/_3$ cup grated Parmesan cheese

3 tablespoons minced parsley, divided

3 tablespoons minced chives, divided

Sea salt

Freshly ground black pepper

Freshly ground nutmeg

1 tablespoon lemon juice

2 tablespoons sugar, divided

1 tablespoon cornstarch

2 tablespoons unsalted butter, plus more for the ramekins

1 pound baby carrots

2 shallots, julienned

$^1/_2$ cup Vegetable Stock (see page 215)

SERVES 8

1. Preheat oven to 400 degrees.

2. Butter 8 (4-ounce) soufflé dishes or ramekins and lightly dust with flour. Refrigerate.

3. In a large mixing bowl, combine the quark, egg yolks, Parmesan, 2 tablespoons parsley, and 2 tablespoons chives. Season to taste with salt, pepper, and nutmeg.

4. In a small mixing bowl or stand mixer, whisk together the egg whites, a pinch of salt, lemon juice, a pinch of sugar, and the cornstarch to form stiff peaks. Carefully fold into the quark mixture just to combine. Remove the soufflé dishes from the refrigerator and fill each two-thirds full with the mixture. Bake in a bain-marie (see Quick Tip page 185) until the soufflé has risen and is golden brown, about 25 to 30 minutes.

5. Meanwhile, melt the butter in a large covered sauté pan over medium heat. Sauté the carrots and shallots until glossy. Add the remaining sugar and melt until liquified. Season to taste with salt and pepper. Pour in stock and cook, covered, until the carrots are softened, about 8 to 10 minutes. Adjust seasoning if necessary and add the remaining 1 tablespoon parsley and 1 tablespoon chives.

PRESENTATION

Remove the soufflés from the oven and, working quickly, place each on a small serving plate. Spoon Glazed Carrots around the ramekins and serve immediately.

Pine Nut–Crusted Soft-Shell Crab with Tomato-Cumin Vinaigrette

We introduced this appetizer at Biró in the spring of 2003, and it immediately became one of the menu's best sellers. The sweet richness of the soft-shell crab is cut by the acidity of the tomato and slight bite of the cumin. The result? Cleaned plates every time.

WINE PAIRING *NV Roederer Estate, Brut, Anderson Valley, California*
2002 Newton Vineyards, Chardonnay Unfiltered, Napa, California

FOR THE PINE NUT–CRUSTED SOFT-SHELL CRABS

1. Mix the flour and pine nuts together and season to taste with salt and pepper. Dredge the soft-shell crabs in the flour mixture.

2. Heat the oil in a sauté pan over high heat and add the coated crabs. Sauté until golden brown, about 3 minutes on each side. Remove from the pan and season with salt.

FOR THE TOMATO-CUMIN VINAIGRETTE

1. In a small mixing bowl, whisk together the cumin, vinegar, and tomato juice. Slowly whisk in the oil to emulsify. Add the chives and season to taste with salt and pepper.

PRESENTATION

Cut each crab in half. Place a small mound of baby greens in the center of each serving plate. Place one crab half, cut side down, atop the greens. Lean the other crab half against it. Drizzle with vinaigrette and garnish the plate with a dusting of cumin.

PINE NUT-CRUSTED SOFT-SHELL CRABS

2 tablespoons flour

1/4 cup toasted pine nuts, ground

Sea salt

Freshly ground black pepper

4 soft-shell crabs

1 1/2 tablespoons extra virgin olive oil

TOMATO-CUMIN VINAIGRETTE

1 tablespoon toasted cumin seeds, ground

1 tablespoon white wine vinegar

1 tablespoon tomato juice

1/2 cup extra virgin olive oil

1 tablespoon chopped chives

Sea salt

Freshly ground black pepper

DISH

Baby greens, for garnish

Ground cumin, for garnish

SERVES 4

White Asparagus Pizzetti with Gravad Lachs, Baby Spinach & Crème Fraîche

This light and versatile German-inspired dish is from Biró's spring menu. While it is excellent as an appetizer, it would also work wonderfully as part of a Champagne brunch. If you make the crusts smaller or simply slice the full-size pizzettis, it would be fantastic as an hors d'oeuvre at an elegantly simple party.

WINE PAIRING *2001 Ferrari-Carano Winery, Fumé Blanc, Sonoma, California*
2000 Domaine R. & V. Dauvissat, Chablis Les Clos, Burgundy, France

PIZZETTI DOUGH

1 pound flour

1 ounce fresh yeast

$1/_8$ teaspoon sea salt

1 cup lukewarm water

1 large egg

2 tablespoons extra virgin olive oil

DISH

8 white asparagus spears, peeled and cooked

7 ounces thinly sliced gravad lachs, torn

1 cup lightly packed baby spinach, stems removed

5 ounces crème fraîche

Extra virgin olive oil

Dill leaves, for garnish

6 cherry tomatoes, halved, for garnish

Wasabi tobiko, for garnish

Aïoli, for garnish (see page 205)

SERVES 4

FOR THE PIZZETTI DOUGH

1. Place the yeast in a large mixing bowl. Sprinkle 1 cup of flour over the yeast. Add the salt and one-half of the lukewarm water and mix to create a starter dough. Allow to rest for 10 minutes.

2. Add the remaining flour, egg, and olive oil. Knead, adding additional lukewarm water as needed, to create a smooth, solid dough. Cover with a cloth and allow to rest for 30 minutes.

3. Cut the dough into four equal pieces. Roll into rounds of about 5 inches in diameter and place on a sheet pan. Allow to rest for 10 minutes. Heat oven to 400 degrees.

4. Bake the pizzetti crusts until lightly golden brown, about 10 to 12 minutes.

PRESENTATION

Place the warm pizzetti crusts on serving plates. Slice the asparagus spears in half diagonally. Layer the gravad lachs, asparagus, and baby spinach atop the crusts and drizzle with crème fraîche and olive oil. Garnish with dill, cherry tomato halves topped with wasabi tobiko, and dollops of Aïoli.

Wild Scottish Salmon with Seven Salts on Mâche

This Scottish salmon is cured in a sweet blend of spices, and then served raw with a mélange of international salts, giving each bite of salmon a unique flavor. You may substitute another variety of salmon for the wild Scottish salmon, and you could sear the edges of the salmon, if you wish. This appetizer is served cold, and the salmon must be prepared one day in advance.

WINE PAIRING *1999 St. Innocent Winery, Pinot Noir, Willamette Valley, Oregon*
2001 Sonoma-Cutrer, Chardonnay, Sonoma, California

FOR THE SALMON

1. Combine the cinnamon stick, anise seed, star anise, cloves, Szechuan peppercorns, black peppercorns, and cardamom seeds in a food processor and finely grind. Transfer to a medium bowl and add the sugar, lemon balm, and dill; blend well.

2. Place the salmon on a plastic wrap–lined sheet pan and liberally coat both sides with the spice mixture. Fold the ends of the plastic wrap over the salmon and place a sheet pan on top of it. Evenly distribute weights or a heavy pan on top of the sheet pan to work the seasoning into the fish. Place in the refrigerator to cure overnight.

3. Remove the salmon from the refrigerator, discard the plastic wrap, and pat the fish dry with paper towels, removing any excess cure. Transfer the salmon to a cutting board and cut into 28 equal cubes.

FOR THE SALAD

In a food processor, combine the parsley and chives and pulse to create a rough paste. With the blender set on low, slowly add the olive oil in a thin, steady stream. Liquefy and season to taste with salt and pepper. Toss with the mâche.

PRESENTATION

I like to serve this dish on rectangular plates, but round will work as well. Line seven salmon cubes down the center of each serving plate if using rectangular plates and around the perimeter if using round plates. If using a rectangular plate, place a small mound of mâche next to each salmon cube and garnish the other side of each cube with a different $1/4$-teaspoon pile of sea salt. If using a round plate, place the salad in the middle and the salt on the outer edge of each salmon cube. You could also place the salts directly on the salmon cubes.

QUICK TIP: INTERNATIONAL SALTS

Anyone who attends my classes, watches my show, or eats at my restaurants quickly learns that I love working with salts from around the world. I favor sea salt, which is extracted from sea water through evaporation, in most of my recipes because it has a pure, clean flavor. I also use kosher salt, tenderizing salt, and house-made seasoned salts on a daily basis, but it's the impressive array of unique salts that have recently found their way to the American marketplace that have me really excited. To find the international salts cited in this recipe and throughout this book, you could scour specialty groceries and beg friends in other countries to send you the goods, like I used to, or simply contact Salt Traders (see page 219), the finest salt purveyor I've found in the U.S. They carry all the salts cited in this recipe and throughout the book. Experiment with different salts and see just how dramatically they can affect the flavor profiles of your favorite foods.

WILD SCOTTISH SALMON
1 cinnamon stick

$1/4$ tablespoon anise seed

$1/4$ teaspoon whole star anise

$1/2$ teaspoon cloves

$1/4$ teaspoon Szechuan peppercorns

$1/4$ teaspoon black peppercorns

$1/2$ teaspoon cardamom seeds

2 tablespoons sugar

$3/4$ ounce lemon balm, chopped

$1/4$ bunch dill, stemmed and chopped

2 pounds Scottish salmon filets, cleaned

MÂCHE SALAD
$1/2$ bunch parsley, stemmed and chopped

$1/2$ bunch chives, chopped

1 tablespoon extra virgin olive oil

Sea salt

Freshly ground black pepper

1 pound mâche

DISH
1 teaspoon Australian Murray River salt flakes

1 teaspoon Danish Viking smoked sea salt

1 teaspoon sel gris with herbs

1 teaspoon sel gris with seaweed

1 teaspoon Hawaiian black lava sea salt

1 teaspoon red alae clay sea salt

1 teaspoon Peruvian pink sea salt

SERVES 4

Napa Cabbage Rolls with Sweetbreads, Prawns & Spicy Mustard Seed Vinaigrette

This appetizer has been extremely popular with both sides of the sweetbread divide: those who know and love sweetbreads, and those who don't quite know what they are but are brave enough to give them a try anyway. (A third group, comprised of those who swear they won't touch sweetbreads, quickly falls into one of the two aforementioned categories after someone at their table tries these delicious rolls and begins to rave.)

Prepare the sweetbreads a day or two ahead of time. Make certain to dice your sweetbreads, prawns, apple, and tomato evenly so the texture of the filling is uniform. If you can't find togarashi, a hot Japanese chile, substitute the chile of your choice.

WINE PAIRING *2001 Domaine Délétang, Montlouis, Loire, France*
2000 Sanford & Benedict Vineyards, Foxen Pinot Noir, Santa Barbara, California

SWEETBREADS
1 pound sweetbreads

1 quart White Veal Stock (see page 215), cold

1 Bouquet Garni (see page 204)

1 small yellow onion, chopped

1 carrot, peeled and chopped

1 stalk celery, chopped

1 tablespoon sea salt

PRAWNS
2 tablespoons extra virgin olive oil

1 pound prawns, peeled and cleaned

1 tablespoon minced garlic

1 tablespoon minced shallots

1 teaspoon saffron seeds

Sea salt

Freshly ground black pepper

SPICY MUSTARD SEED VINAIGRETTE
1 tablespoon mustard seeds

1 tablespoon soy sauce

1 tablespoon white wine vinegar

1 teaspoon cumin

1 teaspoon cayenne pepper

2 teaspoons togarashi

1 tablespoon orange juice

1 teaspoon ground gingerroot

1 tablespoon sesame oil

Sea salt

Freshly ground black pepper

CABBAGE
1 head Napa cabbage

1 tablespoon salt

FILLING
1 Granny Smith apple, peeled and cored

1 teaspoon lemon juice

1 vine-ripened tomato, peeled, seeded, and diced

Diced sweetbreads

Diced prawns

1 tablespoon Spicy Mustard Seed Vinaigrette

SERVES 4

FOR THE SWEETBREADS

1. Soak the sweetbreads in cold water to cover for at least 5 hours, or overnight, until they become white. Change the water two or three times until it remains clear. Rinse the soaked sweetbreads under cold running water.

2. Place the stock, Bouquet Garni, onion, carrot, celery, sweetbreads, and salt in a large stockpot. Over low heat, slowly bring to a boil. Remove the pot from the heat and allow the sweetbreads to infuse in the liquid for 30 minutes.

3. Remove the sweetbreads from the liquid, detach excess membrane from them, and refresh them under cold running water. Dry the sweetbreads and allow them to cool to room temperature. Refrigerate overnight and then dice.

FOR THE PRAWNS

In a large sauté pan, heat the oil over high heat. Add the prawns, garlic, shallots, and saffron seeds and sauté until the prawns are pink and cooked through, about 3 minutes. Season to taste with salt and pepper. Allow to cool and then dice.

FOR THE SPICY MUSTARD SEED VINAIGRETTE

Place the mustard seeds, soy sauce, vinegar, cumin, cayenne pepper, togarashi, orange juice, and gingerroot in a food processor or blender and purée. Add the sesame oil to emulsify. Season to taste with salt and pepper and allow to rest for 10 minutes. Adjust seasoning if necessary.

FOR THE CABBAGE

1. Cut the cabbage into quarters and remove its core. Peel the leaves into a bowl of ice water.

2. Bring a pot of salted water to a boil and blanch the leaves for 10 to 15 seconds. Remove from the water, drain, and immediately plunge into an ice bath. Remove and dry.

FOR THE FILLING

1. Dice the apple and sprinkle with lemon juice to help preserve color.

2. In a small mixing bowl, combine the diced apple, tomato, sweetbreads, and prawns; drizzle with Spicy Mustard Seed Vinaigrette, reserving 1/4 cup. Toss to coat.

PRESENTATION

Center the filling on the cabbage leaves. Tucking in the short ends, roll the cabbage leaves. Cut them on a diagonal and place them on the serving plates of your choice. Drizzle with a bit of the remaining vinaigrette, about 1 tablespoon per serving.

QUICK TIP: WHAT ARE SWEETBREADS?

Sweetbreads are the thymus glands and the pancreas of calves, lambs, and pigs. They have a silky texture and mild flavor, and in this recipe, I use calf sweetbreads. Ask your butcher for just the top portion of the sweetbreads, which is generally referred to as the "heart" lobe. It's much smoother than the lower, or "throat" lobe, though both could be used in this recipe.

Spinach Torte with Parmesan, Thyme & Roasted-Red-Pepper Coulis

This simple appetizer is packed with flavor. It is delicious served warm or cold and is also great for breakfast.

WINE PAIRING *2001 Domaine des Amouriers, Vacqueyras, Rhône, France*
2000 Albert Belle, Crozes Hermitage Cuvee Les Pierrelles, Rhône, France

1. Preheat oven to 350 degrees.

2. Cut each pastry sheet into a 7-inch round and poke holes in it with a fork.

3. In a medium sauté pan, melt the butter over high heat. Add the onions and garlic and sauté until glossy, about 1 minute. Add the spinach and thyme and sauté for 2 additional minutes. Season to taste with salt, pepper, and nutmeg. Remove from heat and allow to cool.

4. Add the ricotta, Parmesan, and 2 eggs to the cooled spinach mixture and mix well to combine. Allow to rest for 5 minutes and adjust seasoning as necessary.

5. Butter a 7-inch-round cake pan and place one of the phyllo rounds into it. Top with one-half the spinach mixture. With the back of a tablespoon, make four indentations in the mixture and fill each with a yolk. Cover with a second phyllo round and the remaining spinach mixture. Make four indentations in the mixture and fill each with a yolk. Cover with the third phyllo round. Lightly brush the pastry with butter and bake on the lowest oven rack until cooked through, about 50 minutes. Turn off heat and allow the torte to cool in the oven.

PRESENTATION

Slice the torte into six equal pieces and place on individual serving plates. Spoon Roasted-Red-Pepper Coulis around the slice and garnish with a sprig of thyme and a sprinkling of pine nuts.

3 sheets phyllo pastry

2 tablespoons unsalted butter, plus more for the pan

2 medium yellow onions, diced

2 cloves garlic, diced

3 pounds baby spinach, stemmed

1 tablespoon chopped thyme

Sea salt

Freshly ground black pepper

Freshly ground nutmeg

1 pound ricotta cheese

$1/4$ cup finely grated Parmesan cheese

2 large eggs

8 large egg yolks

1 cup Roasted-Red-Pepper Coulis (see page 217)

6 sprigs thyme, for garnish

$1/2$ ounce roasted pine nuts, for garnish

SERVES 6

Decorative "Apple" &
"Watermelon" Sushi

Decorative "Apple" & "Watermelon" Sushi

This recipe was featured on my favorite episode of The Kitchens of Biró, *Season One. On this episode, I was joined by my very good restaurateur friend from Germany, Chef Robert Rauh, for the first Sushi Night at Biró. It was Robert who first introduced me to sushi, and it was great to have his expertise and humor in the kitchen on such a busy night. This fun dish lends itself to good times. Kick back with some friends and a glass of sake and enjoy.*

WINE PAIRING *2002 Dr. Loosen Ürzinger Würtzgarten, Riesling Spätlese, Mosel, Germany*
NV Hakutsuru, "Junmai Dai Ginjo" Sake, Kobe, Japan

FOR THE SUSHI RICE

1. Prepare the rice in a rice cooker or covered pot per the package instructions.

2. In a saucepan, bring the sugar, salt, vinegar, and wine to a boil over medium heat. When the sugar is dissolved, remove from heat.

3. Place the cooked rice in a nonreactive bowl and pour the vinegar mixture over it. Mix well and allow to cool.

4. Roll one-half of the rice into balls the size and shape of golf balls. Shape the remaining rice into triangles resembling watermelon wedges.

FOR THE APPLE SUSHI

Cover the rice balls with the sliced salmon.

FOR THE WATERMELON SUSHI

1. Cut the cucumber in half lengthwise. Remove the seeds. Cut it into sections resembling watermelon rinds.

2. Cover the rice wedges with the ahi tuna.

PRESENTATION

Place one mint leaf on top of each salmon ball so that it resembles an apple. Place a cucumber "rind" on the bottom of each tuna wedge. Garnish the wedges with sesame seeds to resemble watermelon seeds. I like to arrange the decorative sushi on either a square white plate or on a footed wooden board and serve with a small bowl of soy sauce for dipping.

QUICK TIP: SUSHI TOOLS

Many people assume that to make sushi they need a lot of special tools and equipment. Not true. In fact, there are only a few items I suggest having on hand to make sushi.

Rice Cooker:
A rice cooker is a good investment. It will keep your rice at the perfect temperature and will produce rice of a consistent quality.

Quality Chef's Knife:
A good, sharp chef's knife is key. It will enable you to slice your fish paper thin and will also ensure nice, even cuts when slicing sushi rolls.

Bamboo Mat:
Bamboo mats are flexible and nonstick. They'll enable you to roll your sushi tightly and effortlessly.

Bamboo Spoon:
A bamboo spoon is an inexpensive investment that will make your job a lot easier. Rice doesn't stick to it, so when seasoning your rice for sushi, the grains stay where they are supposed to.

Paper Fan:
I joke that a cheap paper fan serves two purposes: it enables you to quickly cool your rice to a lukewarm temperature suitable for handling, and it's also good for cooling the chef down when the kitchen gets too hot.

Just remember, nothing is as important to your sushi as fresh ingredients.

SUSHI RICE

$3/4$ cup Boton rice

3 tablespoons sugar

2 teaspoons sea salt

$2/3$ cup sushi vinegar

$1/3$ cup rice wine

APPLE SUSHI

4 ounces smoked salmon, thinly sliced

Small mint leaves, for garnish

WATERMELON SUSHI

4 ounces ahi tuna, minced

1 European cucumber

1 tablespoon black sesame seeds

SERVES 4

Fennel Gratinée with Pears

Robust, anise-flavored fennel is splendidly offset by the sweet, delicate succulence of pears in this elegant presentation. We use Williams' Bon pears, which are more on the tart-sweet side, for this dish, but you can experiment with different varieties. With more than 5,000 to choose from, Fennel Gratinée with Pears can be reinvented many times over!

Whole-milk ricotta cheese can be substituted for the quark in this recipe.

WINE PAIRING *NV Moët & Chandon, White Star, Epernay, France*
2000 Henschke, Keyneton Estate Shiraz, Eden Valley, Australia

$1^3/_4$ pounds fennel

$1^1/_3$ pounds ripe pears

4 tablespoons lemon juice

Unsalted butter

4 eggs, separated

Sea salt

8 ounces quark

5 ounces Gorgonzola cheese

Freshly ground black pepper

SERVES 4

1. Clean the fennel, reserving the greens. Slice the bulbs on a mandoline into $1/_8$-inch-thick slices.

2. Bring a medium stockpot of lightly salted water to a boil over high heat. Add the fennel slices and cook for 5 minutes. Remove and plunge into an ice bath. When cooled, remove and pat dry with paper towels.

3. Cut the pears in half and remove the core. Cut lengthwise into $1/_4$-inch-thick slices. Drizzle with lemon juice.

4. Preheat oven to 400 degrees. Butter a shallow 3-quart casserole.

5. In a mixing bowl or stand mixer, whisk the egg whites with a pinch of salt to form stiff peaks. In a medium mixing bowl, combine the yolks, quark, and Gorgonzola and season to taste with salt and pepper.

6. Carefully fold the egg whites under the yolk-cheese mixture. Mix half of this mixture with the fennel and place in the bottom of the casserole. Layer with the pear slices and spread the remaining half of the yolk-cheese mixture over the pears. Bake uncovered on the second-from-the-top rack of the oven for 30 minutes, or until the gratinée is browned. If it becomes too brown, cover it during the last 10 minutes of cooking.

PRESENTATION

This dish looks lovely served family style or sliced and placed on individual serving plates. Chop the reserved fennel greens and use as a garnish.

Marinated Sea Bass with Avocado–Pearl Onion Ragoût

This sweet-and-sour appetizer is fantastic on its own or served atop crostini.

WINE PAIRING *2002 Newton Vineyards, Chardonnay Unfiltered, Napa, California*
2001 Lucien Albrecht, Tokay Pinot Gris "Vieilles Vignes," Alsace, France

FOR THE MARINADE

Place the soy sauce, mirin, orange juice, rice vinegar, cider vinegar, lemon juice, cayenne pepper, and gingerroot in a food processor or blender and process. Slowly add the sesame oil to emulsify.

FOR THE SEA BASS

1. Rinse the sea bass under cold running water. Pat dry with paper towels and place the filets in the marinade. Allow to marinate at room temperature for 15 minutes.

2. Remove the sea bass from the marinade, reserving $1/4$ cup of the marinade, and pat the fish dry with a paper towel. Dredge the filets in the flour.

3. Heat oven to 350 degrees.

4. Melt the oil and butter in a medium sauté pan over high heat. Sauté the filets for 1 minute on each side. Transfer filets from the sauté pan to a baking rack placed inside a roasting pan, but keep the sauté pan and its drippings for later use. Bake the filets for 5 minutes.

FOR THE AVOCADO–PEARL ONION RAGOÛT

Wipe excess fat out of the pan in which you sautéed the sea bass and add the sesame oil. Heat the pan over high heat. Add the avocado, onions, and pepper and sauté for 1 minute. Add the $1/4$ cup reserved marinade and sauté for an additional 1 minute.

PRESENTATION

Slice the sea bass filet into four equal portions and place on individual serving plates. Top with the Avocado–Pearl Onion Ragoût and garnish with mâche.

MARINADE

$1/2$ cup soy sauce

$1/2$ cup mirin

$1/4$ cup orange juice

$1/8$ cup rice vinegar

$1/8$ cup cider vinegar

1 tablespoon lemon juice

3 tablespoons cayenne pepper

1 tablespoon ground gingerroot

$1/2$ cup sesame oil

SEA BASS

1 (1-pound) sea bass filet

$1/2$ cup flour

1 tablespoon extra virgin olive oil

1 tablespoon unsalted butter

AVOCADO–PEARL ONION RAGOÛT

2 tablespoons sesame oil

1 avocado, diced

8 ounces pickled pearl onions

1 tablespoon diced roasted red pepper

DISH

Mâche, for garnish

SERVES 4

Gorgonzola-Risotto Quenelles with Tomato Glaze

In this delectable appetizer, Gorgonzola—in all its rich, pungent glory—is covered with herbed risotto and then lightly breaded and deep fried. The result is a crunchy and then creamy-tender mouth-feel sure to leave your guests wanting more.

WINE PAIRING *2003 Kiona Vineyard, White Riesling, Yakima Valley, Washington*
2001 Ponzi, Pinot Gris, Willamette, Oregon

3 tablespoons extra virgin olive oil

1 clove garlic, diced

1 shallot, diced

1 cup arborio rice

1 tablespoon chopped rosemary

3 cups Vegetable Stock
(see page 215)

Sea salt

Freshly ground black pepper

4 cups vegetable oil

2 ounces Gorgonzola, cut into
$1/4$-inch-thick dices

1 cup breadcrumbs

Tomato Glaze (see page 218)

Micro greens, for garnish

SERVES 4

1. Heat the olive oil in a medium covered sauté pan over high heat. Add the garlic and shallot and sauté until glossy, about 1 minute. Add the rice and rosemary and sauté for 1 additional minute. Deglaze with the stock. Reduce heat to medium and simmer, covered, for 20 minutes. Season to taste with salt and pepper and allow to cool.

2. Heat vegetable oil to 375 degrees in a deep fryer or deep sauté pan.

3. Press one Gorgonzola dice inside a small mound of cooled rice and form a quenelle (egg) shape with your hands. Press tightly so that the Gorgonzola is completely covered and the rice is compact. You could form it into a ball instead. Repeat the process to form sixteen quenelles.

4. Place the breadcrumbs in a shallow dish and dredge each quenelle in it, completely covering the rice. Tap gently to remove excess breadcrumbs.

5. Fry the quenelles until golden brown, about 4 minutes. Drain on paper towels.

PRESENTATION

Place four quenelles on each serving plate. Spoon Tomato Glaze for dipping onto each plate. Garnish with micro greens. Serve immediately.

Roasted Artichokes with Garlic, Sun-Dried Tomatoes & Goat Cheese

This Mediterranean-inspired dish is simply heavenly. I like to serve it as a rustic appetizer with crusty bread to sop up every last bit of the infused olive oil. If you toss the dish with pasta, it becomes an entrée. Either way, this recipe is sure to become one of your favorites.

If you don't wish to trim the artichokes yourself, use high-quality, unmarinated canned artichokes.

WINE PAIRING *2001 Robert Sinskey Vineyards, Three Amigos Chardonnay, Napa Valley, California*
2001 Newton Vineyards, Chardonnay Unfiltered, Napa Valley, California

1. Preheat oven to 325 degrees.

2. Take the first artichoke and bend the tough outer leaves backward until they break at the point where the tough leaf meets the tender base. Stop when you reach the more tender yellow-green interior leaves. With a serrated knife, cut across the top of the artichoke where the color changes from yellow-green to dark green. Trim the base, removing any discoloration. Halve the artichoke lengthwise and scoop out the hairy choke with a spoon and discard. Place the trimmed artichoke into a large nonreactive bowl and drizzle with lemon juice to prevent oxidation. Repeat the process with the five remaining artichokes, tossing the artichokes in the bowl so they are completely coated in juice.

3. Place the artichokes and juice in a roasting pan. Add the oil, garlic, sun-dried tomatoes, thyme, bay leaf, and salt and pepper to taste. Bring to a boil over medium heat, stirring occasionally. Transfer to the oven and bake until the artichokes are browned in spots and tender when pierced, about 35 minutes. Allow to cool slightly and then cut each artichoke lengthwise into quarters.

PRESENTATION

Divide the Roasted Artichokes, Garlic, and Sun-Dried Tomatoes evenly among the serving plates, removing the bay leaf, and drizzle with the infused oil. Crumble goat cheese atop the servings and broil until the cheese is browned, about 1 minute.

6 medium artichokes

$1/3$ cup lemon juice

$2/3$ cup extra virgin olive oil

1 large head garlic, peeled

$1/2$ cup julienned sun-dried tomatoes

1 teaspoon minced thyme

1 Turkish bay leaf

Sea salt

Freshly ground black pepper

10 ounces goat cheese

SERVES 6

Silky White & Green Asparagus Soup

soups

Chilled Black Cherry Soup with Brandy
& Crème Fraîche

Silky White & Green Asparagus Soup

Lobster Bisque with Pesto

Butternut Squash Soup
with Curried Apple Chutney

Rich Garlic Crème with Croûtons
& Parmesan Crown

Wild Mushroom Consommé
with Duck Ravioli

Gazpacho

Watercress Soup with Fried Leek

Heirloom Tomato Soup with Basil,
Crème Fraîche & Roquefort Crown

Potato Crème with Veal Croûtons
& White Truffle Oil

Beef Consommé with Thyme & Quenelles

Ramp "Cappuccino"

Summer Corn Soup with Sun-Dried Tomato Purée

Spring Pea Soup with Mint & Crème Fraîche

Misó

Carrot-Ginger Soup with Parsley Oil

Sweet-&-Sour Lentil Soup

Roasted-Peach Soup with
Smoked Bacon & Fried Arugula

Braised-Oxtail Soup

Saffron Shrimp-Leek Soup

Chilled Black Cherry Soup with Brandy & Crème Fraîche

This soup is inspired by childhood summers spent at my grandparents' farm outside of Budapest, where black cherries dangle abundantly from gnarled trees. It perfectly captures the sun-drenched flavors of summer and is as simple to make as it is refreshing to eat. It is the ideal prelude to any warm-weather meal, but I especially like it served before pork or filet mignon.

You may use canned cherries for this recipe, but the flavor of your soup will not be as intense, nor the color as vibrant.

WINE PAIRING *NV Iron Horse, Brut, Sonoma, California*
2001 Rene Mure, Pinot Blanc Rouffach, Alsace, France

$1^1/_2$ pounds ripe black cherries, unpitted, divided

$^2/_3$ cup fruity white wine

1 cinnamon stick

$^2/_3$ cup water

2 tablespoons sugar

Zest and juice of 1 lemon

$1^1/_4$ cups crème fraîche, divided

2 tablespoons brandy

SERVES 4

1. Remove the stems and pits from the cherries but do not discard. Place one-half of the pits in a clean kitchen towel or freezer bag and crush them with a mallet. Keep the other half of the pits intact.

2. In a large saucepan, combine the crushed pits, whole pits, stems, wine, cinnamon, water, sugar, lemon peel, and lemon juice. Bring to a boil over medium heat; cover and simmer for 10 minutes.

3. Remove from heat and strain the liquid through a fine-mesh sieve. Return the strained liquid to the pan. Stir in 1 cup of the crème fraîche and all but one-quarter of the cherries. Allow to simmer over medium-low heat for 5 minutes, whisking occasionally.

4. In a food processor or blender, purée the cherry mixture until smooth. Refrigerate until cool, and then whisk in the brandy. Chill until ready to serve.

PRESENTATION

Because of its vibrant color, I suggest serving this soup in a plain white bowl or chilled, clear glass bowl or cup. Drizzle the remaining $^1/_4$ cup crème fraîche over the soup and garnish with the remaining cherries.

QUICK TIP: WHAT IS CRÈME FRAÎCHE?

As you can see in this book, I use crème fraîche a lot. Crème fraîche is a traditional French ingredient made of cultured cream. It is thicker, richer, and more velvety than American sour cream, and has a tangy, slightly nutty flavor. In Europe, we use unpasteurized crème fraîche that is thickened by lactic bacteria culture. In the U.S., a version of crème fraîche is pasteurized by adding a fermenting agent (such as buttermilk or sour cream) to cream. While I'm fortunate to have access to the best crème fraîche, many of my students and restaurant guests tell me they have difficulty finding it at all—or when they do it's simply too expensive. No problem. You can make it yourself (see page 206).

Chilled Black Cherry Soup
with Brandy & Crème Fraîche

Silky White & Green Asparagus Soup

QUICK TIP: WORKING WITH WHITE ASPARAGUS

Not everyone is familiar with white asparagus. Unlike green asparagus, which grows above ground, white asparagus is grown underground and is therefore woodier and requires a bit more preparation:

1. If your asparagus has dirt on it, wash but do not soak it.

2. Peel the asparagus. There are two ways of doing this. If you're afraid of snapping the asparagus spears, you can lay them on a cutting board and peel them in long strips from the tip to the base, rotating the spears as you work. Or you can do it the way I do: hold the asparagus in your hand so the tip is in your fingers and the stalk rests on your hand and wrist. Peel from the tip to the base, rotating the spears as you work. I use an asparagus peeler, as it gives me more control and preserves more of the asparagus than a regular vegetable peeler.

3. Remove the ends from the asparagus spears. You can cut the spears to uniform lengths, or you can let the asparagus tell you where it would like to be cut. The end will break at the point where it is the driest, and therefore the oldest and woodiest. You can simply snap it off and discard.

4. Cleaned asparagus can be kept refrigerated for up to three days in a damp towel, which will keep it moist and white.

Silky White & Green Asparagus Soup

I love watching people eat this soup, because without exception they are surprised at the subtle flavor differences in the two types of asparagus. Some eat one color completely and then start the other, some alternate between the two, and others stir it up to really give their taste buds a workout. If more than one person at the table has ordered it, a debate over which color is better invariably ensues. No matter how they eat it or which type of asparagus they favor, the bowls always come back empty. Try this luxurious soup and I think you'll quickly learn why.

For the White Asparagus Soup, we infused liquid from cooking the asparagus, but not the stalks themselves. Use those as a side dish or as part of a salad.

WINE PAIRING *2003 Robert Sinskey Vineyards, Pinot Blanc of Los Carneros, Napa, California*
2003 Robert Sinskey Vineyards, Vin Gris of Pinot Noir Los Carneros, Napa, California

FOR THE WHITE ASPARAGUS SOUP

1. Peel the white asparagus, reserving the peels. In a large stockpot, combine the water, lemon juice, wine, sugar, and 1 tablespoon of butter and bring to a boil. Add the asparagus. Cook until softened, about 13 minutes. Turn off the heat and remove asparagus from the water, reserving the liquid. Place the asparagus in an ice bath for a minute or two to stop the cooking process. Reserve asparagus to use in another dish preparation.

2. Place the asparagus peels in the reserved liquid and allow to infuse for 10 minutes. Pass the liquid through a fine-mesh sieve, reserving the infused asparagus water. Discard the peels.

3. In a sauté pan, heat the remaining butter and cook until melted but not colored. Add the flour, mixing until all the butter is absorbed. Whisk in the milk, cream, and 2 cups asparagus liquid and bring to a simmer. Reduce heat and cook until the flour flavor has been cooked out, about 15 minutes. Season to taste with salt and pepper.

FOR THE GREEN ASPARAGUS SOUP

1. In a large stockpot, combine the water, lemon juice, wine, sugar, and 1 tablespoon of butter and bring to a boil. Add asparagus and cook until softened, about 5 to 8 minutes. Turn off the heat and remove asparagus from the water, reserving the liquid. Place asparagus in an ice bath for a minute or two to stop the cooking process.

2. In a sauté pan, heat remaining butter until melted but not colored. Add the flour, mixing until all the butter is absorbed. Whisk in the milk, cream, and cooked green asparagus. Bring to a simmer. Reduce the heat and cook until the flour flavor has been cooked out, about 15 minutes. Remove from heat and allow to cool.

3. Pour cooled soup into a food processor or blender. Process until smooth and season to taste with salt and pepper.

PRESENTATION

In a shallow bowl, pour in the white asparagus soup. Using a ladle, carefully pour the green asparagus soup into one side of the bowl so the soup looks half white, half green. You may wish to create a swirl in the soups by inserting a fork into the green asparagus and gently pulling the green soup through the white soup in a circular motion. Garnish with parsley and serve immediately, as asparagus soup forms a "skin" when it cools.

WHITE ASPARAGUS SOUP
2 pounds white asparagus
4 cups water
Juice of $1/2$ lemon
$1/4$ cup white wine
2 tablespoons sugar
$1/2$ cup unsalted butter
1 cup flour
3 cups whole milk, cold
1 cup heavy cream, cold
Sea salt
Freshly ground white pepper

GREEN ASPARAGUS SOUP
4 cups water
Juice of $1/2$ lemon
$1/4$ cup white wine
2 tablespoons sugar
$1/2$ cup unsalted butter
2 pounds green asparagus
1 cup flour
3 cups whole milk, cold
1 cup heavy cream, cold
Sea salt
Freshly ground white pepper

DISH
Chopped parsley, for garnish
SERVES 6

Lobster Bisque with Pesto

This is our take on the traditional lobster bisque. For a variation, you may wish to make this already rich soup even more luxurious by garnishing it with a dollop of crème fraîche.

It's important to remove the meat from a lobster when it is still hot, as the fat in the meat solidifies when cooled, making it difficult to remove from its shell. Work quickly and carefully while performing step two, protecting your hands with a kitchen towel or rubber gloves.

WINE PAIRING *2001 Landmark, Overlook Chardonnay, Sonoma, California*
2002 Verget, Chablis 1er Cru "Montmains," Burgundy, France

2 live lobsters (1 pound each)

2 tablespoons extra virgin olive oil

1 yellow onion, chopped

1 carrot, peeled and chopped

1 celery stalk, chopped

1 garlic head, unpeeled and cut in half crosswise

1 Bouquet Garni with Tarragon (see page 204)

1 Roma tomato, chopped

$^1/_4$ cup tomato paste

4 tablespoons flour

$^1/_2$ cup brandy

$^1/_2$ cup sherry

4 cups Fish Stock (see page 214)

$^1/_2$ cup heavy cream

2 tablespoons unsalted butter

Pesto (see page 217)

SERVES 6

1. Bring a large pot of water to a boil. Add the lobsters headfirst and boil until cooked through, about 8 minutes. Transfer the lobsters to a large bowl and reserve 2 cups of the cooking liquid.

2. Working over a bowl to catch the juices, cut off the lobster tails and claws and reserve the juice. Crack open the tail and claw shells and remove the meat. Dice the meat and then place it in the refrigerator. Coarsely chop the lobster shells and bodies.

3. Heat the oil in a large pot over high heat. Add the lobster shells and bodies and sauté until the shells begin to brown, about 8 minutes. Add the onion, carrot, celery, garlic, Bouquet Garni, and tomato and sauté for an additional 3 minutes. Whisk in the tomato paste and allow to cook for 1 minute. Whisk in the flour until the liquid is bound. Add the brandy, sherry, stock, and reserved lobster-cooking liquid and lobster juices. Decrease heat to low and simmer for 1 hour, stirring occasionally.

4. Strain the soup through a chinoise or fine-mesh sieve into a saucepan, pressing firmly on solids and then discarding them. Simmer over low heat until the soup is reduced to 3 cups, about 15 minutes. Whisk in the cream and simmer an additional 5 minutes.

5. While simmering the soup, sauté the lobster meat on medium heat in butter until warmed.

PRESENTATION

Pour the soup into serving bowls and place a small mound of the meat in the center of the soups. Garnish with a drizzle of pesto.

Butternut Squash Soup with Curried Apple Chutney

This soup is at once sweet, tart, smooth, and spicy. A crisp, tangy apple like a Cortland, or a mix of Granny Smith and Golden Delicious is best for this recipe. For variation, try garnishing the soup with a drizzle of crème fraîche or pumpkin seed oil.

WINE PAIRING *2001 Domaine Trimbach, Riesling Cuvée Frédéric Emile, Alsace, France*
2002 Domaine Bott-Geyl, Gewürztraminer "Beblenheim," Alsace, France

FOR THE BUTTERNUT SQUASH SOUP

1. In a large pot, sauté the squash, apples, and onion in olive oil over medium heat until it just starts to brown. Add the coriander, cumin, and turmeric and stir. Sauté until fragrant, about 1 minute.

2. Pour in the stock, cider, and heavy cream. Add the cinnamon stick, and season to taste with salt and cayenne pepper. Bring to a boil and then reduce heat to medium-low; simmer until the squash and apples are tender, about 15 to 20 minutes.

3. Take off heat and allow to cool slightly. Remove the cinnamon stick, and then pour the soup into a food processor or blender and purée until smooth.

4. Pass the processed soup through a chinoise into a clean pot. Reheat the soup, adjusting seasoning as necessary.

FOR THE CURRIED APPLE CHUTNEY

1. Simmer the water, cider, vinegar, sugar, salt, cloves, mustard seeds, cinnamon stick, and allspice berries in a sauce pan over medium heat for 15 minutes. Allow to cool. Strain through a fine-mesh sieve, reserving the liquid.

2. Combine the reserved liquid, diced squash, and apples in a small pot. Bring just to a boil and then remove from heat. Strain, reserving the chutney for garnish. You may save the liquid in the refrigerator for up to 1 month for other uses.

PRESENTATION

Pour the soup into serving bowls and top with Curried Apple Chutney.

BUTTERNUT SQUASH SOUP

3 cups peeled and coarsely chopped butternut squash

2 cups coarsely chopped apples, unpeeled and cored

1 medium yellow onion, coarsely chopped

2 tablespoons extra virgin olive oil

1 teaspoon coriander

1 teaspoon cumin

1 teaspoon turmeric

6 cups Vegetable Stock (see page 215)

2 cups apple cider

$1/2$ cup heavy cream

1 cinnamon stick

Sea salt

Cayenne pepper

CURRIED APPLE CHUTNEY

$1/2$ cup water

$1/2$ cup apple cider

$1/2$ cup rice wine vinegar

$1/3$ cup plus 2 tablespoons sugar

2 tablespoons kosher salt

4 whole cloves

1 teaspoon mustard seeds

1 cinnamon stick

8 allspice berries

$1/2$ cup peeled and finely diced butternut squash

$1/2$ cup finely diced apples, unpeeled and cored

SERVES 8

Rich Garlic Crème with Croûtons & Parmesan Crown

This luxuriously silky soup is my personal favorite. It was inspired by a garlic soup that Wolfgang Runge, my chef at Kurfürst in Germersheim, Germany, was famous for. He refused to share his prized recipe with me, so I, being a stubborn, hotheaded young chef, spent hours upon hours trying to duplicate—and improve—his recipe. He wasn't particularly happy with my end result, due in no small part, I'm sure, to my friends, family, and guests throughout Europe being quite happy with it. It's become my most-requested recipe and for fourteen years I've shared the exact recipe only with Shannon, whose bribes—which I will keep secret—were, for understandable reasons, the only ones that prevailed.

WINE PAIRING *2002 Gustave Lorentz, Pinot Blanc Reserve, Alsace, France*
2002 Lucien Albrecht, Tokay Pinot Gris "Vieilles Vignes," Alsace, France

4 tablespoons unsalted butter

4 heads garlic, peeled and crushed

2 yellow onions, finely chopped

4 tablespoons flour

1 quart heavy cream, cold

1 quart whole milk, cold

Sea salt

Freshly ground white pepper

2 slices bread

$^1/_2$ cup grated Parmesan cheese

Parsley sprigs, for garnish

SERVES 6

1. In a saucepan, melt the butter over medium heat. Add the garlic and onions and sauté until a light golden brown.

2. Make a roux by stirring in the the flour. Add the cream and milk and bring to a boil. Cook until the flour taste is cooked out, about 15 minutes. Remove from heat.

3. Pass the soup through a food mill fitted with a fine-gauge disk. Pour the milled soup through a chinoise or fine-mesh sieve and season to taste with salt and pepper.

4. Toast the bread slices. Remove crusts and discard, and then cut into croûtons.

PRESENTATION

Pour the soup into serving bowls and sprinkle with croûtons. Sprinkle with Parmesan cheese. Place under a broiler until the cheese becomes golden and bubbly, about 2 minutes. Garnish with a sprig of parsley. Rich Garlic Crème is fantastic served with crusty bread.

QUICK TIP: MORE GARLIC CRÈME SECRETS DIVULGED

Guests, especially non-garlic lovers, often remark that this soup has a surprisingly delicate flavor. For a more intense, earthy flavor, I prefer washing the garlic heads and onions but not peeling them. I cut them in half and prepare the recipe as directed, pressing the onions and garlic with a rubber spatula or the back of a wooden spoon to extract all the flavor during the milling process. The solids are discarded.

To create a lighter soup, substitute Vegetable or White Veal Stock for the milk (see page 215).

Rich Garlic Crème with Croûtons & Parmesan Crown

Wild Mushroom Consommé with Duck Ravioli

When I first came to the United States, I was informed that consommés are weak, colorless soups forced upon hospital patients along with Day-Glo gelatin topped with canned whipped cream. Where I come from, consommés are anything but boring! Start with good-quality ingredients. Cook the consommé slowly, making sure all your ingredients, cookware, and equipment are chilled before use to further slow the cooking process. The slower the consommé begins to cook, the cleaner it will be. And finally, be certain to clarify your consommé. If you follow these steps, you'll be left with a richly-flavored, deep-colored delicacy.

For a vegetarian version of this soup, substitute Vegetable Stock for Chicken Stock (see page 215) and serve plain or with the Wild Mushroom Ravioli (see page 145). Use the ravioli-cutter shape of your choice. Round, square, or triangular, about 2¹/₂ to 3 inches in size—which is what we use for this recipe—all look beautiful.

WINE PAIRING *2001 Domaine de l'Oratoire, Côtes du Rhône, Rhône, France*
2001 Domaine la Buissiere, Gigondas, Rhône, France

WILD MUSHROOM CONSOMMÉ

4 tablespoons extra virgin olive oil

4 tablespoons unsalted butter

1 yellow onion, coarsely chopped

1 cup chopped morels

1 cup chopped portabella mushrooms

1 cup chopped crimini mushrooms

1 cup chopped oyster mushrooms

5 cups cold Chicken Stock (see page 214)

1 Bouquet Garni with Rosemary (see page 204)

2 carrots, peeled and coarsely chopped

2 celery stalks, coarsely chopped

Sea salt

1 recipe Clarification (see page 216)

DUCK RAVIOLI

2 duck breasts (6 ounces each)

1 tablespoon extra virgin olive oil

1 tablespoon unsalted butter

1 shallot, diced

$^1/_4$ cup diced morels

$^1/_4$ cup diced portabella mushrooms

$^1/_4$ cup diced crimini mushrooms

$^1/_4$ cup diced oyster mushrooms

2 teaspoons finely chopped rosemary

Sea salt

Freshly ground black pepper

2 sheets Ravioli Dough (see page 206–207)

Eggwash

DISH

$^1/_4$ cup chopped morels

$^1/_4$ cup chopped portabella mushrooms

$^1/_4$ cup chopped crimini mushrooms

$^1/_4$ cup chopped oyster mushrooms

1 tablespoon extra virgin olive oil

1 tablespoon unsalted butter

Sea salt

Rosemary, for garnish

SERVES 4

FOR THE WILD MUSHROOM CONSOMMÉ

1. In a medium stockpot, melt the olive oil and butter over high heat. Add the onion and sauté until glossy, about 1 minute. Add the mushrooms and sauté for an additional 1 minute.

2. Reduce heat to low. Add the stock, Bouquet Garni, carrots, and celery and bring to a boil. Skim the impurities from the liquid's surface as they rise to the top during the cooking process.

3. Reduce heat to medium and simmer until the liquid has reduced to about 3 cups. Season to taste with salt, and then strain liquid into a bowl through a fine-mesh sieve. Discard the solids, as they will have lost their flavor. Allow the liquid to cool completely and then refrigerate overnight.

4. Clarify the consommé (see page 216).

FOR THE DUCK RAVIOLI

1. Score and then sauté the duck breasts in a sauté pan over high heat, starting skin side down, until medium, about 1 minute each side. Remove from heat and allow to cool. Remove the skins and cut the breasts into small dices.

2. In the same pan in which you sautéed the duck, melt the olive oil and butter over high heat. Add the shallot and sauté until the dices are glossy, about 1 minute. Add the mushrooms and sauté until they have lost all their water and begin caramelizing. Remove from heat.

3. Add the duck breast dices and rosemary. Season to taste with salt and pepper. Remove from heat and allow to cool.

4. Place a sheet of pasta dough on a lightly floured surface. Brush the surface of the dough with eggwash. Using the dull side of the cutter of your choice, create a template for your twelve raviolis by lightly marking the dough, leaving at least $1/2$ inch between them. Center the duck-mushroom filling on the center of each ravioli bottom.

5. Carefully place a second sheet of pasta dough on top of the first sheet, making certain the long ends match up fairly well. Press down between the mounds of duck-mushroom filling, pressing out any air bubbles. Using the tip of a paring knife, gently pierce a small hole in each ravioli. Using the fluted end of your ravioli cutter, cut out the twelve raviolis.

6. Bring a lightly salted pot of water to a boil. Place the raviolis in the water and cook until al dente, about 6 to 9 minutes. Remove from the pot and drain.

PRESENTATION

Sauté the mushrooms in the olive oil and butter until golden. Season to taste with salt. Place two or three raviolis per guest in the serving dishes of your choice. Pour warm consommé over the raviolis and garnish with the sautéed mushrooms and rosemary. Serve immediately.

Gazpacho

Originally a laborer's dish, gazpacho was the standard fare of Andalusian muleteers who carried it in earthen pots on their travels. Today, the soup contains vegetables and differs from city to city within Andalusia—each version claiming to be the original. Arguably, the first recipe came from Córdoba and consisted of bread, garlic, olive oil, and water. Today, Córdoban gazpacho is thickened with cream and cornmeal. In Jerez it is garnished with raw onion rings, and in Malaga it is made with veal bouillon and sometimes garnished with grapes and almonds. In Cadiz, gazpacho is served hot in the winter, and in Segovia it is flavored with cumin, basil, and aïoli.

This recipe is inspired by that of Seville, a city that, of course, also lays claim as home of gazpacho.

WINE PAIRING *2002 Villa Maria, Sauvignon Blanc Reserve, Marlborough, New Zealand*
2003 Bodegas Borsao, Borsao, Borja, Spain

1 pound vine-ripened tomatoes, peeled and chopped

$1/2$ cucumber, peeled and chopped

1 green bell pepper, seeded and chopped

1 red bell pepper, seeded and chopped

1 small yellow onion, chopped

1 garlic clove, chopped

1 cup breadcrumbs

2 tablespoons extra virgin olive oil

2 tablespoons red wine vinegar

2 cups tomato juice

$1/2$ teaspoon dried leaf marjoram

Sea salt

Freshly ground black pepper

SERVES 6

1. Purée all ingredients in a food processor or blender. You may need to process it in two batches. Blend until the soup is the consistency you favor. Some people prefer chunks, while others like a completely smooth soup. I prefer my Gazpacho somewhere in between—with some bite and the consistency of heavy cream.

2. Pour the soup into a large stainless steel bowl, cover, and refrigerate for at least 2 hours. When the soup is well chilled, adjust seasoning with salt and pepper.

PRESENTATION

Gazpacho is traditionally served with a selection of garnishes, including chopped hard-boiled eggs, chopped cucumber, chopped onion, chopped green and black olives, and diced green bell pepper. This soup is best served family style, and I prefer to use earthenware dishes, as the recipe was originally prepared and served in clay bowls.

QUICK TIP: OTHER USES FOR GAZPACHO
I've used Gazpacho leftovers as a pizza sauce, a warm pasta sauce, a sauce for a goat cheese tarte flambée, a cold and warm garnish, and even as a cocktail sauce by adding a bit of horseradish. Be inventive with this versatile soup and know that the longer you keep it, the more complex and intense the flavor will become.

Watercress Soup with Fried Leek

Watercress, a leafy member of the mustard family that grows in cool running water, gives this soup its slightly bitter, peppery flavor and vibrant green color.

WINE PAIRING *2002 Joh. Jos. Prüm, Wehlener Sennenuhr Auslese, Mosel, Germany
2002 Francois Cotat, Sancerre "Les Monts Damnés," Loire Valley, France*

1. In a stockpot, melt the butter over medium heat. Add the leeks and sauté until they are very tender. Sprinkle the flour over the leeks and stir until the butter is absorbed. Cook for 2 minutes, stirring constantly.

2. Reduce heat to low and whisk in the milk. Allow to thicken. Whisk in the vegetable stock and bring to a boil. Continue to cook, stirring frequently, until you can no longer taste the flour, about 10 minutes. Season with the nutmeg, cayenne pepper, salt, and white pepper. Remove from heat and strain into a saucepan.

3. Bring salted water to a boil and blanch the watercress for 2 minutes. Remove the watercress from the hot water and plunge into an ice bath. When the watercress is completely cooled, drain it and then purée it in a blender or food processor until it is smooth. Pour the puréed watercress into a saucepan. Add the strained Vegetable Stock–milk mixture and whisk together. Heat over medium-low heat until warm.

PRESENTATION

Ladle the soup into bowls and garnish with a drizzle of crème fraîche and a small stack of fried leek.

$1/_2$ cup unsalted butter

4 leeks, white and light green parts only, sliced

$1/_2$ cup flour

2 cups whole milk, cold

4 cups cold Vegetable Stock (see page 215)

$1/_4$ teaspoon freshly ground nutmeg

$1/_4$ teaspoon cayenne pepper

Sea salt

Freshly ground white pepper

3 bunches watercress, tied

Crème fraîche, for garnish

Fried Herbs and Greens, for garnish (see page 218)

SERVES 6

QUICK TIP: SAFFRON SHRIMP VARIATION

Saffron shrimp, rather than fried leek, is also delicious on this soup. Feel free to use the shrimp or prawn of your choice. I favor using a pink or red Mediterranean prawn such as a French caramote or Italian gambero rosso. Common North Atlantic prawns or tiger prawns work very well too. If you're using smaller shrimp, use twelve rather than the six called for.

SAFFRON SHRIMP
1 teaspoon extra virgin olive oil
6 prawns, cleaned
1 strand saffron
Sea salt
Freshly ground black pepper

FOR THE SAFFRON SHRIMP
In a small sauté pan, heat the olive oil. Add the shrimp and saffron and sauté until the shrimp are pink and cooked through, about 3 minutes. Season to taste with salt and pepper. Place atop the soup just before serving.

Heirloom Tomato Soup with Basil,
Crème Fraîche & Roquefort Crown

Heirloom Tomato Soup with Basil, Crème Fraîche & Roquefort Crown

Based on availability, you may wish to use Roma tomatoes for this recipe but not vine-ripened tomatoes, as they contain too much water.

WINE PAIRING *1999 Rocca delle Macíe, Chianti Riserva, Italy*
1998 Domaine du Vieux Telegraphe, Châteauneuf-du-Pape, Rhône, France

1. In a large covered saucepan, melt the oil and butter over medium heat. Add the onion and cook until glossy, about 2 to 4 minutes. Add the garlic and cook for an additional 1 minute.

2. Add the tomatoes, sugar, stock, and Bouquet Garni. Bring to a boil, and then cover and reduce heat to medium-low. Simmer for 30 minutes. Uncover and simmer an additional 15 minutes.

3. Pass the soup through a food mill fitted with a fine-gauge disk, or purée in a food processor until smooth. Strain through a chinoise or fine-mesh sieve and discard the skins. Pour the soup back into the saucepan. Stir in the cream and cook, stirring constantly, until the soup becomes creamy, about 5 minutes. Season to taste with salt and pepper and stir in the basil.

PRESENTATION

Pour the soup into serving bowls, preferably plain white ones. Place a dollop of Roquefort cheese in the center of each serving. Heat under a broiler until the cheese bubbles and becomes golden brown. Garnish with basil chiffonades and a drizzle of crème fraîche.

2 tablespoons extra virgin olive oil

2 tablespoons unsalted butter

1 yellow onion, chopped

1 tablespoon minced garlic

$3^1/_2$ pounds heirloom tomatoes

1 teaspoon sugar

2 cups Vegetable Stock
(see page 215)

1 Bouquet Garni (see page 204)

1 cup heavy cream

Sea salt

Freshly ground black pepper

$^1/_2$ cup basil, en chiffonade

$^1/_2$ cup Roquefort cheese

Basil, en chiffonade, for garnish

Crème fraîche, for garnish

SERVES 6

Potato Crème with Veal Croûtons & White Truffle Oil

This is an elegant twist on a classic comfort food. It's even better when reheated, if it lasts that long.

For a lighter vegetarian version of the soup, substitute vegetable stock for the chicken stock and leave off the veal croûtons. It's simply delicious.

WINE PAIRING *2003 Field Stone, Gewürztraminer, Russian River, California*
2002 Mas de Gourgonnier, Mme. Nicolas Cartier, Les Baux de Provence, France

POTATO CRÈME

2 tablespoons extra virgin olive oil

2 tablespoons unsalted butter

2 yellow onions, diced

2 carrots, peeled and diced

1 stalk celery, diced

1 leek, white and light green parts only, diced

$2^1/_2$ pounds Yukon Gold potatoes, unpeeled and diced

6 cups Chicken Stock (see page 214)

2 tablespoons marjoram

4 tablespoons chopped parsley, divided

Sea salt

Freshly ground black pepper

VEAL CROÛTONS

1 (6-ounce) veal filet, diced

Flour

Sea salt

Freshly ground white pepper

1 tablespoon extra virgin olive oil

DISH

White truffle oil

SERVES 4

FOR THE POTATO CRÈME

1. Heat the oil and butter in a large stockpot over medium-high heat. Add the onion, carrot, celery, and leek and sauté until tender but not brown, about 5 minutes. Add the potatoes and sauté for an additional 2 minutes.

2. Pour in the stock and reduce heat to low; bring to a boil. Cook until the potatoes begin to break apart. Add the marjoram and 3 tablespoons of the parsley and season to taste with salt and pepper. Remove from heat.

3. Process the soup in a food processor or blender to the desired consistency. We purée ours slightly so that it's creamy but there are still some small potato pieces that give the soup a bit of bite. If the soup is too thick for your liking, add a bit more stock to thin it.

FOR THE VEAL CROÛTONS

1. Dredge the veal dices in flour and season to taste with salt and pepper. Tap excess flour from the dices.

2. Heat the oil in a sauté pan over high heat. Add the veal and sauté until golden brown, about 30 seconds to 1 minute.

PRESENTATION

Pour the soup into individual serving dishes. Place a small mound of veal croûtons in the center of each serving and drizzle white truffle oil. Garnish all dishes with the remaining of parsley.

Beef Consommé with Thyme & Quenelles

Beef creates one of the most popular consommés, or rich, clear broths. A quenelle is a dumpling made with spiced forcemeat bound with fat and eggs, molded into a small egg shape, and poached in boiling water or stock.

This recipe uses the clarification technique. This means we add a combination of ingredients called a clarification that removes all impurities from your stock to produce a clear, pure consommé. The clarification also enhances the soup's overall flavor. The beef consommé recipe should be prepared a day in advance so it has time to chill.

We tie the leeks in a bundle in this recipe because leeks have a very soft structure that breaks down during long cooking processes. Tying the leeks prevents the leaves from breaking away, becoming mushy, and clouding the soup.

WINE PAIRING *2000 Dehlinger Winery, Pinot Noir Estate, Sonoma, California*
2002 Château de Paraza, Minervois, Minervois, France

FOR THE BEEF CONSOMMÉ

1. Place the lean beef and beef shank with bone into large stockpot and cover with the cold water. Bring to a boil over high heat while carefully skimming off impurities that rise to the surface. Add the vegetables and Bouquet Garni. Reduce heat to low and simmer for 4 hours. It is important that the stock does not boil, as boiling would cause it to become cloudy and gray.

2. Carefully remove the meat and bone from the stock and strain the liquid through a cheesecloth-lined chinoise. Discard the solids and chill the liquid overnight.

3. Clarify the consommé (see page 216).

FOR THE QUENELLES

1. Combine all ingredients and pass through a tamis, or drum sieve. If the dough is too wet, add more breadcrumbs.

2. Bring to a boil in 1 pint salted water.

3. Using two teaspoons, shape one test quenelle into an egg shape by using one teaspoon to hold the quenelle and the other to shape it. Drop it into the boiling water. When the quenelle rises to the surface, it is done. Remove it from the water. If it has broken apart, add more egg and breadcrumbs. Shape all quenelles and continue the process until all the dough has been used.

PRESENTATION

Divide the quenelles among your guests. Place them in clear or white soup bowls and pour the consommé over them. Garnish with parsley and serve immediately.

BEEF CONSOMMÉ
$4^1/_2$ pounds lean beef

$3^1/_4$ pounds beef shank with bone

12 pints cold water

4 large carrots, peeled and coarsely chopped

4 ounces turnips, coarsely chopped

4 ounces parsnips, coarsely chopped

12 ounces leeks, tied in a bundle

2 celery stalks, sliced

1 medium-sized yellow onion pierced with two cloves

1 Bouquet Garni (see page 204)

Sea salt

1 recipe Clarification (see page 216)

QUENELLES
$1^3/_4$ pounds lean beef, minced

1 egg

1 teaspoon chopped thyme

1 teaspoon chopped parsley

2 tablespoons finely chopped carrot

1 tablespoon breadcrumbs

1 pint water

Sea salt

Freshly ground black pepper

DISH
Chopped parsley, for garnish

SERVES 6

QUICK TIP: USING A TAMIS

A tamis consists of a metal mesh or woolen cloth screen stretched across a shallow cylinder of wood or aluminum. It is used to strain liquids and sieve dry ingredients. While turned over, a tamis is also used to incorporate and make moist ingredients silky as you push them through the screen with a pastry scraper or rubber spatula.

Ramp "Cappuccino"

Ramps are wild onions that grow abundantly in wooded areas in the spring. Resembling a scallion, it has a strong, peppery, garlicky-onion flavor and is sometimes referred to as a wild leek. Though we are fortunate enough to be able to pick our own, you can usually find ramps in specialty grocery stores or at farmers markets from about mid-March through the end of June. Based on availability, you may substitute either scallions or leeks—or a combination of the two—in this recipe. We serve it in a cappuccino cup for sipping, but you may wish to serve the frothy soup with a demitasse spoon.

A half hour prior to creating this dish, place two ramps in the heavy cream to impart their flavor in the crèma. Remove the ramps before using the cream in the recipe.

WINE PAIRING *2002 Cloudy Bay, Sauvignon Blanc, Marlborough, New Zealand*
2001 Ponzi, Pinot Gris, Willamette, Oregon

4 cups Vegetable Stock (see page 215)

24 ramps, white and light green parts only

3 teaspoons sherry

Sea salt

Freshly ground white pepper

2 cups ramp-infused heavy cream

Fried Herbs and Greens, for garnish (see page 218)

SERVES 4

1. Bring the stock to a boil. Blanch the ramps until softened, about 1 minute.

2. Pour the blanched ramps and stock into a food processor or blender and process until smooth, about 1 to 2 minutes. Pour the mixture into a saucepan, add the sherry, and reduce by one-half over medium-high heat. Season to taste with salt and pepper.

3. Heat the heavy cream in a medium saucepan over high heat and bring to a boil. Place the cream in a blender and process until it becomes frothy, about 2 minutes. You could also use the frother on an espresso machine or a hand-held blender for this step.

PRESENTATION

Pour the ramp soup into cappuccino cups and spoon the crèma on top. Garnish with fried leek and serve immediately.

Ramp "Cappuccino"

Summer Corn Soup
with Sun-Dried Tomato Purée

This soup is light, flavorful, and easy to make—perfect for summer. The sun-dried tomato purée adds a splash of color and a bright acidity that offsets the sweetness of the corn.

WINE PAIRING *2001 De Loach Vineyards, Chardonnay O.F.S., Russian River, California*
2002 Domaine Bott-Geyl, Pinot d'Alsace, Alsace, France

CORN STOCK
1 quart water

6 ears sweet corn, kernels removed and reserved, cobs reserved

1 small yellow onion, chopped

1 small carrot, peeled and chopped

1 clove garlic

SUMMER CORN SOUP
3 tablespoons unsalted butter

1 small yellow onion, chopped

1 teaspoon chopped garlic

Reserved corn kernels

1 cup heavy cream

2 cups corn stock

Sea salt

Freshly ground black pepper

Cayenne pepper

SUN-DRIED TOMATO PURÉE
$1/2$ cup sun-dried tomatoes

1 clove garlic

1 tablespoon extra virgin olive oil

1 tablespoon tomato juice

Sea salt

Freshly ground black pepper

SERVES 6

FOR THE CORN STOCK

In a medium stockpot, bring the water, corncobs, onion, carrot, and garlic to a boil over high heat. Simmer for 30 minutes. Strain and reserve the liquid.

FOR THE SUMMER CORN SOUP

1. Melt the butter in a medium stockpot over high heat. Add the onion and garlic and sauté until glossy, about 1 minute. Add the corn kernels and sauté for 3 minutes.

2. Add the cream and corn stock. Bring to a boil and then reduce heat to medium. Simmer for 15 minutes. Add salt, black pepper, and cayenne pepper to taste. Purée in a food processor or blender and then pass through a chinoise.

FOR THE SUN-DRIED TOMATO PURÉE

Purée all ingredients in a food processor or blender; season to taste with salt and pepper.

PRESENTATION

Ladle the soup into serving dishes and spoon a dollop of the sun-dried tomato purée onto the center of each soup.

Spring Pea Soup with Mint & Crème Fraîche

Already bright, the sweet pea flavor is invigorated by mint and then refined by crème fraîche in this delectable ode to spring. If you do not have fresh peas, you may substitute three (10-ounce) packages of high-quality frozen peas.

1999 Château Haut-Brion, Graves Blanc, Bordeaux, France
2002 Domaine Lucien Thomas, Sancerre Clos de la Crête, Loire, France

1. Melt the oil and butter in a small stockpot over medium heat. Add the onion and sauté until soft, about 2 to 3 minutes. Add the peas and stock and season to taste with salt and pepper. Simmer for 20 minutes. Add the mint and remove from heat.

2. Purée the soup in a food processor or blender until smooth. Adjust seasoning as necessary.

PRESENTATION

Pour the soup into individual serving dishes. Using a fine-nozzled squeeze bottle, pipe whimsical pea-pod shapes onto each serving with crème fraîche.

2 tablespoons extra virgin olive oil

2 tablespoons unsalted butter

1 yellow onion, chopped

6 cups shelled sweet peas

5 cups Chicken Stock
(see page 214)

Sea salt

Freshly ground black pepper

2 teaspoons chopped mint

Crème fraîche, for garnish

SERVES 4

Misó

Misó

This is our version of the traditional Japanese miso soup. It's as lovely as it is tasty and was a huge hit when we served it for our first Sushi Night at Biró, which was featured on The Kitchens of Biró. *You may add glass noodles to the recipe, if you wish.*

WINE PAIRING *2002 Rudi Pichler, Grüner Veltliner, Wachau, Austria*
2001 Clos Saint Imer, "La Chapelle" Muscat, Alsace, France

In a medium stockpot, combine the stock, ginger, miso, and dashi kombu and bring to a boil over high heat. Reduce heat to low and skim any impurities that have risen to the surface during the cooking process. Simmer for 15 minutes and then add the soy sauce.

PRESENTATION

Place the shallots, onions, enoki mushrooms, shiitake mushrooms, and tofu in plain square or round serving bowls. I like to arrange the mushrooms opposite one another to create balance. Ladle the hot liquid over the vegetables and tofu. In a matter of seconds, the mushrooms will be perfectly cooked. Drizzle with a bit of sesame oil.

5 cups Chicken Stock (see page 214)

1 (1-inch) piece of fresh ginger, peeled and crushed

6 tablespoons miso

2 leaves dashi kombu

2 tablespoons soy sauce

2 tablespoons diced shallots

2 tablespoons chopped green onions

4 ounces enoki mushrooms

8 ounces shiitake mushrooms, thinly sliced

6 ounces firm tofu, cut into 1/2-inch-square dices

Sesame oil, for garnish

SERVES 8

Carrot-Ginger Soup with Parsley Oil

Light and clean, both the carrot and ginger are able to assert themselves in this offering. The parsley oil adds a splash of color and cuts the soup's sweetness.

WINE PAIRING *2001 Hugel, Cuvée Jubilee, Alsace, France*
2003 Coriole, Chenin Blanc, McLaren Vale, Australia

1 tablespoon extra virgin olive oil

$1/2$ pound unsalted butter

5 pounds carrots, peeled and coarsely chopped

1 fresh gingerroot, peeled and coarsely chopped

1 tablespoon curry powder

1 cup flour

4 cups whole milk, cold

4 cups heavy cream, cold

4 cups cold Vegetable Stock (see page 215)

Sea salt

Freshly ground white pepper

Parsley oil, for garnish

SERVES 4

1. Melt the oil and butter in a large stockpot over high heat. Add the carrots and sauté for 30 seconds. Add the ginger and sauté an additional 30 seconds. Stir in the curry.

2. Make a roux by adding the flour. Stir until the liquid is completely bound, and then pour in the milk, cream, and stock.

3. Bring to a boil, whisking steadily, until the flour taste is cooked out, about 15 to 20 minutes. Season to taste with salt and pepper.

4. Purée the soup in a food processor or blender until it is the desired thickness. If it's too thick for your liking, add a bit more stock. If it's too thin, return it to heat and reduce it a bit longer. Adjust seasoning, if necessary.

PRESENTATION

Pour the soup into individual serving bowls and garnish with a drizzle of parsley oil.

QUICK TIP: MAKING A ROUX

A roux is a mixture of equal parts flour and fat and is used to thicken sauces, soups, or ragoûts. There are three types of rouxs—white, blonde, and brown—and the various shades are achieved based on how long the roux cooks before a liquid is added. When adding liquid to a roux, it is crucial that the roux and liquid temperatures are different—hot liquid to cold roux, or cold liquid to hot roux—or your finished product will be lumpy.

Sweet-&-Sour Lentil Soup

This traditional soup recalls childhood memories of Christmas Eve in Germany: the sweet aromas of roasted almonds, warm lebkuchen, and steaming sauces dancing through the kitchen, and the snap of this soup simmering on the stovetop provided the familiar soundtrack for the day's festivities.

Sweet-and-Sour Lentil Soup tastes best reheated, as it allows the flavors to infuse.

WINE PAIRING *1998 Castello di Meleto, Chianti Classico Riserva, Tuscany, Italy*
2002 Bourgogne "Passetoutgrains," Michel Magnien, Burgundy, France

1. Rinse the lentils and place them in a medium-sized bowl. Add enough water to cover lentils by two inches. Allow to rest at room temperature overnight so that the lentils absorb the water. Strain the liquid through a cheesecloth-lined fine-mesh sieve. Reserve the liquid and the lentils.

2. In a stockpot, sauté the bacon and onion over medium-high heat until the bacon is crispy and the onion is glossy. Add the lentils and sauté for 1 minute. Pour in the stock, lentil-soaking liquid, and bay leaf and season with salt and pepper. Reduce heat to medium-low; simmer until the lentils are al dente, about 1 hour.

3. Add the leek, carrots, and potatoes. Simmer until the potatoes are softened, and then add the parsley, thyme, and vinegar. Remove the bay leaf and adjust seasoning with salt and pepper. If the soup is too sour for your liking, add sugar.

PRESENTATION

Ladle the soup into individual serving bowls. It's best served simply, with crusty rye bread.

$1/2$ pound dried lentils

5 slices bacon, coarsely chopped

1 yellow onion, diced

2 cups Beef Stock (see page 214)

1 Turkish bay leaf

Sea salt

Freshly ground black pepper

1 leek, diced

2 carrots, peeled and diced

2 Russet potatoes, peeled and chopped

1 tablespoon chopped parsley

1 tablespoon chopped thyme

2 tablespoons white wine vinegar

SERVES 4

Roasted-Peach Soup with Smoked Bacon & Fried Arugula

This is one very grown-up soup. It's luscious with a smoky depth. Satiny on the tongue. Slightly bitter on the garnish. Try it and learn for yourself why our guests are taken by it.

If you can't find nice fresh peaches, feel free to substitute canned in this recipe.

WINE PAIRING *2002 Domaine Marcel Deiss, Pinot Blanc, Alsace, France*
2003 Coriole, Chenin Blanc, McLaren Vale, Australia

24 peaches, unpeeled

Extra virgin olive oil

$^1/_2$ cup brown sugar

3 cups Chicken Stock
(see page 214)

1 cup heavy cream

4 ounces peach schnapps

Nutmeg

Sea salt

Freshly ground black pepper

2 strips applewood-smoked
bacon, coarsely chopped and fried

Fried Herbs and Greens,
for garnish (see page 218)

SERVES 6

1. Preheat oven to 450 degrees.

2. Cut the peaches in half and remove the pits. On a lightly oiled sheet pan, roast the peaches, skin side down, for 10 minutes. Sprinkle peaches with brown sugar. Bake until the sugar caramelizes and the peaches begin to brown, about 15 additional minutes. Remove from oven and pour the peaches, caramelized sugar, and juices that collected in the pan into a food processor or blender. Process until smooth.

3. Warm the stock, cream, and schnapps in a medium stockpot over high heat for 5 minutes. Pour in the puréed peaches and season to taste with nutmeg, salt, and pepper. Cook, whisking steadily, until it comes to a boil. Pass through a chinoise or food mill fitted with a fine-gauge disk.

PRESENTATION

Ladle the soup into serving bowls. Garnish each serving with Fried Arugula, and then place a small mound of crispy bacon in the center of each serving.

Roasted-Peach Soup with Smoked Bacon & Fried Arugula

Braised-Oxtail Soup

This is our take on a classic. Make certain the oxtails you use are very meaty, and pat them dry before cooking.

WINE PAIRING *1999 Domaine Santa Duc, Gigondas, Rhône, France*
1999 Havens, Merlot Reserve, Napa Valley, California

BRAISED-OXTAIL SOUP

3 tablespoons vegetable oil, divided

3¹/₂ pounds oxtails

Sea salt

Freshly ground black pepper

4 Roma tomatoes

3 cups dry red wine, preferably burgundy

2 yellow onions, chopped

2 leeks, white and pale green parts only, chopped

3 carrots, peeled and chopped

6 garlic cloves, minced

1 gallon Beef Stock (see page 214)

1 Bouquet Garni (see page 204)

2 large Russet potatoes, peeled and cubed

DISH

Thyme sprigs, for garnish

SERVES 8

1. Heat the oil in a large stockpot over high heat. Season the oxtails with salt and pepper and place them in the pot. Add the tomatoes and sauté for 5 minutes. Add the wine and braise until the liquid is reduced by one-third, about 15 minutes. Add the onions, leeks, carrots, and garlic, and sauté until almost all the liquid is gone, about 5 additional minutes.

2. Add the Beef Stock and Bouquet Garni and bring to a simmer. Reduce heat to medium-low and simmer gently, so the simmer is almost imperceptible, until the meat is tender, about 3 hours. Increase the heat to high and add the potatoes; cook until the potatoes are al dente, about 15 to 20 additional minutes.

3. Remove the Bouquet Garni and oxtails from the liquid and season the liquid with salt and pepper to taste. Remove the meat from the oxtails, discarding the bones, and dice the meat.

PRESENTATION

Place the oxtail dices in serving bowls. Ladle the soup into the bowls and garnish with a sprig of thyme.

Saffron Shrimp-Leek Soup

As in many other soups and stocks using shrimp, we use unpeeled shrimp in the preparation of this recipe. Leaving the shells on gives the dish an intense flavor that the shrimp alone could not produce. You may wish to add 2 tablespoons dry white wine to the leeks while sautéing to further enhance this soup's earthy but refined flavor.

WINE PAIRING *2001 Talbott Vineyards, Chardonnay, Monterey, California*
2001 Château Carbonnieux, Graves Blanc, Bordeaux, France

1. In a medium sauté pan, melt the butter over medium heat. Add the shrimp and saffron and sauté until the shrimp become red, about 2 minutes. Do not allow the shrimp to brown or they will become chewy. Remove the shrimp from the pan and bring the pan to medium-high heat. Add the leeks and sauté for 30 seconds.

2. Add enough stock to cover the leeks by about 1^1/$_2$ inches. Bring the stock to a simmer and cook gently until the leeks are tender, about 8 minutes.

3. Carefully peel and clean the sautéed shrimp, discarding the shells.

4. Process the soup in a food processor or blender until smooth. Strain through a chinoise or fine-mesh sieve into a clean pan.

5. Over low heat, stir in the cream. Simmer until the soup is thickened, about 5 minutes. Add the shrimp and season with salt and pepper.

^{1}/$_4$ cup unsalted butter

1 pound shrimp, unpeeled

4 threads saffron

4 large leeks, white and pale green parts only, chopped

3 cups Fish Stock (see page 214)

2 cups heavy cream

2 teaspoons sea salt

^{1}/$_2$ teaspoon freshly ground black pepper

SERVES 6

PRESENTATION

Ladle into the serving dishes of your choice and serve immediately.

QUICK TIP: ABOUT SAFFRON

Saffron is the type of ingredient that the mere mention of makes gourmands salivate and debate, and kitchen novices perspire and quake. I've seen both happen at my culinary school. A foodie may pipe up and say, "The best saffron is from Spain! I paid $60 for a thimble-sized jar of it just the other day!", while someone at the back of the classroom may be wondering, "What is saffron? If it costs that much, I don't think I even want to know."

Here's the deal on saffron: it originated in the East and is a pungent, slightly bitter spice that comes from the dried stigmas of the saffron crocus plant. It is available in yellow-orange powdered and burnt-orange thread forms. Whether you find saffron from Spain, Italy, Greece, Turkey, Morocco, or somewhere else, it's expensive. This is because it takes around 85,000 stigmas to create just over a pound of saffron.

The good news is, because of saffron's strength, a little goes a long way in flavoring and adding color to your soups, stocks, risotto, paella, meats, vegetables, and desserts. But if you don't want to spring for the real thing, no problem. Simply substitute safflower, called "bastard saffron," or turmeric, called "Indian saffron."

Grilled Goat Cheese on Spring Greens with
Citrus Vinaigrette & Iced Olive Oil Shavings

salads

Roquefort-Stuffed Dauphine Violette
Figs à la Bourguignonne

Nut-&-Currant-Stuffed Scallops
of Foie Gras with Madeira & Port Glaze*

Sautéed White Asparagus in Parmesan Tuile with
Summer Greens & Lemon Aïoli

Lobster "Martini"

Mesclun Duck Breast Salad
with Raspberry-Shallot Vinaigrette

Spring Greens with Vine-Ripened Tomato,
Feta, Shallots, Croûtons & Dijon Dressing

Bison Carpaccio on Arugula
with Shaved Parmesan

Mushroom & Spinach Strudel with
Light Champagne Vinaigrette

Crisp Veal Sweetbreads with Port & Ginger

Tarragon Lamb Filet with Micro Greens
& Cranberry Emulsion

Mâche with Smoked Eel & Bacon-Dijon Dressing

Duck Terrine with Black Truffle–Herb Vinaigrette
on Micro Greens

Lentil Salad with Bacon & Frisée

Roasted Striped Beets with Fennel, Mâche
& Yogurt–Walnut Oil Dressing

Trio of Vegetable Sorbets with Spring Salad

Chicory with Red Wine Vinegar, Ricotta,
Gorgonzola, Leeks & Champignons

Heirloom Tomatoes with Tomatillo Salad
& International Salts

Grilled Goat Cheese on Spring Greens with
Citrus Vinaigrette & Iced Olive Oil Shavings

Red Cabbage Salad with Cilantro,
Bulgur, Ham & Dijon

Grilled-Vegetable Salad with Caramelized
Walnuts, Goat Cheese & Pesto

Roquefort-Stuffed Dauphine Violette Figs à la Bourguignonne

The term à la bourguignonne *simply means "cooked in red wine." This salad, with its flavorful contrast of sharp and sweet, is as stunning as it is delicious. Though I like to use a Beaujolais for the wine sauce, you may use the red wine of your preference. For color and flavor, I use the French Dauphine Violette fig, but you may use any sweet variety.*

If you can't locate microgreens, use mesclun greens and cut into chiffonades.

WINE PAIRING *2002 Columbia Crest, Sauvignon Blanc/Semillon, Columbia Valley, Washington*
NV Warre's, Warrior Special Reserve, Oporto, Portugal

12 figs

$1/2$ pound Roquefort cheese

1 tablespoon unsalted butter

1 tablespoon sugar

$1/2$ cup red wine

1 tablespoon port

2 tablespoons balsamic vinegar, divided

Sea salt

Freshly ground black pepper

2 tablespoons water

$1/2$ pound micro greens

SERVES 4

1. Preheat oven to 350 degrees.

2. Cut the tops off the figs and scoop out their insides with a small spoon. Reserve the tops and insides. Pipe or spoon the Roquefort cheese into the figs so that the cheese protrudes slightly from the top of the figs.

3. In a medium ovenproof sauté pan, melt the butter. Place the figs and fig tops in the pan and sprinkle with sugar. Cook over medium heat until the sugar caramelizes, about 2 to 3 minutes. Turn off heat.

4. In a small saucepan, bring the wine to a simmer over low heat. Add the fig insides to the wine. Add the port and reduce by one-half. Stir in 1 tablespoon of the balsamic vinegar and salt and pepper to taste. Remove from heat.

5. Add the water to the pan containing the figs. Pass the wine-vinegar mixture through a fine-mesh sieve. Pour one-half of the mixture over the figs, reserving the remaining mixture, and place into the preheated oven. Bake until the figs are soft and the cheese is melted, about 5 to 10 minutes.

PRESENTATION

Place the greens on the center of each salad plate. Drizzle the remaining wine-vinegar liquid over the lettuce. Place the fig tops back on the figs and set three figs around the greens. Drizzle with the remaining balsamic vinegar. This dish is also great served family style on a rectangular platter.

Nut-&-Currant-Stuffed Scallops of Foie Gras with Madeira & Port Glaze

This dish's classical French foundations and sumptuous flavors and textures have made it one of our guests' favorites. It would make an ideal addition to an elegant dinner party.

The term scallops *in this cases does not refer to the mollusk, but rather to a thin, boneless, round- or oval-shaped slice of meat or fish—in this case foie gras.*

WINE PAIRING *1997 Château Suduiraut, Sauternes, Sauternes, France*
1997 Château Coutet, Barsac, Bordeaux, France

1. In a mixing bowl, combine the currants, walnuts, almonds, and hazelnuts with $1/2$ cup of Port Glaze. Season with salt and pepper and allow to infuse for at least 30 minutes.

2. Combine the Madeira and port in a saucepan and bring to a boil over high heat. Lower heat to medium and reduce mixture until it becomes gelatinous, about 15 minutes. Whisk in the remaining $1/2$ cup Port Glaze. Season with salt and pepper and allow to cool.

3. Season the foie gras scallops with salt and pepper, and then dredge them in flour. Tap off the excess flour and place the scallops in a hot sauté pan. Sear them about 30 seconds on each side. Pat them dry with paper towels and allow to cool to room temperature.

4. Slit each scallop lengthwise through the middle and fill with the currant-nut mixture. Refrigerate until firm, about 10 minutes.

5. Brush the reduced Madeira-port mixture over the scallops. Allow to dry slightly, and then return to the refrigerator. Repeat this process two additional times.

PRESENTATION

In a large mixing bowl, whisk together the vinegar and oils; season to taste with salt and pepper. Add the greens and toss to coat each leaf completely. Slice the stuffed scallops lengthwise into $1/4$-inch-thick slices and fan them on each serving plate. Garnish with a small mound of salad and crushed walnuts.

SCALLOPS OF FOIE GRAS

$3/4$ cup currants, coarsely chopped

$1/2$ cup walnut halves, coarsely chopped

$1/4$ cup almonds, toasted and coarsely chopped

$1/4$ cup hazelnuts, toasted, skinned, and coarsely chopped

1 cup Port Glaze, divided (see page 213)

Sea salt

Freshly ground black pepper

1 cup Madeira

$1/2$ cup port

4 foie gras scallops ($3^{1}/2$ ounces each, $3/4$-inch thick)

Flour

DISH

1 tablespoon red wine vinegar

2 tablespoons peanut oil

1 tablespoon walnut oil

Sea salt

Freshly ground black pepper

2 cups mesclun greens

Crushed walnuts, for garnish

SERVES 4

Sautéed White Asparagus in Parmesan Tuile with Summer Greens & Lemon Aïoli

Unlike green asparagus, which is grown above ground, white asparagus is cultivated underground. I love the flavor and appearance of white asparagus, but green asparagus, lavender-tipped white asparagus, or a combination of all three would work nicely in this salad. If you use green asparagus, however, you needn't blanch it before sautéing. And by the way, it's completely acceptable to eat asparagus with your fingers! Enjoy.

French for "tile," a tuile *is a thin, crisp, sweet or savory cookie or wafer made of dough or cheese. The tuile is placed over a rounded object such as a tea cup, wine bottle, rolling pin, or pepper grinder while hot from the oven. When it cools, it resembles a curved roof tile.*

WINE PAIRING *2001 Les Jamelles, Rose de Cinsault, Vin de Pays, France*
2001 Freie Weingärtner Wachau, Grüner Veltliner Smaragd, Austria

2 cups water

$1/2$ cup white wine

2 tablespoons lemon juice

1 tablespoon sugar

1 pound white asparagus, peeled

1 cup freshly grated Parmesan cheese

1 teaspoon Herb Butter (see page 205)

1 pound spring greens

4 tablespoons Aïoli (see page 205)

Chives, for garnish

2 cherry tomatoes, halved, for garnish

4 strawberries, halved, for garnish

SERVES 4

1. Preheat oven to 350 degrees.

2. Bring the water, wine, lemon juice, and sugar to a boil. Add the asparagus and blanch until tender, about 4 minutes. Remove from the water and immerse in an ice bath to stop the cooking process. Dry on paper towels.

3. Line a baking sheet with Silpat and sprinkle four $1/4$-cup amounts of cheese to create the tuiles. You can use a form-giving round or square mold as a guide or simply sprinkle it by hand. Bake the cheese until golden and melted, about 5 to 7 minutes.

4. Remove the tuiles from the oven and, working quickly but carefully, place them over a rolling pin or wine bottle to create a taco-shell shape. Allow to cool.

5. In a sauté pan, melt the Herb Butter and sauté the asparagus until warm, about 1 to 2 minutes.

PRESENTATION

Place a mound of spring greens on the serving plates. Place a Parmesan tuile atop the greens. Lay sautéed asparagus in the tuile and drizzle with Aïoli. Garnish with whole chives, cherry tomato halves, and strawberry halves.

QUICK TIP: KEEPING YOUR WHITES WHITE
Do you want to keep your white asparagus and cauliflower white like the chefs do? Simply add a bit of sugar to the cooking water and it will stop the oxidation process, sealing in the flavor and color. Immediately after cooking your white vegetables, plunge them into an ice bath to stop the cooking process and further protect the flavor and color. It's that simple.

Sautéed White Asparagus in Parmesan Tuile
with Summer Greens & Lemon Aïoli

Lobster "Martini"

Lobster "Martini"

A restaurant guest eats first with her eyes, and one of the surest ways I've found to dazzle the eyes as well as the taste buds is to present items in vessels intended for another purpose. Our vibrant Lobster "Martini" and frothy Ramp "Cappuccino" (see page 98) are prime examples of this—serving a salad in a martini glass and a soup in a cappuccino cup—and I don't believe it's coincidental that they are among our most popular menu items.

You may substitute whole chives for the lobster antennae garnish, and one sliced lime may be used if you can't locate limequats.

WINE PAIRING *1996 Olivier Leflave, Corton-Charlemagne, Burgundy, France*
2001 Robert Sinskey Vineyards, Three Amigos Chardonnay, Napa, California

FOR THE LOBSTER

1. Bring a saucepan of water to boil and drop in the lobster headfirst. Return to a boil and cook for 1½ minutes, and then drain it. Detach the claws, legs, and antennae. Slice the tail into eight pieces and divide it into two even portions. Cut the claws in half lengthwise. Cut each antenna in quarters.

2. In a sauté pan, melt the oil and butter over high heat. Add the sliced lobster tail, lobster claws, and shallots. Sauté until medium, about 10 seconds. The meat should feel a bit rubbery. Remove from heat and season with salt and black pepper.

FOR THE SALAD

1. In a small mixing bowl, combine the horseradish, tomato paste, mayonnaise, cream, lemon juice, Pernod, orange juice, and cayenne pepper. Add one-half of the sautéed lobster tail meat and blend. Season to taste with salt and pepper.

2. Cut the mesclun greens into chiffonades and divide evenly among 4 martini glasses. Top with the cocktail sauce.

PRESENTATION

Garnish with the remaining lobster tail meat and one halved claw per glass. Prop two antennae segments in the cocktail sauce. Scatter the chopped chives over the sauce and garnish with an olive, a limequat half, and a strawberry half. For added height and dimension, you may wish to serve the martini glass on a small square plate.

LOBSTER
1 large (1½-pound) lobster, antennae attached

1 tablespoon extra virgin olive oil

1 teaspoon unsalted butter

2 shallots, finely diced

Sea salt

Freshly ground black pepper

SALAD
1 tablespoon fresh horseradish, peeled and grated

½ cup tomato paste

2 tablespoons mayonnaise

2 tablespoons heavy cream

1 teaspoon lemon juice

½ teaspoon Pernod

2 tablespoons orange juice, no pulp

⅛ teaspoon cayenne pepper

Sea salt

Freshly ground black pepper

6 ounces mesclun greens

DISH
2 tablespoons chopped chives

4 green colossal olives

2 limequats, halved

2 strawberries, halved

SERVES 4

QUICK TIP: KEEPING LETTUCE FRESH

In a recipe such as this one, where you're using only a small amount of greens, you'll probably have some left over. How do you keep them crisp and colorful? It's actually quite simple. Take a re-sealable plastic bag and place a sheet of paper towel inside. Make sure the paper towel is plain white; teddy bears and flowers may look cute, but the dye doesn't help the flavor or color of your lettuce. The paper towel absorbs any excess moisture that may still be in the lettuce and cause it to wilt. Gently press much of the air out of the bag and seal it. This should keep your lettuce fresh, crisp, and colorful for at least a week.

Mesclun Duck Breast Salad
with Raspberry-Shallot Vinaigrette

This is one of my personal favorites and can be used as a salad or entrée. I love the way the buttery flavor and texture of the duck is balanced with the slightly sweet yet tart acidity of the raspberry vinaigrette.

You may use mixed baby greens for this recipe or create your own mesclun mix by tearing bite-sized pieces of baby red oak leaf, baby arugula, baby mâche, endive, frisée, and radicchio. This recipe is so easy that it takes just 20 minutes to prepare.

WINE PAIRING *2001 Blockheadia Ringnosii, Zinfandel, Napa, California*
2000 Robert Sinskey Vineyards, Four Vineyards Pinot Noir, Napa, California

DUCK BREAST

1 pound Moulard duck breast filets

Sea salt

Freshly ground black pepper

RASPBERRY-SHALLOT VINAIGRETTE

2 tablespoons raspberry vinegar

1 tablespoon sherry vinegar

1/2 teaspoon Dijon mustard

3 shallots, diced

2 teaspoons sugar

Sea salt

Freshly ground black pepper

1/2 cup extra virgin olive oil

DISH

1 pound mesclun greens

Raspberries, for garnish

Raspberry Coulis (see page 216)

SERVES 4

FOR THE DUCK BREAST

1. Preheat oven to 400 degrees.

2. Using a very sharp knife and being careful not to cut into the meat, score the skin of the duck breasts in a crisscross pattern. Season both sides with salt and pepper.

3. Heat a large sauté pan over high heat until very hot. Place the duck breasts in the pan, skin side down, and sear them until some of the fat has melted and the skin is brown and crisp, about 3 minutes. Turn the breasts over and cook them for an additional 3 minutes. Pour off the fat and discard, or chill and use it as a spread for bread and crackers.

4. Place the duck breasts on a baking rack and bake until medium rare, about 8 minutes. Transfer the breasts onto a warm platter, skin side up, and tent loosely with aluminum foil. Allow breasts to rest so the juices that collected in the center during cooking have time to redistribute throughout the meat, making it tender and juicy.

FOR THE RASPBERRY-SHALLOT VINAIGRETTE

1. In a small bowl, combine the raspberry and sherry vinegars, mustard, shallots, sugar, salt, and pepper. Whisk together thoroughly. Slowly whisk in the oil to emulsify. Season to taste with salt, pepper, and sugar, if needed.

2. Let the dressing rest for at least 15 minutes to infuse the vinegar, and then adjust seasoning if necessary.

PRESENTATION

Assemble greens on individual plates and drizzle with dressing. Fan the duck over the salad and garnish with raspberries. Drizzle Raspberry Coulis on the plate.

QUICK TIP: SCORING DUCK BREAST FILETS
Why do I score my duck filets before cooking? There are three reasons:
1. Scoring the filet lets some fat escape from the meat into the pan, allowing you to cook it without additional fat.
2. Scoring allows flavor in, enabling the salt and pepper to be introduced directly to the meat, rather than just to its skin.
3. Most importantly, scoring the filet prevents it from curling up in the pan, which would make it cook unevenly.

Mesclun Duck Breast Salad with Raspberry-Shallot Vinaigrette

Spring Greens with Vine-Ripened Tomato, Feta, Shallots, Croûtons & Dijon Dressing

This is the simplest salad we make at Biró and also one of the most popular, due to its versatility and the fact that it's created with ingredients familiar to everyone. For variation, serve it with the Raspberry-Shallot Vinaigrette from the previous recipe.

WINE PAIRING *2002 Rudi Pichler, Grüner Veltliner, Wachau, Austria*
2003 Bonny Doon Vineyard, Pacific Rim Riesling, Monterey, California

DIJON DRESSING

2 tablespoons Dijon mustard

1 tablespoon sugar

1 cup white wine vinegar

1 cup water

1 cup extra virgin olive oil

Sea salt

Freshly ground black pepper

CROÛTONS

1 tablespoon extra virgin olive oil

1 tablespoon unsalted butter

2 slices white bread, crusts removed and diced

DISH

1 pound spring greens

1 vine-ripened tomato, seeded and diced

10 ounces Feta cheese, diced

4 shallots, diced

Chive Oil, for garnish
(see page 218)

SERVES 4

FOR THE DIJON DRESSING

Whisk the mustard, sugar, vinegar, and water together in a mixing bowl. Slowly whisk in the oil and season to taste with salt and pepper. Add more sugar, if needed.

FOR THE CROÛTONS

Melt the oil and butter in a sauté pan over high heat. Add the diced bread and toast until golden brown. Remove from heat and allow to cool.

PRESENTATION

Place the greens and Dijon Dressing in a mixing bowl and toss to completely coat each leaf. Place the coated greens in individual bowls and sprinkle the salad with tomato, Feta, shallots, and croûtons. Drizzle Chive Oil over the salad.

QUICK TIP: GET YOUR HANDS DIRTY!
When coating leaves with dressing, I do it by hand so I can feel that the dressing has properly made contact with each green, imparting its flavor throughout the dish.

Bison Carpaccio on Arugula with Shaved Parmesan

If you've not yet worked with bison, you should! It is juicy but not fatty, and very flavorful but not "gamey." It's healthy too.

I get my bison from a wonderful farmer in the Northwoods of Wisconsin, and you can just taste his care and the purity of his land in each piece of meat. If you don't have access to bison where you live, ask your butcher if he can get it for you, or simply use beef tenderloin instead.

WINE PAIRING *1994 Tinto Pesquera. Gran Reserva, Ribera del Duero, Spain*
2001 Domaine du Vieux Chêne, "Haie aux Grives," Côtes du Rhône, France

1. Combine the peppercorns, fennel seeds, salt, and lavender in a mortar and coarsely crush with a pestle. You could alternatively pulse the ingredients in a food processor for a few seconds.

2. Rub 1 tablespoon of the oil over the bison, and then coat it with the spice mixture. Let stand 1 hour at room temperature.

3. Heat the remaining 3 tablespoons of oil in a large sauté pan over high heat. Add the bison and sear on all sides, turning every 2 minutes, for about 12 minutes total. The bison should be completely rare in the center. Chill until cold, and then wrap in plastic and freeze for at least 1 hour.

4. Slice the meat as thinly as possible.

PRESENTATION

Place arugula in the center of each serving plate. Surround with bison slices and garnish with Parmesan shavings. You may also wish to garnish it with a drizzle of olive oil.

2 teaspoons whole black peppercorns

1 teaspoon white peppercorns

2 teaspoons fennel seeds

1 teaspoon kosher salt

1½ teaspoons lavender

4 tablespoons extra virgin olive oil

12 ounces trimmed bison tenderloin

2 cups lightly packed arugula

2 ounces Parmesan cheese, shaved

SERVES 8

QUICK TIP: SLICING MEAT PAPER THIN
With a recipe such as this one, you can slice the meat with a very sharp knife, or if you have one, with a meat slicer. Either way, you should freeze the meat before cutting, as it's then much easier to slice. If you're cutting it by hand and the meat is too frozen, wait until it thaws some before proceeding so you don't cut yourself. If it becomes too warm during the cutting process, simply put it back into the freezer until it firms up again. If you've sliced your meat thinly enough, it will thaw before serving. If not, allow it to thaw on the serving plates and then serve.

Mushroom & Spinach Strudel with Light Champagne Vinaigrette

QUICK TIP: COOKING WITH CHAMPAGNE
Because of Champagne's complexity in fruit, tartness, and mouth-feel, it's a great substitute for vinegar. In this recipe, I'm using Champagne because I need tartness, fruitiness, and a bit of sugar. Champagne possesses all three. Equally important, its bubbles provide an effervescence that enlivens the taste buds and balances out the earthy mushroom flavor. Next time you make a dessert, stock, sauce, or dressing, consider giving your dish a bit of bubbly.

Mushroom & Spinach Strudel with Light Champagne Vinaigrette

Strudel conjures up images of flaky, old-world desserts for most Americans, but in Europe, we also fill the thin pastry crust with an array of savory offerings. You may freeze this strudel, unsliced, and simply reheat it for a delicious addition to an impromptu dinner party.

In season, I use wild mushrooms foraged from the Wisconsin countryside, but a blend of store-bought portabella, crimini, shiitake, button, and chanterelle mushrooms will work nicely. This salad may be served cool or warm.

WINE PAIRING *2002 Avila, Pinot Noir, San Luis Obispo, California*
2002 Wild Hog, Estate Pinot Noir, Russian River, California

FOR THE MUSHROOM AND SPINACH FILLING

In a sauté pan, melt the butter with the oil. Add the shallots and garlic and sauté until softened, about 1 minute. Add the mushrooms and sweat, about 2 minutes. Add the spinach, parsley, chervil, and tarragon. Add the wine and reduce until almost dry. Remove from heat and allow to cool.

FOR THE STRUDEL

1. Preheat oven to 425 degrees.

2. Pour the flour into a stand mixer fitted with a paddle attachment. Add the salt, water, and oil and process until combined. Switch to a dough hook attachment and process on medium speed until the dough becomes elastic, about 10 minutes. Form the dough into a ball and brush with a bit of the butter. Wrap the dough with plastic wrap and allow to rest at room temperature for 2 hours.

3. Turn the dough out onto a large kitchen towel sprinkled with flour. Roll it out until it is as thin as possible; you should be able to see through it. Place the dough on a baking sheet lined with Silpat or parchment paper.

4. Pour the mushroom filling vertically down the right-hand side of the dough, leaving the edges clean. Brush the edges with eggwash. Lift up on the long edge of the dough and pull it up toward you until the dough begins folding over itself. Roll completely and brush the top and sides with the remaining butter. Sprinkle with Gruyère and bake until golden brown, about 30 minutes.

FOR THE CHAMPAGNE VINAIGRETTE

Whisk the vinegar, Champagne, mustard, sugar, salt, and pepper together in a mixing bowl. Continue to whisk, adding the oil in a slow, steady stream.

PRESENTATION

Toss the greens with the vinaigrette, making certain that each leaf is completely coated. Place the greens in the center of each serving plate. Slice the strudel into 1$^{1}/_{2}$-inch slices and place three slices on each salad. Drizzle Raspberry Coulis around the salad and garnish with a few fresh raspberries.

MUSHROOM AND SPINACH FILLING
1 tablespoon unsalted butter

1 tablespoon extra virgin olive oil

2 shallots, minced

2 cloves garlic, minced

4 cups assorted mushrooms, sliced

4 cups spinach, stems removed

1 tablespoon chopped parsley

1 tablespoon chopped chervil

1 tablespoon chopped tarragon

$^{1}/_{2}$ cup white wine

STRUDEL DOUGH
1$^{1}/_{2}$ cups flour

Pinch sea salt

$^{1}/_{2}$ cup lukewarm (110-degree) water

1 tablespoon vegetable oil

1 tablespoon Clarified Butter (see page 204)

Flour

Eggwash

$^{1}/_{3}$ cup grated Gruyère cheese

CHAMPAGNE VINAIGRETTE
1 cup white wine vinegar

$^{1}/_{2}$ cup Champagne or sparkling wine

$^{1}/_{4}$ cup Dijon mustard

$^{1}/_{4}$ cup sugar

1 teaspoon sea salt

1 teaspoon freshly ground white pepper

1 cup extra virgin olive oil

DISH
1 pound mesclun greens

Raspberry Coulis (see page 216)

Raspberries, for garnish

SERVES 4

Crisp Veal Sweetbreads with Port & Ginger

I just love this dish. First of all, it looks great. Then you bite into the sweetbreads. Crispiness gives way to a meltingly smooth, rich texture that's perfectly offset by the port and the gentle bite of the ginger. Just fantastic.

You may purchase a high-quality canned pickled ginger or make your own ginger for this recipe. To make your own, purchase a 5-ounce gingerroot, peel and julienne it, and blanching it in boiling water containing 1 tablespoon white wine, 1 teaspoon cumin, and a bit of sugar and sea salt. It adds spectacular flavor to this dish and a flash of pink. You'll need to prepare the sweetbreads one to two days in advance.

WINE PAIRING *2001 Bonny Doon Vineyard, Clos de Gilroy, Santa Cruz, California*
2003 Qupé Vineyard, Bien Nacido Cuvée, Santa Barbara, California

1 pound sweetbreads

1 quart White Veal Stock (see page 215), cold

1 Bouquet Garni (see page 204)

1 small yellow onion, chopped

1 carrot, peeled and chopped

1 stalk celery, chopped

1 tablespoon sea salt

$1/2$ cup flour

Sea salt

Freshly ground black pepper

1 tablespoon extra virgin olive oil

1 tablespoon unsalted butter

1 recipe Port Glaze (see page 213)

2 cups micro greens

4 ounces pickled ginger, julienned

Parsley Oil, for garnish
(see page 218)

SERVES 4

1. Soak the sweetbreads in cold water to cover until they become white, for at least 5 hours or overnight. Change the water two or three times until it remains clear. Rinse the sweetbreads under cold running water.

2. Place the stock, Bouquet Garni, onion, carrot, celery, sweetbreads, and salt in a large stockpot. Over low heat, slowly bring just to a boil. Remove the pot from the heat and allow the sweetbreads to infuse in the liquid for 30 minutes.

3. Remove the sweetbreads from the liquid, removing excess membranes from them, and refresh them under cold running water. Dry the sweetbreads and allow them to cool to room temperature. Refrigerate overnight to firm.

4. Remove the sweetbreads from the refrigerator and slice into four equal pieces. Place the flour in a bowl and dredge the sweetbreads in it, tapping them to remove excess flour. Lightly season with salt and pepper.

5. Melt the oil and butter in a sauté pan over high heat. Add the sweetbreads, smooth side down, and sauté them until golden brown, about 5 minutes. Turn them and cook an additional 1 to 2 minutes. Remove from the pan but reserve the pan and its drippings.

6. Wipe some of the drippings from the pan with a paper towel. Pour in the Port Glaze and warm.

PRESENTATION

Place one sweetbread on the center of each serving plate. Pour the Port Glaze over the sweetbreads, allowing it to drip off and form a vibrant mirror on the plate. Garnish the top of each sweetbread with micro greens and pickled ginger and drizzle Parsley Oil around the plate's perimeter.

Tarragon Lamb Filet with Micro Greens & Cranberry Emulsion

Lamb and cranberry make a delightful cold-weather flavor combination. When selecting lamb for purchase, look for lighter colored meat, as this indicates a younger animal that will have a delicate flavor and moist, tender texture. Darker cuts indicate an older animal, which will have a more pronounced flavor and less-tender flesh.

Micro greens are miniature greens grown specifically to have concentrated flavor and yet remain tiny. If you can't locate them, substitute the greens of your choice. Mesclun greens cut en chiffonade work beautifully for this salad.

WINE PAIRING *1998 Château Bel-Air, St. Émilion, Bordeaux, France*
1999 Havens, Merlot Reserve, Napa Valley, California

FOR THE TARRAGON LAMB FILET

1. Wash the lamb filets and pat dry with paper towels. In a sauté pan, melt the oil and butter over high heat and sear the filets on all sides until lightly golden. Reduce heat to medium and continue to sauté until the meat is golden brown, about 5 minutes, turning the filets over once during the cooking process.

2. Remove the filets to a warmed dish, season with salt and pepper, and cover with the tarragon. Tent loosely with aluminum foil and allow to rest.

FOR THE CRANBERRY EMULSION

1. Heat the vinegar, cranberry juice, and cranberries in a small saucepan over low heat until the cranberries have plumped.

2. Place the plumped cranberries in a food processor or blender and begin to process. Slowly add the oils and lemon juice and process until smooth. Season to taste with salt and pepper.

PRESENTATION

Place the greens in a mixing bowl. Add one-half of the cranberry emulsion and toss to lightly coat each leaf. Thinly slice the lamb filets on an angle. Arrange the slices on the perimemeter of the serving plates and place the salad in the center. Pour the remaining cranberry emulsion over the dish and garnish with the tarragon sprigs.

TARRAGON LAMB FILET

1 pound lamb filets

1 tablespoon extra virgin olive oil

2 tablespoons unsalted butter

Sea salt

Freshly ground black pepper

1/4 cup chopped tarragon

CRANBERRY EMULSION

2 tablespoons sherry vinegar

4 tablespoons cranberry juice

1/3 packed cup dried cranberries

1/3 cup walnut oil

1/4 cup peanut oil

Juice of 1 lemon

Sea salt

Freshly ground black pepper

DISH

2 pounds micro greens

4 sprigs tarragon

SERVES 4

QUICK TIP: ABOUT EMULSIONS

An emulsion is a preparation in which you add one liquid substance to another, but the liquids do not mix. In order to turn the liquids into a smooth blend, or make them stable, you must add an emulsifying, or binding, agent. An example of this is when you disperse droplets of oil into vinegar: the two do not mix. If, however, you add an emulsifier, such as an egg yolk, and whisk them together, they will become stable and form the basis of a vinaigrette. This preparation is also the basis of emulsified sauces such as hollandaise and its derivatives.

Mâche with Smoked Eel & Bacon-Dijon Dressing

This is one of the very first salads I introduced at Biró. It combines rustic, old-world flavors with minimalistic Asian nuances, one of my favorite juxtapositions in cooking. Though this salad is simple in terms of preparation, its elements yield profound flavor. Don't use smoked bacon for the dressing, as it would upstage the smokiness of the eel.

WINE PAIRING *2002 L'Ecole N°41, Fries Vineyard Semillon, Walla Walla Valley, Washington*
2001 Château Carbonnieux, Graves Blanc, Bordeaux, France

BACON-DIJON DRESSING

1/2 cup coarsely chopped bacon

2 tablespoons Dijon mustard

1 tablespoon sugar

1 cup white wine vinegar

1 cup water

1 cup extra virgin olive oil

Sea salt

Freshly ground black pepper

DISH

1 pound mâche

8 ounces smoked eel

1/4 cup crème fraîche

4 cherry tomatoes, halved

Dill leaves, for garnish

SERVES 4

FOR THE BACON-DIJON DRESSING

1. Fry the bacon until crispy and drain on a paper towel.

2. Whisk the mustard, sugar, vinegar, and water together in a mixing bowl. Continue whisking, adding the oil in a slow, steady stream; season to taste with salt and pepper. Add more sugar, if necessary. Add the bacon and mix to combine.

PRESENTATION

In a mixing bowl, place the mâche and pour in the Bacon-Dijon Dressing. Toss to completely coat each leaf. Slice the eel on an angle into 32 equal pieces. Place mounds of the coated mâche in the center of each serving plate. I prefer square plates for this presentation. Place two slices of eel at the 12:00, 3:00, 6:00, and 9:00 plate positions. In each corner of the plate, shape a small quenelle of crème fraîche. Garnish with the cherry tomatoes and dill leaves.

QUICK TIP: FRYING BACON

For extra-crispy bacon, cut it before frying; however, be careful not to cut the bacon too small. Bacon shrinks in size by about one-fifth during the cooking process, and depending on the application, bacon that is chopped too finely prior to cooking may get lost in the finished dish preparation.

Duck Terrine with Black Truffle–Herb Vinaigrette on Micro Greens

Though always elegant, terrines aren't always complicated to create—especially when it comes to mosaic- or pâté-style terrines, which don't contain layers. This is a pâté en terrine of forcemeats, or finely ground meats. You simply need to make the forcemeat, place it in the terrine mold, and sit back and wait for the delectable offering to firm and infuse. Without the salad, the terrine makes a sophisticated amuse-bouche or appetizer. You will need to prepare the terrine 48 hours before serving.

WINE PAIRING *1998 Chateau Canon la Gaffelière, St. Émilion, Bordeaux, France*
2000 Domaine Xavier Besson, Givry "Le Petit Prétans," Burgundy, France

FOR THE DUCK TERRINE

1. Place the bread in a mixing bowl and pour cream over it. Allow to soak for 2 to 3 minutes.

2. Heat the oil in a large sauté pan over high heat. Add the duck, pork neck, and chicken livers and season with the cloves, nutmeg, salt, and pepper to taste. Sauté, stirring constantly, until lightly golden, about 1 minute.

3. Reserving the sauté pan and drippings, pour the sautéed meat cubes into a large mixing bowl. Add the cream-soaked bread and cognac and stir well to combine.

4. In the same pan in which you sautéed the meat cubes, place the shallots and apple and cook over low heat until softened, 1 to 2 minutes. Add the softened shallots and apples to the bowl containing the meat cubes. Mix well to combine and refrigerate until completely cold.

5. Process the cold forcemeat mixture through a meat grinder or food processor until coarsely ground. Season with salt and pepper to taste.

6. Preheat oven to 300 degrees. Line a 12-inch-by-3-inch ovenproof lidded terrine with plastic wrap, leaving three-inch overhangs on the long sides of the terrine. Line the bottom and sides of the terrine with the bacon, reserving one slice. Fill the terrine with the forcemeat mixture, packing it down tightly. Cover the top of the terrine with the reserved slice of bacon. Place the thyme and bay leaves on top, fold over the overhanging plastic, and put on the lid.

7. Bake the terrine in a bain-marie until warmed through, about 1 to 1¹/₂ hours, or until a meat thermometer inserted into the terrine's center indicates a 150-degree internal temperature. Remove from oven and cool the terrine rapidly by submerging it in an ice bath. When the terrine is cold, remove it from the ice bath and remove the lid.

8. Cut a piece of cardboard to fit inside the terrine mold and cover it with aluminum foil. Set the foil-covered cardboard on top of the terrine and evenly distribute weights, such as cans of vegetables, on top of it. Refrigerate for 48 hours.

FOR THE BLACK TRUFFLE–HERB VINAIGRETTE

Whisk together the vinegars, water, mustard, shallot, and chives. Slowly whisk in the oils. Add the truffle and season with sugar, salt, and pepper to taste.

PRESENTATION

Use the plastic wrap to carefully remove the terrine from the mold. Unwrap and cut the terrine into slices about one-quarter inch thick, discarding the thyme and bay leaf. Place one slice on each serving plate and place a mound of salad next to it. Drizzle the plate with Raspberry Coulis.

DUCK TERRINE
6 slices white bread, crusts removed

¹/₂ cup heavy cream

2 tablespoons grapeseed oil

1 pound skinless, boneless duck meat, cut into 1-inch cubes

1 pound pork neck, cut into 1-inch cubes

7 ounces chicken livers, cut into 1-inch cubes

¹/₄ teaspoon ground cloves

¹/₄ teaspoon ground nutmeg

Sea salt

Freshly ground black pepper

¹/₄ cup cognac

4 shallots, finely diced

1 apple, peeled, cored, quartered, and thinly sliced

9 ounces unsmoked-bacon slices

Sprig thyme

2 Turkish bay leaves

BLACK TRUFFLE–HERB VINAIGRETTE
³/₄ cup red wine vinegar

¹/₄ cup balsamic vinegar

¹/₈ cup water

1 teaspoon Dijon mustard

1 shallot, minced

2 teaspoons minced chives

1 cup extra virgin olive oil

1 tablespoon white truffle oil

1 tablespoon minced black truffle

1 teaspoon sugar

Sea salt

Freshly ground black pepper

DISH
1¹/₂ pounds micro greens

Raspberry Coulis, for garnish (see page 216)

SERVES 12

Lentil Salad with Bacon & Frisée

The German and French are quite keen on lentils, so I've prepared countless lentil salads in my career: puy lentil salads, brown lentil salads, warm lentil salads, chilled lentil salads, vegetarian lentil salads, lentil salads with game—you name it. Luckily, they're all delicious, as is this simple variation. It is served at room temperature.

When working with lentils, it's important to first pick them over, discarding any bad ones, and then rinse them under cool running water to clean.

WINE PAIRING *2000 P. Antinori, Chianti Classico Riserva, Tuscany, Italy*
2002 Mas de Gourgonnier, Mme. Nicolas Cartier, Les Baux de Provence, France

1 cup brown lentils

2 strips unsmoked bacon, coarsely chopped

1 small yellow onion, diced

2 carrots, peeled and diced

2 cloves garlic, minced

1 shallot, minced

3 tablespoons red wine vinegar

1 tablespoon Dijon mustard

3 tablespoons extra virgin olive oil

Sea salt

Freshly ground black pepper

1 pound frisée, torn into bite-size pieces

Parsley Oil, for garnish
(see page 218)

SERVES 4

1. Place the lentils in a stockpot and cover with 4 cups cold water. Bring to a boil over high heat and then reduce heat to medium-low. Simmer until the lentils are al dente, about 15 to 20 minutes; drain.

2. While the lentils are simmering, fry the bacon in a medium sauté pan until crisp. Transfer the bacon to a plate lined with paper towels, reserving the pan and the fat.

3. Add the onion and carrots to the pan in which you fried the bacon and sauté over medium-high heat until the carrots are tender, about 15 to 20 minutes. Add the garlic and shallot and sauté an additional 2 minutes.

4. In a mixing bowl, whisk together the vinegar and mustard. Slowly whisk in the oil to emulsify; season to taste with salt and pepper.

5. Place one-third of the vinaigrette in a separate mixing bowl and add the frisée. Toss to coat.

6. In the bowl containing the remaining vinaigrette, place the lentils, sautéed onions, carrots, and fried bacon. Mix well to combine.

PRESENTATION

Place frisée on the center of each serving plate. Top with lentil salad and drizzle Parsley Oil around the plate's perimeter.

Roasted Striped Beets with Fennel, Mâche & Yogurt–Walnut Oil Dressing

This gorgeous salad yields profound flavors and an array of textures: the firm meatiness of the roasted beets, the light crispness of the fennel, the feathery softness of the mâche, the crunchiness of the Parmesan bread, and the silky creaminess of the dressing. I know you'll love it.

WINE PAIRING *2002 Columbia Crest, Sauvignon Blanc/Semillon, Columbia Valley, Washington*
2000 Domaine Ernest Burn, Riesling St. Imer "La Chapelle," Alsace, France

1. Preheat oven to 400 degrees. Wrap the beets tightly in aluminum foil and cook until fork-tender, about 1 hour. Allow the beets to cool slightly, and then slip the peels off under cold running water. Slice the beets into quarter-inch rounds.

2. In a large mixing bowl, whisk together the yogurt, oil, and sage. Add the beets, fennel, and mâche; toss to coat.

3. Place the bread slices on a sheet pan. Coat one side of the slices with oil, and then cover with Parmesan and season with salt and pepper. Broil until the cheese is light golden brown, about 1 minute. Cut each slice in half on a diagonal.

PRESENTATION

Place a mound of beet salad on the center of each serving plate and sprinkle with daikon sprouts. Prop a halved slice of Parmesan bread on opposite sides of each salad.

12 ounces striped beets

1/2 cup plain yogurt

5 tablespoons walnut oil

1 tablespoon chopped sage

1 cup shaved fennel bulb

5 ounces mâche

4 slices rye bread

2 tablespoons extra virgin olive oil

1 cup grated Parmesan cheese

Sea salt

Freshly ground black pepper

1/2 cup daikon sprouts

SERVES 4

QUICK TIP: WHAT ARE DAIKON SPROUTS?

Daikon sprouts are immature daikon radishes, which are sweet, crisp, and juicy Asian radishes with white flesh and a large, bulbous shape. If you can't find daikon sprouts, you may substitute alfalfa sprouts or chives in this recipe.

Trio of Vegetable Sorbets with Spring Salad

Light, clean, and absolutely packed with flavor, this salad is as beautiful as it is easy to make. If you like, you can leave off the diced black truffle in the spring salad; it will still be delicious. Without the salad, one sorbet or just a small serving of each would make a fantastic amuse-bouche.

WINE PAIRING *2001 Sokol Blosser, Pinot Noir, Willamette Valley, Oregon*
2000 Philippe Gavignet, Bourgogne Rouge, Burgundy, France

SORBETS

1 pound carrots, peeled and diced

1$^1/_2$ pounds red beets, cooked, peeled, and diced

1 pound celery, trimmed and diced

Sea salt

Freshly ground white pepper

SPRING SALAD

1 tablespoon diced black truffle

1 tablespoon sherry vinegar

$^1/_8$ teaspoon Dijon mustard

$^1/_4$ cup grapeseed oil

1 tablespoon hazelnut oil

1 tablespoon white truffle oil

Sea salt

Freshly ground black pepper

1 pound spring greens

DISH

Carrot juice

Beet juice

Chive Oil, for garnish
(see page 218)

SERVES 4

FOR THE SORBETS

1. If using an ice cream machine for this recipe, prepare the bowl inserts as per your machine manufacturer's instructions. If you do not have an ice cream machine, place three small stainless steel bowls in the freezer to chill.

2. For each of the sorbets, purée each vegetable separately in a food processor or blender until it is as liquefied as possible. Pass each juice separately through a fine-mesh sieve. Season to taste with salt and pepper. Reserve some of the carrot and beet juices for garnish.

3. Pour the first juice into the bowl of your ice cream machine and process according to your machine's specifications. Repeat the process for the other two sorbets. If using the stainless steel bowl method, place each juice in a separate bowl and remove from freezer every half hour and stir. This process can take up to 2 hours, depending on your freezer and the climate in which you live.

4. Using the edge of a teaspoon, scoop the sorbet into quenelle shapes and place them onto a Silpat- or parchment-lined sheet pan and freeze until ready to serve.

FOR THE SPRING SALAD

In a mixing bowl, whisk together the truffle, vinegar, and mustard. Slowly whisk in the oils in a thin, steady stream. Season to taste with salt and pepper. Add the greens and toss to coat.

PRESENTATION

Place a mound of Spring Salad on each serving plate. Place one quenelle each of the carrot, beet, and celery sorbets atop the salads. Drizzle carrot and beet juices around the plate's perimeter and garnish with Chive Oil.

Chicory with Red Wine Vinegar, Ricotta, Gorgonzola, Leeks & Champignons

This is an elegant salad that can be created quickly—in less than 15 minutes. Chicory is often called Belgian endive in the United States. If you can't find linseed oil, substitute grapeseed oil.

WINE PAIRING *1997 Marqués de Cáceres, Reserva, Rioja, Spain*
2001 Peachy Canyon, Westside Zinfandel, Paso Robles, California

1. Remove the leaves from the chicory and discard the center, which is bitter.

2. Bring a small pot of water to a boil and blanch the leek rounds for 10 seconds. Remove from water and place in an ice bath. Drain.

PRESENTATION

I like to serve this salad layered and family style; so on a simple platter, layer the chicory leaves, champignons, and leeks. Drizzle with vinegar and linseed oil. Crumble the ricotta and Gorgonzola on top of the salad and garnish with oregano. Season to taste with salt and pepper.

4 chicories

5 ounces leeks, white and light green parts only, thinly sliced into rounds

8 ounces champignons, thinly sliced

3 tablespoons red wine vinegar

5 tablespoons linseed oil

4 ounces ricotta cheese

4 ounces Gorgonzola cheese

2 tablespoons coarsely chopped oregano

Sea salt

Freshly ground black pepper

SERVES 4

QUICK TIP: WHAT'S A CHAMPIGNON?

A champignon is a robust French button mushroom. Any good button mushroom would work in this recipe, or feel free to substitute another mushroom of your choice.

Heirloom Tomatoes with Tomatillo Salad & International Salts

This simply elegant dish was created for a special wine dinner just after I had discovered these fantastic salts (see page 219 for sources). I've brought the dish back several times now, and each time it's to great acclaim. Guests are always shocked at just how drastically a different salt can change the flavor profile of a tomato.

If you can't find heirloom tomatoes, use cherry tomatoes, small yellow plum tomatoes, small red plum tomatoes, or a combination of the three. They'll work just fine.

WINE PAIRING *2001 Pojer & Sandri, Palai Müller Thurgaus, Trentino, Italy*
2002 Villa Maria, Clifford Bay Sauvignon Blanc Reserve, Marlborough, New Zealand

HEIRLOOM TOMATOES

1/2 pound yellow grape heirloom tomatoes

1/2 pound red grape heirloom tomatoes

2 tablespoons Danish Viking-smoked salt

1 tablespoon Australian Murray River salt

1 tablespoon fleur de sel

1 tablespoon Hawaiian black lava salt

1 tablespoon Hawaiian red clay salt

1 tablespoon Japanese Nazuna salt

1 tablespoon sel gris with herbs

1 tablespoon Peruvian pink salt

TOMATILLO SALAD

2 tablespoons extra virgin olive oil

1 pound tomatillos, cleaned and quartered, peels reserved

1/2 yellow onion, diced

Danish Viking-smoked salt

Sugar

SERVES 4

FOR THE TOMATOES

Slice each tomato in half lengthwise and top each half with a different salt, about 1/8 teaspoon.

FOR THE TOMATILLO SALAD

In a medium sauté pan, heat the oil. Add the tomatillos and onion. Season to taste with Danish Viking-smoked salt and cook until warmed. Add sugar to cut the acidity if necessary. Allow to cool to room temperature.

PRESENTATION

Open four large tomatillo skins so they resemble flowers. Place one on the center of each serving plate. I use square plates for this dish. Fill with tomatillo salad. Arrange the heirloom tomatoes with salts around the plate's perimeter.

Heirloom Tomatoes with Tomatillo Salad & International Salts

Grilled Goat Cheese on Spring Greens with
Citrus Vinaigrette & Iced Olive Oil Shavings

Grilled Goat Cheese on Spring Greens with Citrus Vinaigrette & Iced Olive Oil Shavings

We introduced this salad in the spring of 2004 and it's been a huge hit, due in no small part, I'm sure, to Shannon raving about it in the dining room every time she eats it—which is nearly every time she sets foot in the building, and usually within ten minutes of doing so.

The salad is simple, flavorful, and fun to make, which is a good thing. If it goes over in your house like it has at Biró, you'll be making it a lot!

WINE PAIRING *2002 Domaine A. Cailbourdin, Pouilly-Fumé "Les Cornets," Loire, France*
1998 Castello di Meleto, Chianti Classico Riserva, Italy

FOR THE GRILLED GOAT CHEESE

1. Heat a grill, grill pan, or nonstick sauté pan to high heat.

2. Slice the goat cheese into 8 (4-ounce) rounds. Dredge the rounds in flour, completely covering the entire surface area. Gently pat the excess flour from the cheese.

3. Grill the goat cheese on both sides until light golden brown. Remove from heat.

FOR THE CITRUS VINAIGRETTE

1. Place the orange, limes, and lemon in a food processor or blender and process until smooth. Add the sugar and oil and pulse. If desired, adjust the flavor with salt and pepper. If vinaigrette is too sour, add more sugar. Reserve about $1/4$ cup of the vinaigrette for garnish.

2. Toss the spring greens with the remaining vinaigrette.

FOR THE ICED OLIVE OIL SHAVINGS

Spread the oil onto a sheet pan and place in the freezer until solid.

PRESENTATION

Place the vinaigrette-coated greens in the center of each serving plate. Top with two pieces Grilled Goat Cheese. Remove the sheet pan containing the olive oil from the freezer. Using the edge of a knife or a vegetable peeler, shave the frozen oil off in sheets. Sprinkle the shavings over the salads. Garnish the plate with orange segments and drizzle the plate with remaining vinaigrette. Serve immediately so your iced olive oil shavings do not melt before your guests see them.

GRILLED GOAT CHEESE

32 ounces goat cheese

Flour

CITRUS VINAIGRETTE

1 navel or blood orange, peeled

2 limes, peeled

$1/2$ lemon, peeled

2 tablespoons sugar

5 tablespoons extra virgin olive oil

1 pound spring greens

ICED OLIVE OIL SHAVINGS

1 cup extra virgin olive oil

DISH

16 orange segments

SERVES 4

Red Cabbage Salad with Cilantro, Bulgur, Ham & Dijon

This is a rustic, German-inspired recipe that's beautiful, affordable, and easy to create. I like to serve it family style.

WINE PAIRING *1998 Marqués de Murrieta, Tinto Crianza, Rioja, Spain*
2002 Casa Castillo, Monastrell, Jumilla, Spain

2 ounces bulgur

5 tablespoons orange juice

8 ounces red cabbage, julienned

$1/2$ red onion, diced

$1/2$ cup cilantro leaves

1 teaspoon honey

2 tablespoons balsamic vinegar

5 tablespoons extra virgin olive oil

1 clove garlic, crushed

$1/2$ teaspoon Dijon mustard

5 ounces cooked ham, thinly sliced

SERVES 4

1. Bring a small pot of water to a boil and blanch the bulgur in it for 1 to 2 minutes. Strain and place the bulgur in a large mixing bowl.

2. Place the juice in a small pan and bring to a boil over high heat. Pour the hot juice over the bulgur and allow to rest until the juice is completely absorbed, about 30 minutes.

3. Add the cabbage, onion, cilantro, honey, vinegar, oil, garlic, and mustard to the bowl containing the bulgur. Mix carefully to combine.

4. Heat a medium sauté pan over high heat. Add the ham and sauté 30 seconds each side.

PRESENTATION

Layer the ham in the center of a serving platter. Spoon Red Cabbage Salad atop the ham and serve immediately.

Grilled-Vegetable Salad with Caramelized Walnuts, Goat Cheese & Pesto

This is a very basic but flavorful salad taken from the basic vegetarian class at the Marcel Biró Culinary School. It also makes a wonderful filling for a sandwich on crusty bread.

WINE PAIRING *2002 Domaine Weinbach, Riesling Schlossberg, Alsace, France*
2001 Domaine du Dragon, "S. Michel" Rouge, Côtes de Provence, France

FOR THE GRILLED VEGETABLES

1. Grill the eggplant, zucchini, peppers, and squash until softened. This can be done on a grill or in a grill pan. Remove vegetables from heat and place in a large mixing bowl.

2. Heat the oil in a medium sauté pan over medium-high heat. Add the onion and sauté until golden brown, about 2 minutes. Add the garlic and tomato purée and cook an additional minute. Add the parsley, basil, and thyme. Pour this mixture over the grilled vegetables, add the Pesto, and toss well to combine.

FOR THE CARAMELIZED WALNUTS

Place the ingredients in a medium sauté pan and cook over high heat until the sugar caramelizes and the nuts become browned, about 5 minutes. Stir occasionally so the nuts do not stick together. Transfer the caramelized nuts to a Silpat- or waxed paper–lined baking sheet to cool.

PRESENTATION

Place the Grilled Vegetable Salad in the center of each serving plate. Sprinkle the goat cheese over the salads and garnish with Caramelized Walnuts.

GRILLED VEGETABLES

1 medium eggplant, sliced into rounds

1 small zucchini, sliced into rounds

1 small red bell pepper, seeded and sliced

1 small green bell pepper, seeded and sliced

1 small yellow squash, sliced into rounds

3 tablespoons extra virgin olive oil

1 small red onion, sliced into rounds

2 teaspoons minced garlic

1 medium vine-ripened tomato, peeled and puréed

3 tablespoons finely chopped parsley leaves

2 tablespoons finely chopped basil leaves

1 tablespoon finely chopped thyme

Pesto (see page 217)

CARAMELIZED WALNUTS

$1/2$ cup walnut halves

2 tablespoons brown sugar

$1/4$ teaspoon sea salt

$1/8$ teaspoon cayenne pepper

1 teaspoon walnut oil

DISH

4 ounces goat cheese, crumbled

SERVES 4

Lamb Loin à la Provençale with Escargot Ragoût,
Smoked Bacon–Wrapped Haricots Verts & Schupfnudeln

entrées

Black Pheasant with Thyme Demi-Glace on Creamed Salsify with Lemon-Parsley Glazed Potatoes

Prosciutto-Wrapped Veal Cutlet with Port Wine–Morel Sauce & Spinach Pasta

Medallions of Pork in Black Cherry–Pepper Sauce with Spätzle & Braised Fennel

Herb-&-Mustard-Crusted Milk Rabbit Loin with Bordelaise Sauce & Sautéed Fingerling Potatoes

Wild Mushroom Ravioli with Sautéed Baby Spinach & Chive-Garlic Velouté

Lamb Loin à la Provençale with Escargot Ragoût, Smoked Bacon–Wrapped Haricots Verts & Schupfnudeln

Filet Mignon Madagascar Flambé in Cognac Crème & Crushed Red Pepper with Garlic Potato Rosettes

Sole en Papillote on Sautéed Baby Spinach with Tomato Fettuccini

Tender Milk Rabbit Loin in Lingonberry Sauce with Poached Williams' Bon Pear & Sage Spätzle

Glazed Moulard Duck Breast Filet with Vichy Carrots & Duchesse Potatoes

Summer Vegetable Tower with Montrachet Cheese Medallion, Spätzle & Tomato Glaze

Lime-Grilled Mahi Mahi with Morel Sauce & Chanterelle-Stuffed Ravioli

Black Pepper–Seared Salmon Filet with Egg Pasta, Sautéed Green Asparagus & Champagne-Lemon Crème

Zucchini-Wrapped Fettuccini with Sun-Dried Tomatoes, Mushrooms, Baby Spinach & Roasted-Red-Pepper Coulis

Ahi Tuna Filet with Lobster-Veal Roulade on Glass Noodle Salad with Sauce Arméricaine

Portabella Schnitzel with Brie & Garlic Mashed Potato Rosettes

Horseradish-Encrusted Sirloin with Roasted Beets & Lyonnaise Potatoes

Ahi Tuna with Wilted Greens, Borlotti Beans, Cumin Toast & Orange-Sherry Vinaigrette

Maltese Baked Swordfish with Lemon-Parsley Glazed Potatoes

Venison Ragoût with Juniper Crème, Napa Cabbage & Garlic Mashed Potatoes

Hanger Steak with Herb-Sautéed Fettuccini, Grilled Blue Prawns, Spinach & Roquefort-Infused Demi-Glace

Rainbow Trout with Sautéed Grapes & Almonds, Summer Vegetables & Garlic-Parsley Potatoes

Capon with Sherry-Chanterelle Sauce on Sautéed Napa Cabbage with Lemon-Parsley Glazed Potatoes

Seared Sea Scallops with Pumpkin-Sage Crème, Wild Mushroom Risotto & Prosciutto Frivolity

Spring Spätzle Gratinée with Sautéed Vegetables and Montrachet Cheese Medallions

Black Pheasant with Thyme Demi-Glace on Creamed Salsify with Lemon-Parsley Glazed Potatoes

In this recipe, black pheasant doesn't refer to a type of game bird but rather a preparation method in which the bird is roasted breast-down in the pan, resulting in a deep, dark skin color. If possible, you should use a hen pheasant for this recipe. The females have more succulent flesh and therefore a more pronounced flavor than the larger males. If you can't find pheasant where you live, feel free to substitute a chicken or guinea hen in its place.

Salsify is a parsnip-shaped root vegetable that is also called oyster plant because of its delicate oyster flavor. You could use fennel, celery root, or even white asparagus in its place in this recipe.

WINE PAIRING *1999 Domaine Guffens-Heynen, Verget Saint-Véran, Burgundy, France*
1999 Domaine Maurice Ecard et Fils, Savigny les Beaune, Les Serpentières, Burgundy, France

BLACK PHEASANT

1 Bouquet Garni (see page 204)

3 cloves garlic

1 medium (3^1/$_2$-pound) pheasant

^{1}/$_3$ cup unsalted butter, melted

Sea salt

Freshly ground black pepper

THYME DEMI-GLACE

^{1}/$_2$ cup Beef Stock (see page 214)

2 tablespoons heavy cream

2 tablespoons Glace de Viande (see page 215)

1 teaspoon finely chopped thyme

Sea salt

Freshly ground black pepper

CREAMED SALSIFY

Juice of ^{1}/$_2$ lemon

10 ounces black salsify

^{1}/$_2$ cup crème fraîche

^{3}/$_4$ cup Chicken Stock (see page 214)

Freshly ground nutmeg

Sea salt

Freshly ground white pepper

DISH

1 recipe Lemon-Parsley Glazed Potatoes (see page 209)

Parsley sprigs, for garnish

SERVES 4

FOR THE BLACK PHEASANT

1. Preheat oven to 450 degrees.

2. Place the Bouquet Garni and garlic cloves inside the pheasant. Brush the skin with a bit of the butter. Season inside and out with salt and pepper.

3. Place the pheasant on one thigh in the roasting pan and roast for 15 minutes. Brush pheasant with more of the butter and turn it onto the other thigh; cook 15 additional minutes. Turn pheasant onto its breast, resting its legs on the edge so the juices run down into the breast, and cook for 30 additional minutes. Baste frequently with the juices and butter during the cooking process.

4. Remove from oven and allow to rest at least 5 minutes.

FOR THE THYME DEMI-GLACE

Place the stock in a large sauté pan and reduce by one-half. Whisk in the cream and add the Glace de Viande. Cook for 1 additional minute. Add thyme and cook, whisking constantly, until combined. Season to taste with salt and pepper.

FOR THE CREAMED SALSIFY

1. Pour the lemon juice into a bowl of cold water. Peel the salsify under cool running water and place it in the bowl of lemon water. Drain the salsify and pat dry with paper towels.

2. Bring a stockpot of salted water to a boil over high heat. Add the salsify and cook until al dente, about 10 to 15 minutes.

3. Meanwhile, place the crème fraîche and stock in a saucepan and bring to a boil over high heat. Reduce heat to medium-low and simmer until reduced by one-half. Season to taste with nutmeg, salt, and pepper.

4. Drain the salsify and place in an ice bath to stop the cooking process. Drain and cut the cooled salsify into ^{1}/$_4$-inch-by-2-inch-long lengths. Add the salsify to the crème fraîche–stock mixture and heat until the salsify is warmed, about 2 minutes. Adjust seasoning as necessary.

PRESENTATION

Place creamed salsify on the center of each serving plate. Slice the pheasant and place the meat on the salsify. Drizzle with Thyme Demi-Glace. Place Lemon-Parsley Glazed Potatoes beside the salsify and garnish with a sprig of parsley.

Prosciutto-Wrapped Veal Cutlet with Port Wine–Morel Sauce & Spinach Pasta

This is saltimbocca Biró style, without sage and with the addition of a seductive Port Wine–Morel Sauce. Spinach Pasta gives the dish a splash of freshness. You're in for a treat!

WINE PAIRING *2002 Eno Zinfandel – Teldeschi Vineyard, "Caught Red Handed," Sonoma, California*
2001 Cosentino Sangiovese, "Il Chiaretto," Yountville, California

FOR THE PROSCIUTTO-WRAPPED VEAL CUTLET

1. Preheat oven to 350 degrees.

2. Wrap a slice of prosciutto around each veal cutlet. Season to taste with salt and pepper.

3. Heat the oil in a medium sauté pan over high heat. Sauté cutlets until golden brown, about 1 minute each side. Transfer to a baking rack, and reserve the pan and drippings. Place in the oven and cook until medium, about 5 to 10 minutes. Remove from oven and tent loosely with aluminum foil.

FOR THE PORT WINE–MOREL SAUCE

1. Remove excess fat from the sauté pan in which you sautéed the Prosciutto-Wrapped Veal Cutlets. Add oil and heat pan over high heat. Add the shallots and garlic and sauté until glossy, about 1 minute. Deglaze and flambé with the port. Add the morels and sauté until all the liquid is absorbed, about 1 minute. Reduce heat to medium.

2. Pour in the cream and reduce by one-third. Whisk in the Glace de Viande and stock. Simmer, whisking frequently, for 5 minutes. Season to taste with salt and pepper.

PRESENTATION

Sauté the pasta in butter until warmed. Season to taste with salt and pepper. Wind the pasta into four equal portions and place in the center of each serving plate. Slice the Prosciutto-Wrapped Veal Cutlets on an angle and fan around the pasta. Drizzle the sauce around the plate's perimeter.

PROSCIUTTO-WRAPPED VEAL CUTLET

4 large slices prosciutto, thinly sliced

4 (5-ounce) portions veal inside rounds

Sea salt

Freshly ground black pepper

2 tablespoons extra virgin olive oil

PORT WINE–MOREL SAUCE

2 tablespoons extra virgin olive oil

1 tablespoon diced shallots

1 teaspoon minced garlic

1 tablespoon white port

8 ounces fresh morels, sliced

1 cup heavy cream

2 tablespoons Glace de Viande (see page 215)

$1/2$ cup Chicken Stock (see page 214)

Sea salt

Freshly ground black pepper

DISH

2 tablespoons unsalted butter

Spinach Pasta, cooked al dente (see page 206)

Sea salt

Freshly ground white pepper

SERVES 4

Medallions of Pork in Black Cherry–Pepper Sauce with Spätzle & Braised Fennel

This German-inspired dish is one of my personal favorites. The sweet tartness of the black cherries perfectly offsets the flavor of the pork, and the black pepper adds just the right amount of bite. The deep colors of the pork and Black Cherry–Pepper Sauce look lovely with spätzle, and braised fennel is a delicately flavored accompaniment.

WINE PAIRING *2002 Urziger Würzgarten, Riesling Kabinett, by Alfred Merkelbach, Germany*
2001 Domaine Carneros, Pinot Noir, Napa, California

PORK MEDALLIONS

1¹/₂ pounds pork tenderloins

Sea salt

Freshly ground black pepper

BLACK CHERRY–PEPPER SAUCE

1 cup sugar

3 cups water

1 pound fresh pitted cherries or ¹/₂ pound canned pitted cherries in juice, divided

1 tablespoon cognac

1 teaspoon Glace de Viande (see page 215)

Sea salt

1 tablespoon freshly ground black pepper

BRAISED FENNEL

2 fennel bulbs with greens

1 tablespoon unsalted butter

2 shallots, diced

¹/₂ cup heavy cream

Sea salt

Freshly ground white pepper

1 teaspoon Pernod

DISH

¹/₂ recipe Spätzle (see page 209)

SERVES 4

FOR THE PORK MEDALLIONS

1. Cut the tenderloins into pieces about 1 inch thick. Season with salt and pepper.

2. Heat a grill or grill pan over high heat. Grill the tenderloins until golden brown, about 2 minutes each side.

FOR THE BLACK CHERRY–PEPPER SAUCE

1. Place sugar and 2 tablespoons of water in a medium-sized stockpot and caramelize the sugar over low heat. Add two-thirds of the cherries, the remaining water, cognac, and Glace de Viande. Cook until the cherries are soft then remove from heat.

2. Place the cherry mixture in a food processor or blender and process until smooth. Pass through a fine-mesh sieve into a saucepan. Reduce over medium-low heat until it becomes syrupy, about 2 minutes. Add salt to taste and the black pepper.

FOR THE BRAISED FENNEL

1. Remove the greens from the fennel bulbs and reserve. Cut the bulbs into quarters. Remove the root, as it is bitter. Using a mandoline, cut the fennel into fine strips. If you do not own a mandoline, cut the fennel into juliennes.

2. In a sauté pan, melt the butter. Add the shallots and cook until glossy, about 1 minute. Add the fennel and cook until tender. Add the cream and reduce until it has a coating consistency. Season with salt and pepper. Add Pernod. Chop and add the reserved fennel greens.

PRESENTATION

Place the Spätzle on the center of each serving plate. Place the pork medallions around the Spätzle and drizzle with Black Cherry–Pepper Sauce. Using two tablespoons, shape the Braised Fennel into quenelles and place them in between the pork medallions. Slice the remaining ¹/₃ cup cherries in half and use as garnish.

QUICK TIP: WHAT'S A MANDOLINE

A mandoline is a manual slicer with adjustable stainless steel blades that allow you to slice fruits and vegetables into various shapes and thicknesses, from juliennes to dices, waffle cuts, and beyond. Mandolines not only cut down on your prep time, they give you beautiful slices that cook evenly because of their uniformity. You can find mandolines at any good kitchen supply store.

**Medallions of Pork in Black Cherry–Pepper Sauce
with Spätzle & Braised Fennel**

Herb-&-Mustard-Crusted Milk Rabbit Loin with Bordelaise Sauce & Sautéed Fingerling Potatoes

Milk rabbit is not a type of rabbit, but rather a preparation method in which the rabbit is placed in a buttermilk bath. Soaking wild game or poultry in buttermilk tenderizes the meat and extracts any bitterness it may contain. Buttermilk baths also work well for tenderizing tough cuts of beef.

WINE PAIRING *2001 Chateau Ste. Michelle, Canoe Ridge Vineyard Merlot, Colombia Valley, Washington*
2000 Beaujolais Moulin à Vent, Domaine du Granit, Burgundy, France

HERB-&-MUSTARD-CRUSTED RABBIT LOIN

4 rabbit loins, 8 ounces each

2 cups buttermilk

Sea salt

Freshly ground black pepper

Flour

2 tablespoons unsalted butter

1 tablespoon herbes de Provence

2 teaspoons diced shallots

2 teaspoons minced garlic

3 cups breadcrumbs

1 cup Dijon mustard

2 large eggs

BORDELAISE SAUCE

1¹/₂ tablespoons finely chopped shallots

8 white peppercorns, crushed

1 cup red wine

1¹/₂ cups White Veal Stock (see page 215)

1 Bouquet Garni (see page 204)

¹/₄ pound beef marrow, soaked in ice water for 4 hours

Sea salt

Freshly ground black pepper

1 tablespoon unsalted butter, chilled and diced

FINGERLING POTATOES

2 tablespoons unsalted butter

1 pound fingerling potatoes, quartered and boiled

Sea salt

Freshly ground black pepper

¹/₂ tablespoon chopped parsley

SERVES 4

FOR THE HERB-&-MUSTARD-CRUSTED RABBIT LOIN

1. Soak the loins in buttermilk at room temperature for at least 1 hour. Remove from the buttermilk and pat dry. Season lightly with salt and pepper. Dredge in the flour.

2. Preheat oven to 400 degrees.

3. Melt the butter in a medium ovenproof sauté pan over high heat. Sauté the loins until golden brown, about 4 to 5 minutes each side. Remove from heat.

4. In a small bowl, whisk together the herbes de Provence, shallots, garlic, breadcrumbs, mustard, and eggs. Season to taste with salt and pepper. Spoon the mixture onto each loin and press it down with your hands to completely cover the top. Place in the oven and bake until the crust is golden brown and the meat is medium, about 5 to 10 minutes.

FOR THE BORDELAISE SAUCE

1. Place the shallots, peppercorns, and wine in a medium saucepan and cook over high heat until reduced by one-third. Add the White Veal Stock and Bouquet Garni and simmer gently until the sauce coats the back of a spoon, about 20 minutes. Pass through a fine-mesh sieve into a clean saucepan.

2. Drain the beef marrow and slice into thin rounds. Place in a small saucepan with enough cold water to cover, and salt lightly. Bring just to a boil over medium heat. Turn off heat and allow the marrow to rest for 30 seconds before draining it through a chinoise or fine-mesh sieve. Discard the liquid.

3. Season the wine sauce to taste with salt and pepper. Whisk in the butter and add the beef marrow.

FOR THE FINGERLING POTATOES

Melt the butter in a medium sauté pan over medium heat. Add the boiled potatoes and sauté until lightly golden. Season to taste with salt and pepper. Sprinkle with parsley.

PRESENTATION

Pour a mirror of Bordelaise sauce on the center of each serving plate. Place potatoes on the sauce. Slice the loins on an angle into ¹/₄-inch-thick slices, being careful to keep the crusts intact. Fan around the potatoes.

Wild Mushroom Ravioli with Sautéed Baby Spinach & Chive-Garlic Velouté

A flavor-packed dish that combines earthy tones and ethereal textures, Wild Mushroom Ravioli with Sautéed Baby Spinach & Chive-Garlic Velouté may be used as at Biró—as an entrée—or you may add a piece of fish to make it an even more substantial main course. For variation, you may wish to add ¹/₂ cup shredded Parmesan or Gruyère to the Velouté sauce, whisking it in with the chives.

WINE PAIRING *2002 Avila, Pinot Noir, San Luis Obispo, California*
2001 Domaine d'Andézon, Côtes du Rhône, Rhône, France

FOR THE CHIVE-GARLIC VELOUTÉ

1. Melt the butter in a medium saucepan over medium-high heat. Add the garlic and sauté until glossy, about 15 to 30 seconds. Reduce heat to low. Add the flour and whisk until all the fat is absorbed.

2. Add the stock and bring to a simmer, whisking frequently. Simmer until thickened and the flour taste is gone, about 5 to 10 minutes. Season to taste with salt and pepper. Add the chives. If the sauce is too thick for your liking, add more stock.

PRESENTATION

Place six raviolis on the center of each plate. Drizzle the sauce around the plate's perimeter and place a mound of Sautéed Baby Spinach in the center of the raviolis. Garnish with a sprinkling of chives and cherry tomato halves.

CHIVE-GARLIC VELOUTÉ

2 tablespoons unsalted butter

1 tablespoon minced garlic

3 tablespoons flour

1¹/₂ cups White Veal Stock, cold (see page 215)

Sea salt

Freshly ground white pepper

1 tablespoon minced chives

DISH

3 recipes Wild Mushroom Ravioli (see page 208)

Sautéed Baby Spinach (see page 211)

Minced chives, for garnish

4 cherry tomatoes, halved, for garnish

SERVES 4

QUICK TIP: CLEANING MUSHROOMS

Most people use salt or water to clean mushrooms, and neither is a good idea. Salt dehydrates mushrooms, leaving them dry. Water is absorbed by mushrooms, leaving them spongy and diluted in flavor. I clean my mushrooms with flour, which acts as a dry cleanser and also removes excess moisture without dehydrating. Simply pour some flour into a large mixing bowl and add the mushrooms you wish to clean. Briskly rotate the bowl—make those mushrooms dizzy—and then remove them from the flour, brushing lightly with a dry pastry brush.

Lamb Loin à la Provençale with Escargot Ragoût, Smoked Bacon–Wrapped Haricots Verts & Schupfnudeln

Dishes from Provence are called à la Provençale and are characterized by the use of olive oil, tomato, and garlic. This recipe is one of the most popular at Biró, and its Provençal sauce—with or without the escargot—is wonderful served with pasta.

Haricots verts are French string beans. You may use any slender green bean in this recipe.

WINE PAIRING *2002 Chateau Ste. Michelle, Canoe Ridge Estate Merlot, Columbia Valley, Washington*
1997 Ruffino, Chianti Classico Riserva Ducale, Italy

LAMB LOIN
1 lamb loin (1$^1/_2$ pounds), cleaned and silver skin removed

Sea salt

Freshly ground black pepper

1 tablespoon extra virgin olive oil

PROVENÇAL SAUCE WITH ESCARGOT RAGOÛT
2 tablespoons extra virgin olive oil

8 ounces escargot

$^1/_2$ yellow onion, diced

1$^1/_2$ pounds vine-ripened tomatoes, peeled, seeded, and crushed

2 crushed garlic cloves

1 Bouquet Garni (see page 204)

$^3/_4$ cup dry white wine

1 teaspoon Pernod

2 teaspoons Glace de Viande (see page 215)

Sea salt

Freshly ground black pepper

1 tablespoon basil, en chiffonade

BACON-WRAPPED HARICOTS VERTS
8 ounces haricots verts

12 slices applewood-smoked bacon

1 tablespoon unsalted butter

Freshly ground white pepper

SCHUPFNUDELN
3 Russet potatoes

1 large egg, lightly beaten

2 egg yolks, lightly beaten

Freshly ground nutmeg

Sea salt

Freshly ground white pepper

1$^1/_2$ – 2 cups flour, plus more for dusting

1 tablespoon unsalted butter

SERVES 4

FOR THE LAMB LOIN

1. Preheat oven to 425 degrees.

2. Season the lamb loin generously with salt and pepper.

3. In an ovenproof sauté pan, heat the oil over high heat. Sear the loin on all sides until golden brown.

4. Place the pan in preheated oven and cook until medium, about 10 minutes.

5. Remove the lamb from oven and allow to rest at room temperature for about 3 to 5 minutes.

FOR THE PROVENÇAL SAUCE

1. Heat the oil in a covered saucepan over medium heat. Add the escargot and onion, and sauté until softened but not browned, about 2 to 3 minutes.

2. Add tomatoes and simmer for 15 minutes.

3. Add the garlic, Bouquet Garni, wine, Pernod, and Glace de Viande. Cover and cook for 15 minutes. Remove the lid and season to taste with salt and pepper. Allow to cook, uncovered, until the sauce is reduced by half.

4. Add fresh basil just before serving.

FOR BACON-WRAPPED HARICOTS VERTS

1. Preheat oven to 400 degrees. In a small saucepan, bring salted water to a boil. Add haricots verts and blanch until al dente, about 2 to 4 minutes.

2. Remove the haricots verts from the water and place in an ice-water bath until cooled. Remove from water and dry with a white paper towel.

3. Lay bacon strips out on a flat surface. Center a bundle of about ten haricots verts on each strip. Wrap bacon around the haricots verts. You may wish to slice the ends from beans so the bundles are uniform in size.

4. In a large ovenproof sauté pan, heat butter over high heat until melted. Add the bacon-wrapped haricots verts, making certain there is enough room in between bundles so the bacon does not stick together. Turn until all sides are golden brown.

5. Place the pan in the oven and cook until the bundles become crispy, about 4 minutes. Season to taste with pepper.

FOR THE SCHUPFNUDELN

1. Preheat oven to 375 degrees. Bake the potatoes until they are soft all the way through, about 1 hour. Allow to cool slightly.

2. Peel off the skins and process the potatoes through a food mill into a mixing bowl.

3. Add the egg, egg yolks, and nutmeg, salt and pepper to taste and stir. Add enough flour to form a stiff dough. Turn the dough out onto a floured surface and knead, continuing to add flour until the dough no longer sticks.

4. Roll the dough into a log about an inch in diameter; cut into half-inch-thick sections. Roll the sections into cigar-shaped dumplings about $2^1/_2$ inches long. Bend the dumplings into a half-moon shape so the ends are tapered and curved. Allow to rest about 20 minutes.

5. Melt the butter in a sauté pan over medium heat. Add the schupfnudeln and sauté until golden brown, about 2 minutes.

PRESENTATION

Slice the lamb loin on an angle. Fan the meat onto round plates and drizzle with the escargot ragoût. Arrange two schupfnudeln each at the 12:00, 4:00 and 8:00 positions on the plates. Each pair should form an X shape. Place the Bacon-Wrapped Haricots Verts at the 2:00, 6:00 and 10:00 plate positions. (See a photograph of this dish on page 138.)

QUICK TIP: GETTING THE MOISTEST MEAT

You may wonder how your favorite restaurant always gets their meats perfectly moist and tender. The secret is this: they allow their meat to rest at room temperature before cooking and then allow it to rest again before serving.

On *The Kitchens of Biró* I demonstrated with two duck breasts why you must never take your meat directly from the refrigerator to the pan. The first duck breast came directly from the refrigerator. It was inflexible and lightly colored. This is because, as we do when we're cold, meat in the refrigerator constricts, preserving all the blood in the center. Cooking this breast would have resulted in a tough, dry piece of meat. The second duck breast had been removed from the refrigerator 25 minutes earlier. It was flexible and colorful, which means the juices were distributed throughout the breast, making the muscle tissue soft. Cooking this duck breast would have resulted in a perfectly tender piece of meat.

After you've cooked your meat, let it rest before serving or cutting it. This allows the juices, which once again collected in the center during the cooking process, to redistribute throughout the meat.

Filet Mignon Madagascar Flambé in Cognac Crème & Crushed Red Pepper with Garlic Potato Rosettes

This very popular dish is our take on the traditional steak au poivre, or steak with pepper. We serve it with our Bacon-Wrapped Haricots Verts (recipe can be found in the previous lamb loin recipe.)

WINE PAIRING *1999 DeLille Cellars D2, Bordeaux Blend, Yakima Valley, Washington*
2000 Newton, Claret Bordeaux Blend, Napa, California

FILET MIGNON MADAGASCAR FLAMBÉ

6 (6 to 8 ounces each) filet mignons

Sea salt

Freshly ground black pepper

2 tablespoons Clarified Butter (see page 204)

2 tablespoons extra virgin olive oil

2 tablespoons unsalted butter, divided

1 shallot, diced

1 tablespoon green peppercorns, drained

$^1/_2$ cup cognac

1 cup heavy cream

1 tablespoon Glace de Viande (see page 215)

1 teaspoon red peppercorns

DISH

1 recipe Garlic Potato Rosettes (see page 210)

Crushed red peppercorns, for garnish

SERVES 6

FOR THE FILET MIGNON MADAGASCAR FLAMBÉ

1. Preheat oven to 375 degrees.

2. Thoroughly dry the steaks with paper towels. Season both sides with salt and pepper.

3. Heat a large sauté pan over high heat. Add Clarified Butter and oil. Add the steaks and sear until caramelized and brown, about 2 minutes each side.

4. Place a baking rack inside a roasting pan. Transfer the steaks to the rack and finish cooking in the oven until the desired doneness is achieved. Keep the sauté pan for later use.

5. Place steaks on a warm platter and tent loosely with aluminum foil. Allow to rest for 5 to 6 minutes.

6. Add 1 tablespoon of the butter and the shallot to the sauté pan and cook over medium heat for 30 seconds. Add the green peppercorns and cook for an additional 30 seconds.

7. Pour the cognac into the sauté pan and deglaze it, scraping up the brown bits that have formed in the pan. Allow to reduce for 1 to 2 minutes, and then add the cream and Glace de Viande.

8. Turn up the heat and bring to a boil. Boil until the sauce is thickened and reduced by two-thirds, about 4 to 5 minutes.

9. Decrease the heat to medium-low; add any steak drippings from the roasting pan and the remaining 1 tablespoon butter. Whisk thoroughly until the butter is incorporated. Add the red peppercorns and warm gently.

PRESENTATION

Pipe Garlic Potato Rosettes onto the serving plates. If serving with Bacon-Wrapped Haricots Verts, arrange three bundles on each plate. Place the filet in the center of the plate and top with Cognac Crème. Garnish with crushed red peppercorns.

QUICK TIP: DONENESS TEST FOR MEAT

Did you ever wonder how to tell the right temperature of your meat, seafood, or poultry? It's actually very simple: shake your hand to relax it then press between your thumb and index finger with your other hand. Now press your meat. If it feels like the spot between your thumb and index finger, your meat is rare. If your meat feels like the spot between your thumb and index finger when your hand is fully extended, your meat is medium. If your meat feels like the same spot on your hand when you make a fist, your meat is well done.

Sole en Papillote on Sautéed Baby Spinach with Tomato Fettuccini

En papillote is a preparation in which food is wrapped, cooked, and served in foil or grease-proof paper, such as parchment or wax paper. This is our version of a classical French recipe, and without exception, my guests and students are surprised at just how flavorful such a light preparation can be.

When purchasing sole for this recipe, make certain that it's true sole. There is no sole in American waters, and quite often what is sold as sole here is actually flounder. We use Dover sole for this dish.

WINE PAIRING *2003 Robert Sinskey Vineyards, Los Carneros Pinot Blanc, Napa, California*
2002 Cape Mentelle, Semillion/Sauvignon Blanc, Margaret River, Australia

FOR THE SOLE EN PAPILLOTE

1. Preheat oven to 400 degrees.

2. Fold the pieces of parchment paper in half lengthwise and cut into a heart shape. Butter the inside of each sheet, stopping 2 inches from the perimeter.

3. Place one sole filet, skin side down, on one-half of each heart. In order to achieve even cooking, tuck the thin edges of the filet under the thicker center.

4. Season with salt and pepper. Divide the zest, chives, and fennel greens evenly and place on top of the filets. Place one lemon slice on each filet and drizzle the sole with lemon juice.

5. Fold the uncovered half of parchment over the filet and align the edges. Fold the edges over by $1/2$ inch and carefully crimp the edges together, making certain that they are airtight.

6. Place the packages on a sheet pan and bake until the parchment puffs and becomes browned around the edges, about 10 minutes.

PRESENTATION

This dish must be served immediately, as the parchment paper can deflate as its contents cool. Place the papillotes on serving plates. Place the Sautéed Baby Spinach and Tomato Fettuccini onto the plates next to the papillotes. Allow your guests to open their own papillotes, as the fragrant steam that will be released is an important part of their dining experience. They can do this with two forks or with their hands if they're careful.

SOLE EN PAPILLOTE

6 sheets (12-inch-x-18-inch) parchment paper

Unsalted butter

6 (10-ounce) sole filets

Sea salt

Freshly ground white pepper

Zest of 3 oranges

$1/2$ cup chopped fresh chives

$1/2$ cup chopped fennel greens

1 small lemon, finely sliced

2 tablespoons fresh lemon juice

DISH

1 recipe Sautéed Baby Spinach (see page 211)

1 recipe Tomato Fettuccini (see page 206–7)

SERVES 6

Tender Milk Rabbit Loin in Lingonberry Sauce with Poached Williams' Bon Pear & Sage Spätzle

This is one of the most popular cold-weather entrées at Biró, much to the delight of Craig Wolf, our executive sous chef, who loves working with rabbit and presides over the meat station. Milk rabbit is a term used in Europe to describe a young rabbit, not a cook preparation using milk. Young rabbits have tender, delicately flavored flesh. Older rabbits have darker flesh and a stronger, gamy flavor.

Lingonberries are small, tart berries that make a delicious sauce for a variety of meats or for Baked Brie (see page 56). It is fine to use canned lingonberries for this recipe. If you are using fresh lingonberries, you will first need to crush the berries and then caramelize them over medium heat with 2 tablespoons sugar and 1 teaspoon water. I use Williams' Bon Pears for this recipe, but you may use any pear available.

WINE PAIRING *2001 Valley of the Moon, Pinot Noir, Sonoma, California*
2002 Wild Hog, "Saralee's Vineyard" Pinot Noir, Russian River, California

POACHED PEAR
2 cups water

$1/4$ cup white wine

$1/2$ lemon

1 cup sugar

1 cinnamon stick

2 Williams' Bon pears, peeled, halved, and cored

MILK RABBIT LOIN
2 tablespoons extra virgin olive oil, divided

2 tablespoons unsalted butter, divided

1 yellow onion, diced

1 cup tightly packed baby spinach, stems removed

16 sun-dried tomato halves

2 rabbit loins, butterflied

Sea salt

Freshly ground black pepper

LINGONBERRY SAUCE
$1/2$ cup Glace de Viande (see page 215)

$1/8$ cup heavy cream

$1/4$ cup lingonberries

DISH
1 recipe Sage Spätzle (see page 209)

Lingonberries, for garnish

SERVES 4

FOR THE POACHED PEAR

1. Place the water and wine in a medium stockpot. Squeeze in the lemon juice and add the squeezed lemon. Add the sugar and cinnamon stick and bring to a boil.

2. Add the pears and return to a boil. Reduce the heat to a simmer.

3. Cut a circular piece of parchment paper to fit inside the stockpot. Place the paper directly over the pears and cook for 15 minutes. Remove the pot from the heat and allow the pears to infuse for at least 15 minutes.

FOR THE MILK RABBIT LOIN

1. Preheat oven to 400 degrees.

2. Melt 1 tablespoon of the oil and 1 tablespoon of the butter in a sauté pan. Add the onion and sauté until glossy, about 1 to 2 minutes. Add the spinach and tomatoes and sauté for an additional 1 to 2 minutes. Remove from heat and allow to cool.

3. With a mallet, pound the butterflied rabbit loins until they are even in thickness. Season the tops of the loins with salt and pepper, then spread the onion, spinach, and tomato mixture on it. Roll the loins tightly and secure with butcher's twine or toothpicks. Season the outside of the rabbit rolls with salt and pepper.

4. Melt the remaining oil with the remaining butter over high heat in an ovenproof sauté pan. Place rabbit rolls in the pan and sear on all sides until golden brown.

5. Place the pan in the oven and cook for 10 to 15 minutes. Remove from oven and allow to rest for 5 minutes. Cut the strings or remove the toothpicks. Slice each loin into ten pieces.

FOR THE LINGONBERRY SAUCE

Bring the Glace de Viande and cream to a boil in a small saucepan. Add the lingonberries and reduce by one-third. Strain through a fine-mesh sieve and discard the berry solids.

PRESENTATION

Pour the Lingonberry Sauce onto the center of each plate. Cover the center with Sage Spätzle. Keeping the top of the pears intact, slice each into quarter-inch-thick slices and fan on top of the Spätzle. Place five slices of rabbit around the Spätzle. Garnish the pear with fresh or canned lingonberries.

Tender Milk Rabbit Loin in Lingonberry Sauce
with Poached Williams' Bon Pear & Sage Spätzle

Glazed Moulard Duck Breast Filet with Vichy Carrots & Duchesse Potatoes

The Moulard duck is a cross-breed of the French Nantes and Barbary ducks and is highly prized for its succulent, berry-flavored meat and exceptional foie gras. It's important when working with this lean duck that you score the skin and not overcook it, otherwise you'll get a dry, chewy filet—definitely not what you're looking for.

Vichy carrots are traditionally sliced and then slow-cooked with sugar, bicarbonate of soda (Vichy salt), and mineral water from Vichy Saint-Yorre, France, until all the liquid is absorbed. I'm guessing you don't have Vichy salt or water crowding your pantry shelves, so let's improvise and just stick with the sugar and some sparkling mineral water. They'll still taste delicious.

WINE PAIRING *2001 Cimicky, "Trumps" Grenache/Shiraz, Barossa Valley, Australia*
1999 Domaine Clos du Caillou, Châteauneuf-du-Pape, Rhône, France

DUCK BREAST
1 pound Moulard duck breast filets

Sea salt

Freshly ground black pepper

VICHY CARROTS
4 tablespoons unsalted butter

1 medium yellow onion, diced

1 tablespoon sugar

2 pounds young carrots, peeled and thinly sliced

$2^1/_4$ cups Vichy or sparkling mineral water

2 tablespoons chopped parsley

Vichy or sea salt

Freshly ground black pepper

DUCHESSE POTATOES
3 pounds Russet potatoes, peeled and chopped

Sea salt

$1/_2$ cup unsalted butter

$1/_2$ cup plus 2 tablespoons grated Gruyère cheese, divided

7 large egg yolks

Freshly ground nutmeg

Eggwash

DISH
Parsley sprigs, for garnish

SERVES 4

FOR THE MOULARD DUCK BREAST FILETS

1. Preheat oven to 400 degrees. Using a very sharp knife and being careful not to cut into the meat, score the skin of the duck breasts in a crisscross pattern. Season both sides with salt and pepper.

2. Heat a large ovenproof sauté pan over high heat until very hot. Place the duck breasts in the pan, skin side down, and sear them until some of the fat has melted and the skin is brown and crisp, about 3 minutes. Turn the breasts over and cook for an additional 3 minutes, glazing (basting) the breasts with fat from the bottom of the pan.

3. Place the pan in the oven and cook for 3 minutes. Glaze the breasts with the fat from the bottom of the pan and cook for an additional 2 minutes. Transfer the breasts onto a warm platter, skin side up, and tent loosely with aluminum foil. Allow them to rest so the juices that collected in the breast's center during cooking have time to redistribute throughout the meat, making it tender and juicy.

FOR THE VICHY CARROTS

Melt butter in a medium stockpot over high heat. Add onion and sauté until glossy, about 1 minute. Add sugar and cook until it liquefies but does not color. Add the carrots and stir. Add the sparkling mineral water and cover. Cook until the carrots are soft and have absorbed most of the water, about 10 minutes. Add parsley and season to taste with salt and pepper.

FOR THE DUCHESSE POTATOES

1. Bring the potatoes to a boil in a pot of lightly salted water. Cook until fork-tender, about 15 to 20 minutes. Drain and pass through a ricer. Allow to cool slightly.

2. Preheat oven to 350 degrees.

3. Place the cooled, riced potatoes in a stand mixer fitted with a paddle attachment. Process on low speed until the potatoes look smooth. With the motor running, add the butter and $1/_2$ cup of the Gruyère. Slowly add the yolks and mix until combined. Season to taste with salt and nutmeg.

4. Using a pastry bag fitted with a star tip, pipe the potatoes onto a Silpat- or parchment-lined baking sheet. Brush with eggwash and sprinkle with the remaining 2 tablespoons Gruyère. Bake until the edges are golden brown, about 20 to 25 minutes.

PRESENTATION

Slice the duck breasts on an angle and fan them on the serving plates. Place the Duchesse Potatoes and Vichy Carrots beside the duck and garnish with parsley sprigs.

Summer Vegetable Tower with Montrachet Cheese Medallion, Spätzle & Tomato Glaze

For this great vegetarian recipe that was featured on our organic food and wine episode with Rob Sinskey, you will need four three-inch timbales. A timbale is a high-sided, drum-shaped mold. If you don't have timbales, use ramekins or ovenproof teacups. It is important to leave the Montrachet cheese in the refrigerator until ready to use, as it will otherwise become too soft and break apart when breaded.

WINE PAIRING *1999 Gevrey-Cambertin, Vieilles Vignes Geantet-Pansiot, Burgundy, France*
2001 Schlumberger, Riesling "Les Princes Abbès," Alsace, France

FOR THE SUMMER VEGETABLE TOWER

1. Preheat oven to 400 degrees.

2. Brush timbales with 1 tablespoon Herb Butter and place on a sheet pan. Cut parchment paper to fit the inside bottom of the timbales and place inside timbales.

3. In a small sauté pan, melt the remaining Herb Butter with 1 tablespoon of the oil. Add onion juliennes and caramelize.

4. In a large sauté pan, heat the remaining 1 tablespoon olive oil and sauté the celery root, eggplant, zucchini, garlic, and squash on both sides until golden brown. Add the tomatoes and sauté on each side. Add the basil and season with salt, pepper, and nutmeg. Allow to cool on a parchment-lined sheet pan.

5. To assemble the towers, place one celery root slice in the bottom of each timbale. Layer with one slice eggplant, one-eighth of the onions, one slice each zucchini, squash, and tomato. Repeat the process and cover with the roasted peppers. Place timbales on a sheet pan, and bake for about 10 minutes. To check for doneness, stick a metal skewer into the center of the timbales. If the skewer is warm, the timbales are done.

6. Invert timbales on serving plates. If the vegetable towers do not slide out easily, carefully run a knife around the inside edges of the timbales.

PRESENTATION

Place the Montrachet Cheese Medallions on top of the vegetable towers. Arrange Spätzle around the towers and drizzle plates with Tomato Glaze. Garnish with basil.

SUMMER VEGETABLE TOWER

2 tablespoons Herb Butter, divided (see page 205)

2 tablespoons extra virgin olive oil, divided

2 medium yellow onions, julienned

1 celery root, cut into 8 ($1/_2$-inch-thick) slices

1 medium eggplant, cut into 8 ($1/_2$-inch-thick) slices

1 medium zucchini, cut into 8 ($1/_2$-inch-thick) slices

2 cloves garlic

1 medium yellow squash, cut into 8 ($1/_2$-inch-thick) slices

2 plum tomatoes, cut into 8 ($1/_2$-inch-thick) slices

1 ounce fresh basil, en chiffonade

Sea salt

Freshly ground black pepper

1 tablespoon freshly ground nutmeg

2 roasted red bell peppers

DISH

1 recipe Montrachet Cheese Medallions (see page 210)

1 recipe Spätzle (see page 209)

Tomato Glaze, for garnish (see page 218)

Basil leaves, for garnish

SERVES 4

Lime-Grilled Mahi Mahi with Morel Sauce
& Chanterelle-Stuffed Ravioli

Lime-Grilled Mahi Mahi with Morel Sauce & Chanterelle-Stuffed Ravioli

This stunning dish is a guest favorite. Moist, meaty filets of mahi mahi are marinated in lime and herbs, which counterbalance the sweetness of the fish. Tender wild mushroom ravioli are blanketed in a silky Morel Sauce, rounding out this glorious combination of flavors.

WINE PAIRING *2000 Domaine Drouhin, Pinot Noir, Willamette Valley, Oregon
2001 Landmark, Overlook Chardonnay, Sonoma, California*

FOR THE LIME-GRILLED MAHI MAHI

1. In a mixing bowl, combine the oil, juice, rosemary, thyme, bonito flakes, salt, and pepper. Whisk until combined. Add fish filets and allow to marinate at room temperature for at least 20 minutes. Remove the fish from marinade, allowing some of the liquid to run off the fish.

2. Prepare a hot grill or grill pan. Grill the mahi mahi until medium, about 2–3 minutes on each side, making certain to turn the filets to create crisscross grill marks.

FOR THE MOREL SAUCE

1. Heat oil in a medium sauté pan over high heat. Add the shallots and garlic and sauté until glossy, about 1 minute. Deglaze and flambé with the port. Add the morels and sauté until all the liquid is absorbed, about 1 minute.

2. Pour in the cream and reduce by one-third. Whisk in the Glace de Viande and stock. Simmer, whisking frequently, for 5 minutes. Season to taste with salt and pepper.

PRESENTATION

Place lemon slices in the center of each plate. Top with the Lime-Grilled Mahi Mahi and arrange the raviolis around the fish. Drizzle the Morel Sauce over the raviolis and garnish with cherry tomato halves and baby spinach leaves.

LIME-GRILLED MAHI MAHI
1/2 cup extra virgin olive oil

Juice of 1 lime

1 sprig rosemary

1 sprig thyme

1/2 teaspoon bonito flakes

Sea salt

Freshly ground black pepper

4 mahi mahi filets, 6 ounces each

MOREL SAUCE
2 tablespoons extra virgin olive oil

1 tablespoon diced shallots

1 teaspoon minced garlic

1 tablespoon white port

8 ounces fresh morels, sliced

1 cup heavy cream

2 tablespoons Glace de Viande
(see page 215)

1/2 cup Chicken Stock
(see page 214)

Sea salt

Freshly ground black pepper

DISH
1 lemon, thinly sliced, for garnish

1 recipe Wild Mushroom Ravioli
(see page 208)

8 cherry tomatoes, halved,
for garnish

Baby spinach, for garnish

SERVES 4

Black Pepper–Seared Salmon Filet with Egg Pasta, Sautéed Green Asparagus & Champagne-Lemon Crème

Comprised of familiar flavors, this dish is great for nearly any occasion, from a simply elegant dinner party to a casual night in. Champagne-Lemon Crème, with or without the addition of sautéed vegetables, can be served with pasta as an entrée.

WINE PAIRING *1999 Domaine Joseph Drouhin, Chambolle - Musigny Les Amoureuses, Burgundy, France*
2001 Louis Latour, Puligny - Montrachet "Les Folatières," Burgundy, France

BLACK PEPPER–SEARED SALMON FILET

4 (6-ounce) salmon filets

Sea salt

4 tablespoons cracked black pepper

2 tablespoons extra virgin olive oil

1 tablespoon unsalted butter

SAUTÉED GREEN ASPARAGUS

2 tablespoons unsalted butter

1 tablespoon minced shallots

16 spears green asparagus, blanched

1 teaspoon lemon juice

Sea salt

Freshly ground black pepper

CHAMPAGNE-LEMON CRÈME

1 teaspoon lemon zest

Juice of 1 lemon

4 whole white peppercorns

1 Turkish bay leaf

2 cups Champagne or sparkling wine

1 cup heavy cream

Sea salt

Freshly ground white pepper

1 tablespoon unsalted butter

DISH

1 recipe Egg Pasta (see page 206), cooked al dente

2 tablespoons unsalted butter

Sea salt

Freshly ground white pepper

SERVES 4

FOR THE BLACK PEPPER–SEARED SALMON FILET

1. Preheat oven to 350 degrees.

2. Season the filet with salt.

3. Place the pepper in a shallow dish, and place the first filet skin side down into the pepper and press to coat. Repeat the process with the remaining three filets.

4. Heat the oil and butter in a medium ovenproof sauté pan over high heat. Place the filets in the pan, pepper side down, and sauté for 1 minute. Turn over and sauté for 1 additional minute. Place in the oven and bake until medium, about 4 to 5 minutes.

FOR THE SAUTÉED GREEN ASPARAGUS

Melt the butter in a medium sauté pan over high heat. Add the shallots and sauté until glossy, about 30 seconds. Add the blanched asparagus and sauté for 1 to 2 minutes. Drizzle with lemon juice and season to taste with salt and pepper.

FOR THE CHAMPAGNE-LEMON CRÈME

Place the zest, juice, peppercorns, bay leaf, and Champagne in a medium saucepan; reduce to a glaze over high heat, about 5 to 10 minutes. Add the cream and reduce by one-half, about 5 minutes. Turn off heat and season to taste with salt and pepper. Whisk in the butter. Pass through a fine-mesh sieve, discarding the solids, before serving.

PRESENTATION

Sauté the pasta in the butter until warm. Season to taste with salt and pepper. Place pasta in the center of each serving plate. Place the salmon, peppercorn side up, on top of the pasta and drizzle Champagne-Lemon Crème around the plate's perimeter. Place the asparagus spears around the plate's perimeter.

Zucchini-Wrapped Fettuccini with Sun-Dried Tomatoes, Mushrooms, Baby Spinach & Roasted-Red-Pepper Coulis

This dish is a veritable celebration of spring's garden harvest—and it looks as fantastic as it tastes. You may wish to prepare the Zucchini-Wrapped Fettuccini one day in advance, baking it just before serving. Boxed fettuccini works just fine if you don't have time to make homemade.

WINE PAIRING *2001 Eno Teldeschi Vineyard, "Little Miss Dangerous" Zinfandel, Sonoma, California*
2000 Robert Sinskey Vineyards, Pinot Noir Los Carneros, Napa, California

FOR THE ZUCCHINI-WRAPPED FETTUCCINI

1. Heat oven to 375 degrees.

2. In a large bowl, mix together the basil, baby spinach, sun-dried tomatoes, garlic, shallots, mushrooms, and salt and pepper to taste. Add the oil and cooked Fettuccini; allow to marinate for at least 10 minutes.

3. Bring lightly salted water to a boil and blanch the zucchini and squash until al dente, about 30 seconds. Immediately submerge in an ice bath to stop the cooking process. Remove and pat dry with paper towels.

4. Lightly butter four shallow ovenproof bowls or cups about 8 ounces each. Fan out the blanched zucchini and squash in the bowls, alternating colors and making sure that the strips overlap the bowl's edge by at least two inches.

6. Place the fettuccini mixture inside the bowl and fold the overlapping edges of the zucchini and squash over it. Bake for 10 to 15 minutes.

PRESENTATION

Invert the Zucchini-Wrapped Fettuccini on individual serving plates and spoon Roasted-Red-Pepper Coulis around the plate perimeters. Garnish with sprigs of lavender, leaves of baby spinach, and cherry tomato halves; serve immediately.

ZUCCHINI-WRAPPED FETTUCCINI

2 tablespoons fresh basil, julienned

1 cup lightly packed baby spinach, stems removed

2 tablespoons diced sun-dried tomatoes

2 cloves minced garlic

1 tablespoon minced shallots

$1/2$ cup shiitake mushrooms, finely sliced

Sea salt

Freshly ground black pepper

2 tablespoons extra virgin olive oil

16 ounces Fettuccini
(see page 206)

2 zucchinis, sliced very thinly lengthwise

2 yellow squash, sliced very thinly lengthwise

Unsalted butter

DISH
Roasted-Red-Pepper Coulis
(see page 217)

6 sprigs lavender for garnish

Baby spinach for garnish

2 cherry tomatoes, halved, for garnish

SERVES 4

Ahi Tuna Fillet with Lobster-Veal Roulade on Glass Noodle Salad with Sauce Américaine

If you've seen the episode of The Kitchens of Biró *featuring this Asian-inspired dish, you know it's stunning. But just wait until you taste it! It's truly even more dazzling to the taste buds than to the eye.*

Américaine is a delicious sauce prepared with lobster, white wine, cognac, tomatoes, and butter that perfectly complements the flavors of the fish, lobster, and veal. To further the Asian feel of this recipe, you may wish to serve it in plain white bowls with chopsticks.

WINE PAIRING *2002 Thibert, Les Cras Pouilly-Fuisse (100% Chardonnay), France*
2000 Beaux Frères, Pinot Noir, Yamhill County, Oregon

AHI TUNA FILET WITH LOBSTER-VEAL ROULADE ON GLASS NOODLE SALAD

2 (1.8-ounce) packages glass noodles

1 tablespoon rice wine

1 tablespoon chopped chives

1 teaspoon fresh grated ginger

$1/2$ teaspoon red pepper flakes

2 tablespoons soy sauce

1 tablespoon sesame oil

Sea salt

Freshly ground white pepper

6 ounces veal tenderloins, butterflied

$1/2$ cup tightly packed baby spinach, stems removed

1 lobster tail

2 tablespoons unsalted butter, divided

2 tablespoons extra virgin olive oil, divided

1 pound ahi tuna filets

1 teaspoon paprika

SAUCE AMÉRICAINE

1 ($1^1/2$ pound) live lobster

Cayenne pepper

Sea salt

Freshly ground black pepper

$1/2$ cup peanut oil

4 tablespoons diced carrots

2 tablespoons minced shallot

2 garlic cloves, unpeeled and crushed

$1/3$ cup cognac or Armagnac

$1^1/2$ cups Chablis or other dry white wine

$1/2$ cup Fish Stock (see page 214)

$1/4$ pound Roma tomatoes, peeled, seeded, and chopped

1 Bouquet Garni (see page 204)

6 tablespoons heavy cream

1 tablespoon unsalted butter

2 tablespoons flour

SERVES 4

FOR THE AHI TUNA FILET WITH LOBSTER-VEAL ROULADE ON GLASS NOODLE SALAD

1. Preheat oven to 400 degrees. In a stockpot, bring the amount of water indicated on glass noodle package and rice wine to a boil. Add the glass noodles and cook until al dente, about 1 to 2 minutes. Remove from heat, drain, and allow to cool.

2. Place the chives, ginger, pepper flakes, soy sauce, sesame oil, salt, and pepper to taste in a small bowl. Add the glass noodles; stir and allow to infuse.

3. Pound the butterflied veal tenderloin with a mallet so it is even in thickness. Layer the spinach leaves on top of it.

4. Sauté the lobster tail in 1 tablespoon melted butter until red, about 5 minutes. Season with sea salt. Cut the lobster tail into thin slices and place those on the spinach leaves. Roll the tenderloin and secure with butcher's twine or toothpicks.

5. In an ovenproof sauté pan, melt 1 tablespoon of the olive oil and the remaining 1 tablespoon butter. Sauté the roulade until golden brown on each side. Finish cooking in the preheated oven for 5 minutes.

6. Cut the tuna filets into four 2-inch-thick strips. Season with paprika. Sear the filets in a very hot pan with the remaining olive oil. Cook until rare but golden brown on the edges, about 1 to 2 minutes each side.

FOR THE SAUCE AMÉRICAINE

1. Bring a large stockpot of water to a boil. Rinse the lobster under cold running water and drop it headfirst into the water for 45 seconds.

2. While the lobster is still hot, carefully separate the head from the body using a large knife. Cut the claw joints and tail into rings across the articulations. Split the head lengthwise and remove the gritty sac close to the antennae. Remove all white membranes. Scrape out the greenish coral from inside the head and reserve. Season the lobster to taste with cayenne pepper, salt, and black pepper.

3. Heat the oil in a medium sauté pan over high heat. Add the lobster pieces and sauté until the shell turns bright red and the flesh is brightly colored. Remove the lobster pieces with a slotted spoon and set aside. Reserve the pan and drippings, removing much of the excess fat.

4. Return the pan to high heat. Place the carrots and shallots in the pan and sauté for 1 minute. Add the garlic and return the lobster pieces to the pan. Flambé with the cognac, carefully tipping the pan sideways until it flames, if it doesn't ignite on its own. Add the wine, stock, tomatoes, and Bouquet Garni and season with salt. Bring to a boil and then reduce heat to medium. Simmer for 15 minutes. Remove and reserve the claws and rings of lobster tail. Simmer the sauce for an additional 30 minutes, skimming impurities as they rise to the surface.

5. Using a fork, mash together the reserved lobster coral, butter, and flour; slowly add the mixture to the sauce. Cook for another 5 minutes and then pour in the cream. Pass through a chinoise or fine-mesh sieve, pressing the solids with the back of a spoon to extract all the liquid. Season to taste with salt and pepper. Remove the reserved lobster meat from the shells and dice it, adding it to the sauce just before serving.

PRESENTATION

Pour the sauce Américaine on the center of shallow individual bowls or plates. Place the glass noodles on the center of the sauce. Drizzle the chive–soy sauce mixture over the noodles. Slice the lobster roulade, removing the string or toothpicks, so that each person gets two to three pieces; place roulade on the glass noodles. Cut each sliced ahi tuna filet on an angle into four equal pieces and place, rare side up, beside the lobster roulades.

Portabella Schnitzel with Brie & Garlic Mashed Potato Rosettes

The first time Shannon traveled to Hungary to meet my paternal grandparents, they didn't share a common language—that is, until my nagymama, or grandmother, learned that my future wife was a vegetarian. She then picked wild mushrooms to make Shannon a veggie version of the Wiener schnitzel we were eating. Suddenly the two were talking a mile a minute, through me, of course, Shannon trying to charm the recipe out of her and Nagymama trying to charm her way out of giving it—which translated to me having to try to duplicate it once back home. Thus my version of Nagymama's breaded portabellas was born. I stuff my mushroom caps with a blend of cheeses, cream, onion, chives, and garlic, and they've been a big hit with both our vegetarian and nonvegetarian guests. I've not yet had the heart to ask Shannon whose are better.

WINE PAIRING *1999 Domaine Michael Lefarge, Volnay, Burgundy, France*
2001 Van Duzer, Pinot Noir, Willamette Valley, Oregon

PORTABELLA SCHNITZEL

8 ounces Brie cheese, rind removed, at room temperature

1 ounce grated Parmesan cheese

1 ounce grated Gruyère cheese

3/4 cup sour cream

1 small yellow onion, diced

1 teaspoon minced garlic

1 tablespoon minced chives

1 teaspoon Hungarian paprika

Sea salt

Freshly ground black pepper

4 large portabella mushroom caps, peeled and gills removed,

1 cup flour

4 large eggs

1 teaspoon heavy cream

1 cup breadcrumbs

2 tablespoons extra virgin olive oil

2 tablespoons unsalted butter

DISH

1 recipe Garlic Mashed Potato Rosettes (see page 210)

12 baby spinach leaves, for garnish

12 cherry tomatoes, for garnish

SERVES 4

FOR THE PORTABELLA SCHNITZEL

1. Preheat oven to 350 degrees.

2. Place the Brie in a large mixing bowl. Add the Parmesan, Gruyère, sour cream, onion, garlic, chives, paprika, and salt and pepper to taste. Combine with your hands, as your body temperature will melt the cheese and make the mixture smoother. The mixture should be thick, about the texture of cream cheese. If it's too thin, add more Parmesan or Gruyère. If it's too thick, add heavy cream.

3. Season the portabellas with salt and pepper. Spread one-quarter of the cheese mixture inside each cap and press firmly.

4. Place the flour in a shallow dish. Whisk together the eggs and heavy cream in a second shallow dish to make an eggwash. Place the breadcrumbs in a third shallow dish. Dredge the stuffed portabellas in the flour, tapping gently to remove excess. Place them in the eggwash and cover completely, shaking gently to remove excess. Place the eggwashed portabellas into the breadcrumbs and coat completely. Repeat the process to double bread.

5. Heat the oil and butter in a large ovenproof sauté pan over high heat. Place the portabellas in the pan, stuffed side down, and sauté until golden brown, about 2 minutes. Turn and sauté until golden brown. Place the pan in the oven and bake until the mushrooms are tender, about 5 to 10 minutes. Remove from oven and let cool slightly, allowing the cheese to rest before slicing.

PRESENTATION

Slice the mushrooms into quarters. Stack the slices in the center of each serving plate and pipe Garlic Mashed Potato Rosettes onto the plate at the 12:00, 4:00, and 8:00 positions. Place a leaf of baby spinach at the 2:00, 6:00, and 10:00 plate positions and garnish with one cherry tomato per leaf.

Portabella Schnitzel with Brie & Garlic Mashed Potato Rosettes

Horseradish-Encrusted Sirloin with Roasted Beets & Lyonnaise Potatoes

Horseradish-Encrusted Sirloin with Roasted Beets & Lyonnaise Potatoes

This beautiful entrée is a new spin on the old-world tradition of pairing beef, beets, and Lyonnaise potatoes. The horseradish crust is coarse and substantial, giving each bite a spicy crunch.

WINE PAIRING *2000 Monticello Vineyards, Jefferson Cuvée Cabernet Sauvignon, Napa, California*
2001 Whitehall Lane Winery, Cabernet Sauvignon, Napa, California

FOR THE HORSERADISH-ENCRUSTED SIRLOIN

1. Preheat oven to 400 degrees.

2. Season the sirloins with salt and pepper. Heat the oil in a medium ovenproof sauté pan over high heat. Sear the sirloins until golden brown, about 2 to 4 minutes on each side. Remove from heat.

3. In a medium mixing bowl, combine the horseradish, crème fraîche, egg, yolks, parsley, paprika, and salt and pepper to taste. The mixture should be thick. If it is runny, add breadcrumbs. Divide the horseradish mixture evenly and spread it over the tops of the sirloins. Place in the oven and bake until the crust is golden brown and the sirloin is medium, about 5 to 10 minutes. Remove from oven and tent loosely with aluminum foil.

4. Place the cream, Glace de Viande, and stock in a small saucepan and reduce by one-half over high heat. Season to taste with salt and pepper.

FOR THE ROASTED BEETS

1. Preheat oven to 400 degrees. Salt the beets and wrap them tightly in aluminum foil; cook until fork-tender, about 1 hour. Allow the beets to cool slightly, then slip the peels off under cold running water. Slice the beets into thin rounds.

2. Melt the butter in a small saucepan over high heat. Add the beets and caraway and sauté to coat. Season to taste with salt and pepper.

FOR THE LYONNAISE POTATOES

1. Preheat oven to 400 degrees.

2. Peel the potatoes and cut into 1/2-inch-thick slices. Place the potatoes in a stockpot and add water to cover. Bring to a boil and boil for 2 minutes; drain.

3. Heat the oil in a large casserole dish over medium-high heat. Add the onions and sauté until lightly caramelized, about 8 to 10 minutes. Add garlic and sauté until the onions are deep brown and the garlic is soft, about 2 additional minutes. Transfer the mixture to a bowl, reserving the casserole dish and its drippings.

4. Place the butter in the casserole and allow to melt. Cover the bottom of the pan with one-third of the potato slices. Season to taste with salt and pepper. Cover the potatoes with one-half of the onion mixture. Cover with one-half of the remaining potatoes and season to taste with salt and pepper. Spread the remaining onion mixture over the potatoes. Place a layer of the remaining potatoes on top of the onions and season to taste with salt and pepper.

5. Bake until the potatoes are tender and browned on top, about 10 to 12 minutes. Sprinkle with parsley.

PRESENTATION

Slice the sirloins on an angle, being careful to keep the crust intact. Place in the center of each serving plate. Cut the Lyonnaise Potatoes in squares and then in half diagonally. Place one triangle of potatoes on each side of the sirloin. Spoon a bit of sauce in each corner and top with beets.

HORSERADISH-ENCRUSTED SIRLOIN

4 (6-ounce) beef sirloins

Sea salt

Freshly ground black pepper

2 tablespoons extra virgin olive oil

1 cup shredded fresh horseradish

1/4 cup crème fraîche

1 large egg

2 large egg yolks

1/2 tablespoon chopped parsley

1/8 teaspoon Hungarian paprika

2 tablespoons heavy cream

1 tablespoon Glace de Viande (see page 215)

1/4 cup Beef Stock (see page 214)

ROASTED BEETS

12 ounces red beets, leaves removed

Kosher salt

2 tablespoons unsalted butter

1/2 teaspoon ground caraway seeds

Sea salt

Freshly ground black pepper

LYONNAISE POTATOES

2 pounds Russet potatoes

2 tablespoons extra virgin olive oil

4 onions, thinly sliced into rounds

2 tablespoons chopped garlic

1/2 cup unsalted butter

Sea salt

Freshly ground white pepper

1 tablespoon minced parsley

SERVES 4

Ahi Tuna with Wilted Greens, Borlotti Beans, Cumin Toast & Orange-Sherry Vinaigrette

I use this restaurant recipe in classes and demonstrations quite often because it features an array of techniques: sautéing, deglazing, blanching, pan-toasting, and reducing. It also has various steps, which challenge my students, but is not overly complicated, which helps build their confidence when they've successfully re-created it for themselves. Most importantly, it yields exceptional results. See for yourself.

If you can't find Borlotti beans, substitute another white bean.

WINE PAIRING *1996 Storybook Mountain Vineyard, Estate Zinfandel, Napa, California*
1999 Domaine Maurice Ecord, Savigny-Les-Beaune Les Serpentières, Burgundy, France

ORANGE-SHERRY VINAIGRETTE

1/4 cup brown sugar

1/2 cup orange juice

Pinch sea salt

1 teaspoon ground cumin

1 teaspoon freshly ground black pepper

1/4 teaspoon ground coriander

1/4 cup sherry vinegar

1/2 cup extra virgin olive oil

BORLOTTI BEANS

1/4 cup Borlotti beans

1 tablespoon extra virgin olive oil

1/4 cup diced yellow onion

1/4 cup diced celery

1/4 cup peeled and diced carrots

Sea salt

Freshly ground white pepper

CUMIN TOAST

1 tablespoon unsalted butter

1 tablespoon extra virgin olive oil

4 ounces white bread, diced

1 teaspoon cumin

Sea salt

Freshly ground black pepper

AHI TUNA

1 pound ahi tuna

1 tablespoon cayenne pepper or Hungarian paprika

1 tablespoon extra virgin olive oil

Freshly ground black pepper

1 pound mesclun greens

1/8 cup caramelized onion

1/8 cup diced tomatoes

DISH

16 orange fillets, for garnish

SERVES 4

FOR THE ORANGE-SHERRY VINAIGRETTE

1. In a sauté pan, add the brown sugar. Cook over medium-low heat until the sugar melts. Add orange juice and deglaze the pan. Add the salt, cumin, pepper, and coriander and allow to reduce by one-half.

2. Add the vinegar and oil and cook until reduced. Whisk and set aside.

FOR THE BORLOTTI BEANS

1. Soak the beans in cold water overnight. Blanch until al dente, about 1 minute, in an uncovered pot filled with just enough water to cover.

2. Heat the oil in a sauté pan over medium heat. Add the beans, onion, celery, and carrots and sauté until softened. Season to taste with salt and pepper. Remove from heat and set aside.

FOR THE CUMIN TOAST

1. Heat the butter and oil in a sauté pan over high heat. Add the bread dices and toast, adding cumin, salt, and pepper as you go, until the dices are a deep golden brown.

FOR THE TUNA

1. Slice the tuna into four individual pieces. Gently rub with the cayenne pepper or paprika.

2. Heat the oil in a sauté pan over high heat. Sear the tuna on all sides until medium-rare or to your desired temperature. Season with black pepper.

3. Remove tuna from the pan but do not discard the drippings. In the same pan, place the mesclun greens and wilt them with the onions and tomatoes.

PRESENTATION

Place the Borlotti Beans on the center of each serving plate. Place wilted greens on top of the beans. Slice each tuna section into four pieces and position around the plate at the 1:00, 4:00, 7:00, and 10:00 positions. Place the orange segments at the 12:00, 3:00, 6:00, and 9:00 plate positions. Drizzle the vinaigrette around the plate's perimeter.

Maltese Baked Swordfish with Lemon-Parsley Glazed Potatoes

Maltese cuisine is characterized by its use of blood oranges in both sweet and savory offerings. In this case, we're making a blood orange, navel orange, Roma tomato, and aromatic herb concassé to enhance the fantastic flavor of swordfish. If you can't get swordfish, use tuna, as its flesh is similar in taste and texture.

WINE PAIRING *1997 Paul Hobbs, Chardonnay, Sonoma, California*
1999 Domaine Fontaine-Gagnard, Chassagne-Montrachet, Burgundy, France

FOR THE MALTESE-BAKED SWORDFISH

1. Preheat oven to 350 degrees.

2. Season both sides of the swordfish filets with salt and pepper, then sprinkle with the lime juice.

3. In a large ovenproof sauté pan, melt 1 tablespoon of the oil with the butter over high heat. Add the swordfish and sauté for 2 minutes on each side. Remove from heat.

4. Cut one-half of the blood orange and one-half of the navel orange segments into dices. Reserve the remaining segments.

5. Add the tomatoes and orange dices to the pan with the swordfish. Add the rosemary, thyme, basil, and remaining oil. Finish cooking in the oven for 4 minutes. Season to taste with salt and pepper.

PRESENTATION

Arrange blood and navel orange segments around each plate's perimeter. Place the tomato concassé on the center of the plate and top with swordfish. Garnish with Lemon-Parsley Glazed Potatoes, rosemary, thyme, and orange oil.

MALTESE BAKED SWORDFISH

4 (6-ounce) swordfish filets

Sea salt

Freshly ground black pepper

Juice of 1 lime

4 tablespoons extra virgin olive oil, divided

1 tablespoon unsalted butter

1 blood orange, zested, segmented, and divided

1 navel orange, zested, segmented, and divided

3 Roma tomatoes, diced

1 teaspoon chopped rosemary

1 teaspoon chopped thyme

1 tablespoon fresh basil, en chiffonade

DISH

1 recipe Lemon-Parsley-Glazed Potatoes (see page 209)

Rosemary sprigs, for garnish

Thyme sprigs, for garnish

Orange oil, for garnish

SERVES 4

QUICK TIP: WHAT'S A CONCASSÉ
Concassé is a coarsely chopped or ground mixture most often used when referring to chopped or diced tomatoes or tomato mixtures.

Venison Ragoût with Juniper Crème, Napa Cabbage & Garlic Mashed Potatoes

With its earthy flavors and rich texture, this cold-weather dish proves that comfort food can have an elegant touch. The Venison Ragoût is fantastic served on its own or over butter-sautéed egg pasta, spätzle, or schupfnudeln.

WINE PAIRING *1999 E. Guigal, Côte-Rôtie Château d' Ampuls, Rhône, France*
2000 Domaine de Michelle, Châteauneuf-du-Pape, Rhône, France

VENISON RAGOÛT WITH JUNIPER CRÈME

$1/8$ cup vegetable oil

2 pounds venison, cut into
1- x 1-inch cubes

2 carrots, peeled and diced

1 stalk celery, diced

1 medium yellow onion, diced

2 cups button mushrooms

$1/2$ cup tomato paste

1 cup Bordeaux

1 Bouquet Garni (see page 204)

1 cup Beef Stock (see page 214)

$1/4$ cup dried juniper berries

Sea salt

Freshly ground black pepper

1 cup heavy cream

4 tablespoons lingonberries

DISH

1 recipe Garlic Mashed Potatoes
(see page 210)

1 recipe Sautéed Napa Cabbage
(see page 213)

4 sprigs thyme, for garnish

SERVES 4

FOR THE VENISON RAGOÛT WITH JUNIPER CRÈME

1. Heat the oil in a large stockpot over high heat until very hot. Brown the venison, stirring to ensure even cooking. Remove venison from the pot, reserving the pot and drippings.

2. In the same pot, add the carrots, celery, onion, and mushrooms; sauté over high heat until golden brown. Add the tomato paste and stir. Deglaze the pan by adding the Bordeaux. Add the Bouquet Garni, Beef Stock, browned venison, juniper berries, and salt and pepper to taste. Cover and simmer over medium-low heat until the venison is softened, about 1 to $1^1/2$ hours. Remove from heat and allow to cool. Remove the venison chunks from the ragoût and reserve.

3. Strain the remaining sauce through a chinoise into a fresh saucepan, reserving the vegetables and discarding the juniper berries. Add the cream to the sauce and reduce over medium-low heat until it becomes thick and brown. Stir in the lingonberries. Add the venison and vegetables back into the sauce and combine. Reheat before serving.

PRESENTATION

Ladle the ragoût onto the center of each serving plate. Arrange the Garlic Mashed Potatoes and Sautéed Napa Cabbage around the ragoût and garnish with a sprig of thyme.

Hanger Steak with Herb-Sautéed Fettuccini, Grilled Blue Prawns, Spinach & Roquefort-Infused Demi-Glace

Also known as Scottish tender, hanger steak is a fantastic cut of beef that is often overlooked in the United States. It has a pronounced flavor, and when prepared correctly, is quite succulent. Here it is paired with Grilled Blue Prawns and a sumptuous Roquefort-Infused Demi-Glace, which adds a harmonious complexity to the dish.

You could substitute another steak in this recipe if you can't find hanger steak.

WINE PAIRING *1999 Pezzi King, Cabernet Sauvignon, Dry Creek, California*
2000 Chateau Chatain, Montagne St. Emilion, Bordeaux, France

FOR THE HANGER STEAK

1. Preheat oven to 350 degrees.

2. Melt the oil and butter in a medium saucepan over medium-high heat. Season the steaks with salt and pepper and sear until golden brown, about 2 minutes on each side. Reserving the pan and drippings, transfer the steaks to a baking rack and bake until medium rare, about 5 to 8 minutes. Tent loosely with aluminum foil.

FOR THE GRILLED BLUE PRAWNS

1. Heat a grill or grill pan over high heat.

2. Place the prawns in a bowl and drizzle with the lemon juice. Season to taste with salt and pepper.

3. Grill prawns until cooked through, turning once, about 2 minutes on each side.

FOR THE ROQUEFORT-INFUSED DEMI-GLACE

In the same pan in which you seared the steaks, place the stock and reduce by one-half. Whisk in the cream and add the Glace de Viande. Cook for 1 additional minute. Add 2 tablespoons of the Roquefort and cook, whisking constantly, until melted, about 1 minute. Season to taste with salt and pepper.

PRESENTATION

Sauté the pasta in the butter until warm. Add the thyme and rosemary and season to taste with salt and pepper. Drain the spinach and place on one-half of the plate's perimeter. Place the Fettuccini opposite the spinach. Place the Hanger Steak in the center of the plate. Place two Grilled Blue Prawns atop the spinach and drizzle the sauce over steak. Garnish with the remaining 2 tablespoons Roquefort.

HANGER STEAK
1 tablespoon extra virgin olive oil

2 tablespoons unsalted butter

4 (6-ounce) hanger steaks

Sea salt

Freshly ground black pepper

GRILLED BLUE PRAWNS
8 blue prawns, cleaned

1 teaspoon lemon juice

Sea salt

Freshly ground black pepper

ROQUEFORT-INFUSED DEMI-GLACE
1/2 cup Beef Stock (see page 214)

2 tablespoons heavy cream

2 tablespoons Glace de Viande (see page 215)

4 tablespoons crumbled Roquefort cheese, divided

Sea salt

Freshly ground black pepper

DISH
1 pound Fettuccini (see pages 206–7)

2 tablespoons unsalted butter

1 teaspoon chopped thyme

1 teaspoon chopped rosemary

Sea salt

Freshly ground black pepper

1 recipe Sautéed Spinach (see page 211)

SERVES 4

Rainbow Trout with Sautéed Grapes & Almonds, Summer Vegetables & Garlic-Parsley Potatoes

This is a casual and flavorful German-inspired dish, perfect for any time of year. You could also prepare the trout on a grill.

WINE PAIRING *2002 Hogue Cellars, Dry Johannisberg Riesling, Yakima Valley, Washington*
2002 Domaine Cailbourdin, Pouilly-Fumé Les Cornets, Loire, France

RAINBOW TROUT WITH SAUTÉED GRAPES & ALMONDS

4 rainbow trout, cleaned and scaled

Sea salt

Freshly ground white pepper

1 tablespoon lemon juice

1 cup flour

2 tablespoons extra virgin olive oil

3 tablespoons unsalted butter, divided

4 ounces green seedless grapes, halved

4 ounces red seedless grapes, halved

1/4 cup sliced roasted almonds

1/4 cup Chablis or other dry white wine

1 tablespoon chopped parsley

1 tablespoon chopped dill

DISH

1 recipe Garlic-Parsley Potatoes (see page 209)

1/2 recipe Sautéed Vegetables (see page 211)

4 sprigs dill, for garnish

4 slices lemon, for garnish

SERVES 4

FOR THE RAINBOW TROUT WITH SAUTÉED GRAPES & ALMONDS

1. Preheat oven to 350 degrees.

2. Rinse the trout inside and out under cold running water. Pat dry with paper towel and then season inside and out with salt and pepper. Season inside with the lemon juice. Dredge in flour, tapping the trout to remove excess.

3. Heat the oil and 2 tablespoons of butter in a large sauté pan over high heat. Sauté, turning once, until golden brown on each side. Reserving the pan and drippings, remove the trout and place on a sheet pan. Bake until cooked through, about 5 to 10 minutes.

4. Meanwhile, remove excess fat from the pan in which you sautéed the trout. Add the remaining 1 tablespoon butter and melt over high heat. Add the green and red grapes and sauté for 1 minute, then add the almonds. Deglaze with the wine. Reduce for 2 minutes, then add the parsley and dill.

PRESENTATION

Place the Garlic-Parsley Potatoes on the center of each serving plate. Place a trout on top of the potatoes. Scatter the Sautéed Vegetables around the plate's perimeter and drizzle with the sauce. Garnish with dill sprigs and a lemon slice.

Capon with Sherry-Chanterelle Sauce on Sautéed Napa Cabbage with Lemon-Parsley Glazed Potatoes

Capon is a young, castrated rooster that has succulent, flavorful breasts. Sherry-Chanterelle Sauce adds a delicious touch of elegance to the bird, while the cabbage and potatoes provide an earthy flair.

Don't let the term airline breasts conjure images of bland airplane food! Airline is actually a boneless breast cut of poultry in which the wing bone is still attached. If you can't find capon breasts, Amish chicken, duck, or pheasant breasts make wonderful substitutions.

WINE PAIRING *1999 Luigi Viberti, Barbera d'Alba, Piedmont, Italy*
2003 Kiona Vineyards, White Riesling, Yakima Valley, Washington

FOR THE CAPON

1. Preheat oven to 300 degrees.

2. Melt the oil and butter in a medium ovenproof sauté pan over high heat. Season the capon with salt and pepper and dredge in the flour, tapping it to remove excess. Sauté the capon, skin side down, until golden brown, about 2 minutes. Turn over and place in the oven. Bake until cooked through, about 12 minutes.

FOR THE SHERRY-CHANTERELLE SAUCE

1. In a large saucepan, melt the oil and 2 tablespoons of the butter over high heat. Add the shallots and sauté until glossy, about 30 seconds. Add garlic and sauté 15 additional seconds. Add the chanterelles and sauté until lightly golden. Deglaze with the sherry and reduce by one-half.

2. Add the stock, cream, and salt and pepper to taste. Reduce heat to medium-high and reduce sauce by one-half, stirring occasionally. Whisk in the remaining 1 tablespoon butter to smooth the sauce and prevent it from forming a skin.

PRESENTATION

I like to use square plates for this dish. Slice the Capon on an angle. Place the Sautéed Napa Cabbage in the center of each serving plate and top with a breast of capon, skin side up. Place Lemon-Parsley Glazed Potatoes in the corners and drizzle sauce in between the potatoes.

CAPON

1 tablespoon extra virgin olive oil

2 tablespoons unsalted butter

4 (6- to 8-ounce) airline capon breasts

Sea salt

Freshly ground black pepper

Flour

SHERRY-CHANTERELLE SAUCE

1 tablespoon extra virgin olive oil

3 tablespoons unsalted butter, divided

1 tablespoon minced shallots

1 teaspoon minced garlic

1 cup quartered chanterelles

$1/4$ cup sherry

2 cups Chicken Stock (see page 214)

$1/2$ cup heavy cream

Sea salt

Freshly ground black pepper

DISH

1 recipe Sautéed Napa Cabbage (see page 213)

1 recipe Lemon-Parsley Glazed Potatoes (see page 209)

SERVES 4

Seared Sea Scallops with Pumpkin-Sage Crème, Wild Mushroom Risotto & Prosciutto Frivolity

Sage and pumpkin are great accompaniments to scallops in the fall or early winter. When choosing fresh scallops, make certain they have a sweet scent and moist sheen. Avoid what I call "pumped" scallops—large scallops that have been injected with a solution of water and tripolyphosphate to make them more plump. These scallops have a compromised flavor and will shrink in the pan up to 50 percent. All fresh scallops should be used within a day or two of purchase.

Choose a small pie pumpkin for this recipe, rather than a large variety, as they are too dry and aren't as flavorful.

WINE PAIRING *2003 Wild Horse Winery, Central Coast Chardonnay, San Luis Obispo, California*
2002 Qupé Winery, Viognier, Santa Barbara, California

SEARED SEA SCALLOPS WITH PUMPKIN-SAGE CRÈME

1 small (about 16 ounces) pie pumpkin

3 tablespoons unsalted butter, divided

2 tablespoons extra virgin olive oil, divided

1/4 cup chopped yellow onion

1 tablespoon flour

1 cup heavy cream, cold

1 tablespoon Chablis or other dry white wine, cold

1/2 cup Fish Stock, cold (see page 214)

1/4 cup sage, en chiffonade

Sea salt

Freshly ground white pepper

1 pound (about 18–20 pieces) Gulf or diver scallops

WILD MUSHROOM RISOTTO

3 tablespoons extra virgin olive oil

3 tablespoons unsalted butter

2 shallots, chopped

4 ounces crimini mushrooms, sliced

4 ounces portabella mushrooms, sliced

4 ounces shiitake mushrooms, sliced

4 ounces oyster mushrooms, sliced

1 cup arborio rice

1/2 cup sherry

5 1/2 cups Vegetable Stock, divided (see page 215)

1/2 cup grated Parmesan cheese

3/4 teaspoon chopped thyme

Sea salt

Freshly ground black pepper

PROSCIUTTO FRIVOLITY

6 ounces prosciutto, cut into 1/8-inch-thick slices

DISH

Fried Herbs and Greens, for garnish (see page 218)

SERVES 6

FOR THE SEARED SEA SCALLOPS WITH PUMPKIN-SAGE CRÈME

1. Preheat oven to 350 degrees.

2. Peel the pumpkin and remove the seeds and pulp. Slice the flesh into wedges. Place the wedges in a baking dish and cover tightly with aluminum foil. Cook in preheated oven to release the pumpkin's flavors and to soften. This will take $1\frac{1}{2}$ hours. Coarsely chop the pumpkin wedges.

3. In a large saucepan, melt 2 tablespoons of the butter with 1 tablespoon of the oil. Add the pumpkin wedges and onion and sauté until the onion is soft and glossy, about 2 to 3 minutes. Whisk in the flour until the liquid is absorbed. Add the cream, wine, and stock and reduce by one-third, whisking frequently. Add the sage and season to taste with salt and pepper.

4. Pass the pumpkin crème through a food mill fitted with a fine-gauge disk, and then strain it through a fine-mesh sieve. Place back in the saucepan and reheat. Thin with additional cream and wine, if necessary. Adjust seasoning as needed.

5. Pat the scallops dry with a paper towel. Season lightly with salt.

6. In a sauté pan, melt the remaining 1 tablespoon butter and oil. Add the scallops and cook until lightly golden, about 2 to 3 minutes per side. They should be medium and therefore spring back slightly when touched.

FOR THE WILD MUSHROOM RISOTTO

1. Melt the oil and butter in a large sauté pan over high heat. Add the shallots and sauté until glossy, about 30 seconds.

2. Add the mushrooms and cook until tender and the juices are released, about 8 minutes. Stir in the rice. Deglaze with the sherry and simmer, stirring frequently, until the liquid is absorbed.

3. Add 1 cup of the Vegetable Stock and simmer, stirring frequently, until absorbed. Add the remaining stock, one cup at a time, allowing it to be completely absorbed before adding the next cup. Cook until the rice is tender and the mixture is creamy, about 20 minutes. Stir in the Parmesan and thyme. Season to taste with salt and pepper.

FOR THE PROSCIUTTO FRIVOLITY

Preheat oven to 350 degrees. Place prosciutto on a parchment-lined sheet pan and bake until much of the fat has been cooked out and the prosciutto is crispy like a potato chip, about 5 to 10 minutes.

PRESENTATION

Pour the Sage-Pumpkin Crème on the center of each serving plate. Place the Wild Mushroom Risotto on the Sage-Pumpkin Crème and prop two pieces of Prosciutto Frivolity in the risotto. Arrange the Seared Sea Scallops around the plate's perimeter and garnish each with a piece of fried sage.

Spring Spätzle Gratinée with Sautéed Vegetables & Montrachet Cheese Medallions

This is one of the most popular vegetarian dishes we serve at Biró, but meat-eaters love it, as well. After sautéing the Spätzle as explained on page 209, leave it in the pan and proceed with this recipe.

If you're not able to locate Bull's Blood lettuce, which is an exceptional baby green with deep red leaves, substitute another red lettuce, such as baby oak leaf.

WINE PAIRING *2000 Ojai Vineyard, Syrah, Ventura County, California*
2001 De Loach Vineyards, Chardonnay O.F.S., Russian River Valley, Sonoma, California

SPRING SPÄTZLE GRATINÉE

4 tablespoons Clarified Butter (see page 204), plus more for the dishes

$1/2$ cup heavy cream

1 recipe Spätzle (see page 209)

Freshly ground nutmeg

Sea salt

Freshly ground black pepper

1 cup shredded Gruyère cheese

8 tablespoons breadcrumbs

DISH

Bull's Blood lettuce, for garnish

$1/2$ recipe Sautéed Vegetables (see page 211)

1 recipe Montrachet Cheese Medallions (see page 210)

Tomato Glaze, for garnish (see page 218)

SERVES 4

FOR THE SPRING SPÄTZLE GRATINÉE

1. Preheat oven to 350 degrees. Lightly butter 4 small bowls or cups.

2. Add the cream to the warm sautéed Spätzle. Season to taste with nutmeg, salt, and pepper and cook for 1 minute. Add the Gruyère and stir until melted. Place in the bowls or cups and press down so the Spätzle takes on the shape of the dish. Place on a baking sheet and bake until warmed through, about 10 minutes.

3. Meanwhile, melt the Clarified Butter in a medium sauté pan over high heat. Add the breadcrumbs and sauté, stirring frequently, until golden brown.

PRESENTATION

I like to use square plates for this dish. Invert the Spätzle Gratinée onto one corner of the plate. Sprinkle with the breadcrumbs and garnish with a bit of Bull's Blood lettuce. Place the Sautéed Vegetables in the opposite corner. Place one Montrachet Cheese Medallion in the remaining two corners and spoon Tomato Glaze on the plate as garnish.

Berry-Custard Cake with Fruit Coulis

desserts

Double Mousse au Chocolat
with Apricot & Raspberry Coulis

Rich Grand Marnier Chocolate Cake with
Shiny Chocolate Icing & Vanilla Gelato

Iced Strawberry Soufflé with Mint-Orange Sabayon

Caramel-Crème Berries in Tuile Cup
with Vanilla Gelato

Chocolate & Chilled-Mango Pyramid
with Raspberry Coulis

Alsatian Rhubard Tartlets with Black Walnut Gelato

Chocolate–Dulce de Leche Crêpe Torte

Pumpkin Pot de Crème with Pumpkin-Seed Wafer

Chocolate Feuillantine with Poached Pears, Caramel
& Pistachio Mousse

Baked Peach with Lavender Gelato

Topfenpalatschinken

Lemon Mousse with Coconut Crisps
& Espresso Syrup

Tarte Flambée with Peaches, Crème Fraîche
& Grand Marnier

Pineapple "Ravioli" with Strawberry-Mint Crème

Champagne Parfait with Poached Cherries, Whipped
Vanilla Crème Fraîche & Black Pepper Cake

Heirloom Black Cherries in Port Gelée

Berry-Custard Cake with Fruit Coulis

Chocolate Tartlets with Caramelized Raspberries
& Lime Gelato

Green Tea Crème Brûlée

Sachertorte

Double Mousse au Chocolat with Apricot & Raspberry Coulis

These sensuous dark and white chocolate mousses are a sure bet when you're looking for a delicious yet uncomplicated dessert. They are excellent served with whipped cream, crème fraîche, and fresh berries, or you may use them as a filling for a pie, tart, or puff pastry.

WINE PAIRING *1999 d'Arenberg, Shiraz Port, McLaren Vale, Australia*
1998 M. Chapoutier, Banyuls "Vin Doux Naturels," Languedoc, France

DARK CHOCOLATE MOUSSE
7 ounces semi-sweet chocolate

5 large egg yolks

$1/_4$ cup sugar

2 cups heavy cream

3 large egg whites

Pinch sea salt

WHITE CHOCOLATE MOUSSE
$8^1/_2$ ounces white chocolate

5 large egg yolks

$1/_4$ cup sugar

2 leaves gelatin, bloomed

2 cups heavy cream

3 large egg whites

Pinch sea salt

DISH
Apricot Coulis (see page 216)

Raspberry Coulis (see page 216)

Fresh berries, for garnish

Sliced grapes, for garnish

Pistachios, for garnish

Roasted shaved almonds,
for garnish

Whipped cream or crème fraîche,
for garnish

SERVES 6

FOR THE DARK CHOCOLATE MOUSSE

1. In a double boiler, melt the chocolate. Meanwhile, combine the egg yolks and sugar in a bowl and stir until the sugar crystals are no longer visible. Allow the chocolate to cool slightly and then add it to the egg mixture and blend.

2. Either in a mixer fitted with a wire whisk attachment or by hand, whip the cream until stiff peaks form.

3. Either in a mixer fitted with a wire whisk attachment or by hand, whisk the egg whites with a pinch of salt until stiff peaks form.

4. Slowly fold the whipped cream into the chocolate mixture with a rubber spatula. Carefully fold the egg-white mixture into the chocolate–whipped cream mixture with a rubber spatula. Chill at least 2 hours prior to serving.

FOR THE WHITE CHOCOLATE MOUSSE

1. In a double boiler, melt the white chocolate. Meanwhile, combine the egg yolks and sugar in a bowl and stir until the sugar crystals are no longer visible. Allow the chocolate to cool slightly and then add it to the egg mixture and blend. Add the gelatin.

2. Either in a mixer fitted with a wire whisk attachment or by hand, whip the cream until stiff peaks form.

3. Either in a mixer fitted with a wire whisk attachment or by hand, whisk the egg whites with a pinch of salt until stiff peaks form.

4. Slowly fold the whipped cream into the chocolate mixture with a rubber spatula. Carefully fold the egg-white mixture into the chocolate–whipped cream mixture with a rubber spatula. Chill at least 2 hours prior to serving.

PRESENTATION

Using a teaspoon, shape the mousses into quenelle, or egg, shapes by dipping the spoon into a cup of very hot water and then placing the spoon, rounded bottom up, into the mixture with the far edge of the spoon. With the edge nearest you close to but not touching the mousse, drag the spoon toward you, twisting your wrist upward until the mousse folds over itself into a quenelle shape.

Immerse your spoon in hot water before shaping each new quenelle. Place the mousse quenelles at opposite sides of the plate. Drizzle the plate with Raspberry and Apricot Coulis and garnish with fresh berries, sliced grapes, pistachios, almonds, and whipped cream or crème fraîche.

Double Mousse au Chocolat wtih Apricot & Raspberry Coulis

Chocolate's my friend, so you see me use a lot of it on our television series and in the restaurant and school. But how do I decide which dark chocolate to use? It's actually very simple. I buy the chocolate, I taste the chocolate, and if I like the chocolate, I use the chocolate. But there is a guideline you can use in selecting dark chocolate for your dishes, and that's by checking its cocoa butter content.

We use dark chocolate that contains a minimum of 66 percent cocoa butter. It's shiny, it breaks cleanly, it doesn't contain any clumps or air bubbles, and it has a great flavor. Many of the dark chocolates you find in a grocery store have just 35 to 58 percent cocoa butter (and some as little as 10 percent!) and therefore contain vegetable fat, cocoa powder, or chocolate liqueur as main ingredients. These chocolates don't melt as well, don't taste as good, can be greasy or sticky to the touch, and may even have grainy white flecks in them. Unless you're using them for specialty drinks, as we do with a spice-infused Mexican chocolate in our bar, steer clear of them. High-quality chocolate yields high-quality desserts, and you should make sure your time and efforts are well spent.

Rich Grand Marnier Chocolate Cake with Shiny Chocolate Icing & Vanilla Gelato

Orange and chocolate have enjoyed a long and glorious relationship on the dessert plate for a reason: they are absolutely delicious together.

This is our take on a French classic, and we use only Valrhona chocolate for it. You may use the high-quality chocolate of your choice.

WINE PAIRING 1997 Niepoort, Vintage Ruby Port, Portugal
2001 Robert Sinskey Vineyards, Zinskey Late Harvest Zinfandel, Napa, California

RICH GRAND MARNIER CHOCOLATE CAKE

Butter for baking form

$1/2$ cup unsalted butter, at room temperature

4 ounces semi-sweet chocolate, finely chopped

$1/2$ cup sugar

Zest of 2 oranges

3 large eggs, separated, at room temperature

2 tablespoons Grand Marnier

$1/2$ cup minus 1 tablespoon cake flour

Pinch sea salt

SHINY CHOCOLATE ICING

$2/3$ cup heavy cream

7 ounces semi-sweet chocolate, finely chopped

7 tablespoons clarified butter, at room temperature

DISH

Vanilla Gelato (see page 212)

Raspberry Coulis (see page 216)

Raspberries, for garnish

Mint leaves, for garnish

MAKES 1 (9-INCH) CAKE

FOR THE RICH GRAND MARNIER CHOCOLATE CAKE

1. Preheat oven to 350 degrees.

2. Butter your baking form and line its bottom with parchment paper.

3. In a double boiler, melt the chocolate. Allow to cool slightly.

4. Meanwhile, in a mixing bowl, cream the butter and sugar until it is a uniform pale yellow color. Add the orange zest, egg yolks, and Grand Marnier and mix together.

5. Pour the melted chocolate into the mixture. Add the flour and blend. Set aside.

6. Whisk the egg whites with a pinch of salt until they reach the stiff-peak stage. Very carefully fold the egg whites into the chocolate mixture with a rubber spatula.

7. Pour the batter into a prepared baking form and bake for 25 minutes, or until a toothpick inserted into the cake's center comes out clean.

8. Invert cake onto a cooling rack. Allow to cool at least 10 minutes and then apply icing.

FOR THE SHINY CHOCOLATE ICING

1. Bring cream to a simmer over high heat. When it begins to simmer, remove it from the heat. Add the finely chopped chocolate. Stir until all the chocolate is melted and evenly incorporated into the cream. Allow it to come to room temperature.

2. Add the clarified butter to the chocolate-cream mixture and blend well. Use immediately.

PRESENTATION

Slice the cake into thin slices; it's quite rich and a little goes a long way. Place a slice on each serving plate and serve with a scoop of Vanilla Gelato. Garnish with Raspberry Coulis, a few fresh raspberries, and a mint leaf.

QUICK TIP: WHISKS VS. RUBBER SPATULAS

In this recipe, a whisk is used to bring egg whites to the stiff-peak stage, but a rubber spatula is used to fold them into the chocolate. Why? Whisks are used to create volume as quickly as possible. This is because the metal or silicone strands cut through the product you're whisking, introducing air pockets that create volume. Over-whisking has the opposite effect, so whisked items are blended with other ingredients with a rubber spatula. Fold from the bottom of the bowl to the top, being careful not to "cut" into the ingredients with the side of the spatula.

Iced Strawberry Soufflé with Mint-Orange Sabayon

Traditional soufflés are airy, sweet or savory egg-based hot preparations that rise, while baking, above the dish in which they are cooked. Iced soufflés are frozen desserts, usually made of ice cream, that mimic this look. Their height is achieved by placing a collar of wax or parchment paper inside each soufflé dish or ramekin. This one, I think you'll agree, is quite tasty, and the sensation of the cold soufflé and the warm sabayon is really pleasant. We serve it in 4-inch ramekins.

WINE PAIRING *NV Gruet, Blanc de Noir, Albuquerque, New Mexico*
1999 Domaine Mas Amiel, Plenitude Muscat d'Alexandrie, Roussillon, France

FOR THE ICED STRAWBERRY SOUFFLÉ

1. Remove the Strawberry Gelato from the freezer and allow to sit at room temperature until softened.

2. Cut 4 collars of parchment or waxed paper double the height of your ramekins and long enough to overlap the inside circumference of the ramekin by about $1/2$ inch. Place a collar inside the first ramekin and spoon the gelato into the middle of the ramekin without disturbing the collar. Once you have filled the ramekin itself with gelato, press the gelato firmly into the mold with a spoon. Spoon in enough gelato so that it is level with the top of the collar. Smooth with a palette knife and repeat the process with the remaining ramekins.

3. Place the soufflés in the freezer and chill until completely hardened, at least 2 hours. Remove from the freezer and gently slide the collars out of the ramekins, leaving the gelatin behind.

FOR THE MINT-ORANGE SABAYON

1. In a large metal bowl, whisk together the yolks, sugar, orange juice, and $1/2$ cup of the cream. Cook in a double boiler, whisking constantly, until the mixture becomes frothy and the whisk leaves distinct marks. Place the mixture in an ice bath to stop the cooking process, stirring gently with a rubber spatula to cool.

2. In a mixer fitted with a whisk attachment, pour in the remaining cream and beat until stiff peaks form. Gently fold the cream into the cooled yolk mixture until well incorporated. Fold in the mint.

PRESENTATION

To further mimic the look of a traditional soufflé, we use a blowtorch to brown the surface of the gelato. This also helps soften the soufflé, as gelato contains less air and is therefore denser than ice cream. Remove the soufflés from the ramekins and place on the center of each serving plate. Pour the Mint-Orange Sabayon around the soufflé and garnish each with two strawberry halves, placed cut side up. Serve immediately.

ICED STRAWBERRY SOUFFLÉ

4 cups Strawberry Gelato (see page 212)

MINT-ORANGE SABAYON

4 large egg yolks

$1/4$ cup sugar

$1/4$ cup orange juice

1 cup heavy cream, divided

1 tablespoon mint, en chiffonade

DISH

4 strawberries, halved, for garnish

SERVES 4

Caramel-Crème Berries in Tuile Cup with Vanilla Gelato

Caramel-Crème Berries in Tuile Cup with Vanilla Gelato

A few years back, my mother assumed cooking duties for the Christmas dinner—a bounty of traditional German fare for sixteen guests. Just following the entrée, she burned the chocolate cake she had made and summoned me to the kitchen for help. Finding only frozen berries, flour, sugar, orange juice, eggs, cream, and butter, I quickly whipped up this dessert while standing in a cloud of black smoke. Her guests were none the wiser.

I now make the dish with fresh rather than frozen berries, but frozen berries work fine. Feel free to cut this recipe by half, but it's been my experience that guests will want more than one. If you have leftovers, the tuiles keep nicely in a sealed plastic storage container, and the caramel-crème berries can simply be reheated.

WINE PAIRING *Yalumba, 50-Year-Old Tawny Port, Barossa Valley, Australia*
2000 Domaine Mas Amiel, Muscat "Collection", Roussillon, France

FOR THE TUILES

1. Preheat oven to 350 degrees.

2. Sift the flour, sugar, and salt into a small mixing bowl. Add the egg whites and melted butter; whisk to combine. Set the batter aside to rest for $1^1/_2$ hours before using, or cover and refrigerate for up to 3 days.

3. Line three sheet pans with Silpat or heavily buttered pieces of parchment paper. Using $1^1/_2$ tablespoons per tuile, spoon the batter onto the sheet pans, five per sheet. The tuiles, or cookies, should be at least 2 inches apart, as they spread during baking. Dipping a spoon in milk first, spread each cookie into a 3-inch round. To ensure even baking, make the edges no thinner than the centers.

4. Bake the tuiles until the edges are golden and the centers are just beginning to color, about 8 to 10 minutes. Remove the cookies from the oven. As soon as they are cool enough to handle, remove the tuiles from the sheet pans and drape them around rolling pins, wine bottles, or tea cups to form a shape to hold the filling. If the tuiles become too cool and stiff to bend, return them to the oven for 1 minute to soften.

FOR THE CARAMEL-CRÈME BERRIES

1. In a sauté pan over low heat, heat the sugar with the water (this prevents the sugar from browning too fast and ensures even cooking). When the sugar caramelizes, add one-half of the berries.

2. Add the orange juice and reduce until the caramel sauce becomes syrupy and the berries break apart, about 2 minutes. Add the heavy cream and Grand Marnier and reduce for an additional minute, whisking to ensure a smooth consistency. Add the remaining half of the berries and stir. Remove from heat and allow to cool slightly.

PRESENTATION

Place 1 teaspoon of whipped cream onto the center of each serving plate to hold the tuile into place. Place 2 scoops of Vanilla Gelato into each tuile. Drizzle with warm Caramel-Crème Berries and garnish with mint leaves, shaved almonds, crushed pistachios, and whipped cream. Serve immediately, as you don't want the ice cream to melt before your guests see your creation.

TUILES

$1/_3$ cup flour

$1/_2$ cup plus 2 tablespoons granulated sugar

1 pinch salt

3 large egg whites

$2^1/_2$ tablespoons melted unsalted butter

2 tablespoons milk

CARAMEL-CRÈME BERRIES

$1/_3$ cup unrefined sugar

1 tablespoon water

1 cup strawberries, divided

1 cup raspberries, divided

1 cup blackberries, divided

$1/_3$ cup orange juice

$1/_2$ cup heavy cream

1 teaspoon Grand Marnier

DISH

$1/_2$ cup whipped cream, divided

Vanilla Gelato (see page 212)

10 mint leaves, en chiffonade

Shaved almonds, for garnish

Crushed pistachios, for garnish

MAKES 15 TUILES

Chocolate & Chilled-Mango Pyramid with Raspberry Coulis

If you're looking for a dessert to impress but don't have a lot of time, this is your recipe. Served cold, it layers the decadent crunch of chocolate-cornflake disks with the refreshing, satiny sensation of puréed mangoes. Simply delicious.

WINE PAIRING *2001 Robert Sinskey Vineyards, Zinskey Late Harvest Zinfandel, Napa, California*
2000 Domaine du Mas Blanc, Banyuls Cuvée Dr. André Parcé, Banyuls, France

10 ounces semi-sweet chocolate, chopped

1 teaspoon cocoa powder

1 teaspoon unsalted butter

³/₄ cup cornflakes, crushed

1 cup mangoes, peeled, seeded, sliced, and divided

2 tablespoons condensed milk

1 teaspoon grated ginger

2 leaves gelatin

Raspberry Coulis, for garnish (see page 216)

SERVES 4

1. Melt the chocolate in a double boiler. Add the cocoa powder and butter, stirring until well blended. Remove from heat and allow to cool slightly.

2. Pour the chocolate mixture into a medium-sized bowl. Pour in the cornflakes and stir.

3. On a sheet pan lined with parchment paper, spoon the chocolate-cornflake mixture into eight small disks, 3 to 4 inches in diameter. Allow to cool at room temperature, or place in refrigerator until hard.

4. Place two-thirds of the mangoes in a food processor or blender and purée until smooth. With the machine running, add the condensed milk and ginger. Bloom the gelatin and add it to the mango mixture. Allow to set in refrigerator.

PRESENTATION

Place one disk on the center of each serving plate. Spoon mango purée onto it. Top with a disk. Garnish with the remaining mango slices and a drizzle of Raspberry Coulis.

Alsatian Rhubarb Tartlets with Black Walnut Gelato

I always wait for rhubarb season to roll around, as it's one of my favorite warm-weather ingredients. These tartlets are elegant enough for a dinner party, yet simple enough for a picnic. I like mine served lukewarm with plenty of Black Walnut Gelato. You could substitute tart apples or pears for rhubarb in this recipe.

WINE PAIRING *1994 Domaine Suronde, Quartz de Chaume, Loire, France*
1990 Le Mont, Vouvray Moelleux, Loire, France

FOR THE TARTLETS

1. Blend the flour, sugar, and salt in the bowl of a stand mixer fitted with a whisk attachment. Add butter and beat at medium-low speed for 3 minutes. Add crème fraîche and beat until moist clumps form, about 1 minute.

2. Butter 6 (4-inch) tart forms.

3. Turn dough out onto a clean work surface. Gather the dough into a smooth ball and flatten into a 6-inch-diameter disk. Wrap dough in plastic and refrigerate until cold, at least 2 hours. You may wish to perform this step one day ahead of time and refrigerate the dough. Allow the dough to soften slightly before rolling it out. Roll out onto a lightly floured surface until about $1/8$ inch thick. Using a tart form, cut out a piece of pastry and press the pastry into the bottom of the form. Repeat with the remaining forms. Pierce the pastry with a fork and place in the refrigerator to firm for about 15 minutes.

FOR THE RHUBARB FILLING

1. Preheat oven to 350 degrees.

2. Remove the tartlets from the refrigerator and arrange the rhubarb atop the chilled pastry in each form. Place the tartlets back in the refrigerator.

3. Combine the sugar, cream, and eggs in a bowl and whisk until well combined. Pour over the rhubarb and sprinkle with sugar.

4. Bake until the crust is golden brown and the filling is solid, about 20 minutes.

PRESENTATION

Remove tartlets from their forms and place one on the center of each serving plate. Drizzle crème fraîche over the tartlets and serve lukewarm with a scoop of Black Walnut Gelato.

TARTLETS

$1^1/_2$ cups flour, plus more for dusting

2 tablespoons sugar

$1/_2$ teaspoon salt

$3/_4$ cup chilled unsalted butter, cut into $3/_4$-inch pieces, plus more for the tartlets

6 tablespoons chilled crème fraîche

RHUBARB FILLING

4 stalks rhubarb, peeled, halved, sliced, and sugared

$1/_2$ cup sugar

1 cup heavy cream

6 whole eggs

DISH

Crème fraîche, for garnish

Black Walnut Gelato
(see page 212)

SERVES 6

Chocolate–Dulce de Leche Crêpe Torte

Warm, chilled, and frozen layered versions of the traditional Spanish dulce torte abound, and this one is particularly delicious. With its gorgeous layers of sweet cream, decadent chocolate, and airy crêpes, this torte should be served sliced.

Dulce de leche is sold under the name "sweetened condensed milk" in the United States.

WINE PAIRING *2000 Romariz, Vintage Porto, Portugal*
Iron Horse Vineyards, Wedding Cuvée, Sonoma, California

2 cups flour

2 tablespoons sugar

Pinch sea salt

2$\frac{1}{2}$ cups plus 2 tablespoons milk

1 teaspoon vanilla extract

6 large eggs, lightly beaten

4 tablespoons melted butter, plus more for brushing

1 cup plus 2 tablespoons heavy cream

10 ounces bittersweet chocolate, chopped

1 teaspoon cinnamon

4 large egg yolks

1$\frac{1}{2}$ cups sweetened condensed milk

Confectioners' sugar, for dusting

Mint leaves, for garnish

Berries, for garnish

MAKES 1 (9-INCH) TORTE

1. In a medium bowl, whisk together the flour, sugar, and salt. Whisk in the milk, vanilla, whole eggs, and 4 tablespoons melted butter; let batter rest for 30 minutes.

2. Heat a 10-inch nonstick skillet and brush lightly with melted butter. Pour $\frac{1}{3}$ cup crêpe batter into the skillet and immediately swirl until it reaches halfway up the side. Pour any excess batter back into the bowl. Cook the crêpe over moderate heat until golden at the edge and set in the center, about 1 minute. Flip the crêpe and cook for about 15 seconds longer, or just until the bottom is browned in spots. Repeat with the remaining batter, brushing the skillet with the butter only as needed.

3. In a medium saucepan, bring 1 cup of the cream to a boil. Remove the pan from the heat and add the chocolate and cinnamon. Let stand for 5 minutes to allow chocolate to melt and the flavors to infuse, and then whisk until smooth. Whisk in two egg yolks. In a medium bowl, whisk the sweetened condensed milk with the remaining 2 tablespoons cream and the remaining egg yolks.

4. Preheat the oven to 350 degrees. Butter a 9-inch round cake pan, line the bottom with parchment paper, and butter the paper. Fit a crêpe in the bottom of the pan, pressing to flatten it. Halve two crêpes and line the sides of the pan with them, placing the cut sides down and slightly overlapping the bottom crêpe; the rounded part of the halved crêpe will hang over the edge of the pan.

5. Spoon a slightly heaping $\frac{1}{2}$ cup of the chocolate filling into the pan and spread to the edge of the crêpe. Top with another crêpe, pressing to flatten it. Spoon a slightly heaping $\frac{1}{2}$ cup of the sweetened condensed milk filling on top, spread it to the edge, and top with a crêpe. Repeat this layering with the remainder of the fillings and four more crêpes, ending with a crêpe. Fold the overhanging crêpes over the top. Gently press a round of buttered parchment paper directly onto the torte and cover the pan with foil.

6. Bake the torte until puffed, about 1 hour. Remove the foil and let cool for 1 hour. Remove the parchment and run a knife around the edge of the pan to loosen the torte. Invert onto a plate and remove the parchment paper. Allow to cool.

PRESENTATION

Slice the torte into your desired number of pieces—it's quite rich, so a small sliver goes a long way. Place each slice on a serving plate, standing the pieces up so that your guests can see the beautiful layers in the torte. I like to serve this dish lukewarm; to do so, place the slices in a 300-degree oven for a few minutes to soften the chocolate. Dust the plates with confectioners' sugar and garnish with mint leaves and berries.

Pumpkin Pot de Crème with Pumpkin-Seed Wafer

French for "pot of cream," pot de crème is a rich, creamy custard that is served in pot-shaped cups or ramekins. Though it is classically flavored with vanilla, it is also excellent flavored with citrus, chocolate, or coffee. Pumpkin makes the perfect autumn pot de crème, as you'll see in this delicious dessert.

WINE PAIRING *2000 InnisKillin, Icewine, Ontario, Canada*
2003 Nivole Muscato d'Asti, Michele Chiarlo, Piedmont, Italy

FOR THE PUMPKIN POT DE CRÈME

1. Preheat oven to 325 degrees.

2. Whisk together the cream, milk, sugar, vanilla, and pumpkin purée in a heavy pot. Bring the mixture to a simmer over medium heat.

3. In a medium-sized bowl, whisk the remaining ingredients together. Slowly pour mixture into the pumpkin mixture and whisk to form a custard. Pour this through a strainer into a large glass measuring cup.

4. Set 8 (6-ounce) ramekins in a bain-marie. Pour equal amounts of the pumpkin custard into ramekins. Bake in the bain-marie until the custards are firm but jiggle slightly, about 45 minutes to 1 hour.

FOR THE PUMPKIN-SEED WAFERS

1. Preheat oven to 350 degrees.

2. In a food processor, process the pumpkin seeds and one-half of the sugar to a fine meal.

3. Combine the egg and vanilla in a small bowl. With the machine running, add it to the pumpkin meal and process until the mixture comes together to create a dough.

4. Pour the remaining $1/4$ cup sugar into a wide, shallow bowl. Drop the pumpkin-seed dough by rounded teaspoon into the sugar and completely coat. Using a fork, pick up the rounds and place onto a sheet pan lined with Silpat or parchment paper. Flatten slightly with the fork.

5. Bake until pale golden, about 15 minutes. Allow to cool on the pan to prevent breakage.

PRESENTATION

Place a ramekin on the center of each serving plate. Place a pumpkin-seed wafer in each pot de crème.

POT DE CRÈME

2 cups heavy cream

$1^1/_2$ cups milk

$^3/_4$ cup sugar

2 teaspoons vanilla

1 cup pumpkin purée

14 egg yolks

1 teaspoon cinnamon

1 teaspoon allspice

$^1/_8$ teaspoon freshly ground nutmeg

$^1/_2$ teaspoon ginger

$^1/_4$ teaspoon salt

PUMPKIN-SEED WAFERS

$^1/_2$ cup plus 2 tablespoons green pumpkin seeds

$^1/_2$ cup sugar, divided

1 egg, beaten

$^1/_2$ teaspoon pure vanilla extract

SERVES 8

QUICK TIP: MAKING YOUR OWN BAIN-MARIE

A bain-marie, or water bath, means "Mary's bath" in French and is used for keeping delicate food or dishes warm without allowing them to break, curdle, or continue cooking. Most believe it's named after Marie Antoinette, who took her baths at approximately 120 degrees.

Bain-maries are also used to melt or slow-cook items, such as in this recipe. You may purchase a bain-marie, which resembles a double-boiler pan in which the lower pan contains hot water and the upper pan contains the food, or you may easily fashion one yourself by placing a container such as a gratin dish, ramekin, or soufflé dish holding food in a large, shallow pan of warm water and cooking or warming the food in an oven or on the stovetop.

I often see people filling their bain-maries with water and the item to be cooked or warmed and then carefully trying to maneuver their way to the stove. It's much easier—and safer—to fill your bain-marie after you have placed it on the stovetop or in the oven. You don't want any water to get into the item you're making. To facilitate even cooking, make certain there is water and space surrounding each individual vessel within the larger pan.

Chocolate Feuillantine with Poached Pears, Caramel & Pistachio Mousse

This decadent but not cloyingly sweet dessert was originally created for one of the wine and cuisine groups that frequently dine at Biró. It was the perfect conclusion to their elegant meal, and I'm confident it will be for yours as well. We use Williams' Bon pears for this dish, but Anjou, Bartlett, or Bosc pears would also work well. If you can't find pistachio paste, you can make your own by combining $^1/_4$ cup pistachios with 2 teaspoons sugar in a food processor and process until smooth.

WINE PAIRING *2000 d'Arenberg, Port Shiraz, McLaren Vale, Australia*
2000 Domaine Mas Amiel, Muscat "Collection," Roussillon, France

CHOCOLATE SQUARES
8 ounces semi-sweet chocolate, chopped

POACHED PEARS
2 cups ruby port

$^2/_3$ cup sugar

$^1/_2$ cup water

4 star anise

3 firm Williams' Bon pears, peeled, halved, and cored

CARAMEL
1 cup heavy cream

$^1/_2$ cup packed dark brown sugar

$^1/_4$ cup unsalted butter

PISTACHIO MOUSSE
$^1/_2$ cup whole milk

$^1/_2$ cup heavy cream

2 tablespoons sugar

1 tablespoon pistachio paste

4 large egg yolks

1 cup whipped cream

DISH
Chopped pistachios, for garnish

Raspberry Coulis, for garnish (see page 216)

Berries, for garnish

Mint, for garnish

SERVES 4

FOR THE CHOCOLATE SQUARES

1. Melt the chocolate in a double boiler.

2. Pour the melted chocolate onto a parchment-lined baking sheet and, with a palette knife, smooth to about $^1/_8$ inch thick. Refrigerate until completely hardened, about 20 minutes. The chocolate may curl at the edges during the cooling process; this is normal.

3. Remove the chocolate from the refrigerator and let sit at room temperature for 45 seconds to 1 minute. Using a $2^1/_2$-x-$2^1/_2$-inch-square cutter, cut eight squares into the chocolate but do not remove the squares from the parchment. Place back in the refrigerator.

FOR THE POACHED PEARS

1. Cut a circle of parchment that is slightly smaller than the opening of the saucepan in which you will poach the pears. Cut a hole about 1 inch in diameter into the center of the parchment.

2. Place all ingredients in a saucepan. Place the parchment directly over the ingredients so that the pears stay completely submerged in the liquid. Bring to a boil over high heat. Turn off heat and allow pears to infuse for 25 to 30 minutes. Remove parchment.

FOR THE CARAMEL

Place all the ingredients in a medium saucepan and bring to a boil over medium-high heat, stirring frequently. Reduce heat to medium-low and simmer, stirring frequently, until the sauce is reduced to about $^3/_4$ cup, about 15 minutes.

FOR THE PISTACHIO MOUSSE

1. Bring the milk, cream, sugar, and pistachio paste to a boil in a large saucepan over high heat. Reduce heat to medium and simmer.

2. In a medium bowl, whisk the yolks until smooth. Whisk a bit of the hot mixture into the yolks to temper them and then whisk the tempered yolks into the hot mixture. Reduce until the mixture coats the back of a spoon, about 5 to 10 minutes. Remove from heat and pour the mixture into a large mixing bowl resting in an ice bath. Cool completely.

3. Fold the whipped cream into the cooled cream mixture.

PRESENTATION

Spoon a mirror, or thin layer, of Caramel on the center of each serving plate. Leaving the tops intact, slice the Poached Pears into fans and place atop the Caramel. Remove the chocolate squares from the refrigerator and gently peel them from the parchment. Place one square on top of each pear and cover with pistachio mousse. Place a second square on top of the mousse. Garnish with chopped pistachios, Raspberry Coulis, berries, and mint. Serve immediately.

Baked Peach with Lavender Gelato

For centuries, gardeners have awaited the blooming of fragrant lavender. Not only prized for its aroma and beauty, lavender has for centuries been cultivated in mountainous regions in the western Mediterranean, France, Italy, England, and Norway for use as a tonic against faintness, heart palpitations, toothaches, rheumatism, sprains, poor spirits, and colic. Today, lavender is used widely throughout the world in aromatherapy and in cooking. Though we can't be sure it will heal what ails you, this recipe's delicate blend of flavors is sure to delight your taste buds.

This recipe is always a hit at the culinary school, and students invariably fight over the caramel left over in the baking dish. I suggest scooping what you can out of the pan and distributing it evenly among your guests—or sneaking it all for yourself before a fight ensues.

WINE PAIRING *Iron Horse Wedding Cuvée, Brut, Sonoma, California*
2002 Beaumalric Muscat de Beaumes de Venise, Vin Doux Naturel, France

FOR THE BAKED PEACH

1. Preheat oven to 450 degrees.

2. Prick peaches with a fork and set them close together in a baking dish. Place a pat of butter on each peach, sprinkle with sugar, and add just enough water to cover the bottom of the dish. Bake until soft, 20 to 30 minutes, depending on the ripeness of the peaches.

PRESENTATION

Place one peach on a small plate and serve with one or two large scoops of Lavender Gelato. Garnish with berries, mint, and whipped cream.

BAKED PEACH

6 fresh peaches

$1/2$ cup granulated sugar

6 teaspoons butter

Water

DISH

Lavender Gelato (see page 212)

Berries, for garnish

Mint, for garnish

Whipped cream, for garnish

SERVES 6

Topfenpalatschinken

Palatschinken are filled pancakes similar to crêpes but with less egg and more flour.

This traditional Hungarian dessert makes me smile—not just because I love it, but also because it reminds me of being a rambunctious kid. When spending summers on our paternal grandparents' farm in Hungary, I'd beg my grandmother to make Palatschinken because it was one of my favorite dishes and the only one my little sister Nicole hated worse than peas. I'd eat all of my Palatschinken and then down all of hers, telling our grandmother that neither of us could get enough of her great creation. She'd keep the Palatschinken coming and my sister would beg me in our native German, which our grandmother couldn't understand, to ask her to stop. At that point I'd usually stop eating. Knowing that food left on plates wasn't tolerated in our grandparents' home, my sister would either accept any bribe presented her or be forced to cram fistfuls of the filled pancakes down the crack between the kitchen bench and wall. Either way, I was happy and well fed.

Despite what my sister may tell you, palatschinken are fantastic—especially when baked with a topping, or topfen, *as in this dessert. Use ricotta for the filling if you can't find quark.*

WINE PAIRING *1998 Domaine des Baumard, Quarts de Chaume, Loire, France*
2003 Nivole Muscato d'Asti, Michele Chiarlo, Piedmont, Italy

PALATSCHINKEN

1¹/₂ cups whole milk

2 large eggs

1¹/₄ cups flour

Pinch sea salt

2 teaspoons sugar

Unsalted butter, for sautéing

FILLING

1 pound quark

1¹/₂ cups heavy cream

6 eggs, separated

8 tablespoons raisins

Zest of ¹/₂ lemon

4 tablespoons sugar

TOPPING

1¹/₂ cups whole milk

2 eggs

4 tablespoons sugar

DISH

Whipped cream, for garnish

Berries, for garnish

SERVES 8

FOR THE PALATSCHINKEN

1. In a medium mixing bowl, whisk together the milk and eggs. Slowly whisk in the flour. Add a pinch of salt and the sugar and whisk to combine.

2. Heat an 8¹/₂-inch crêpe pan over high heat. Add a bit of butter to the heated pan and let it melt and then pour about 2 tablespoons of batter into the center of the pan. Rotate the pan in a circular motion so the batter distributes evenly throughout the bottom. Cook until the bottom of the pancake is lightly browned and spotted, about 30 to 45 seconds. Flip and cook for an additional 10 to 15 seconds. Transfer the prepared pancake, nice side down, to a plate. Repeat this process, adding more butter to the pan as necessary, until all the batter is used.

FOR THE FILLING

1. Combine the quark, cream, yolks, raisins, and zest in a large mixing bowl and stir until smooth.

2. Whip the egg whites with the sugar until stiff. Carefully fold the whites under the quark mixture.

FOR THE TOPPING

Place the ingredients in a mixing bowl and whisk together to combine.

PRESENTATION

Spoon about 2 tablespoons filling onto the center of each pancake and roll tightly. Place them, seam side down, into a baking dish. Pour the topping over the rolled pancakes and bake until golden brown, about 20 minutes. Slice the Palatschinken into squares and place on individual serving plates. Serve warm, garnished with whipped cream and berries.

Lemon Mousse with Coconut Crisps & Espresso Syrup

This dessert is easy to make and equally easy to fall in love with. It made its debut on Biró's summer 2004 menu and quickly developed a following. Its devotees were captivated by the luxurious texture of the mousse, which is perfectly counterbalanced by the flaky crunch of the crisps and grounded by the rich Espresso Syrup. I know they'd be pleasantly surprised at just how easy the dessert is to re-create at home.

WINE PAIRING *2001 Robert Sinskey Vineyards, Zinskey Late Harvest Zinfandel, Napa, California*
NV Egly-Ouriet, Brut Rose, Champagne, France

FOR THE LEMON MOUSSE

1. Whisk the egg yolks and sugar together in a medium saucepan. Whisk in the lemon juice and zest. Place the pan on the stovetop and heat over medium-low. Slowly whisk in one piece of butter at a time, adding another piece when the piece before it has completely melted. Whisk the mixture constantly until it reaches the boiling point; immediately remove from heat.

2. Strain the mixture through a fine-mesh sieve into a chilled bowl and stir in the bloomed gelatin. Stir occasionally until the mixture is room temperature.

3. Whisk the cream until soft peaks form. Fold the cream into the lemon mixture, one-third at a time. Chill for at least 1 hour.

FOR THE COCONUT CRISPS

1. Preheat oven to 375 degrees.

2. Brush the Tarte Flambée Crust with melted butter.

3. In a small mixing bowl, combine the coconut, sugar, and coriander. Sprinkle the coconut mixture over the tarte dough sheet. Press the toppings into the dough to adhere. Cut the Tarte Flambée Crust into the shapes you desire with a knife or cookie cutter, and bake for 7 minutes. Reduce heat to 250 degrees and bake until crispy and lightly browned, about 8 to 10 additional minutes.

FOR THE ESPRESSO SYRUP

Reduce the ingredients in a small pan over high heat until syrupy, about 5 minutes. Remove from heat and allow to cool slightly.

PRESENTATION

Place the Lemon Mousse on the serving dishes of your choice. Prop a Coconut Crisp in each portion and garnish with a drizzle of Espresso Syrup.

LEMON MOUSSE

10 large egg yolks

$1^1/_4$ cups sugar

$^3/_4$ cup lemon juice

1 tablespoon lemon zest

$^1/_2$ cup unsalted butter, cut in pieces

2 leaves gelatin, bloomed

$1^1/_4$ cups heavy cream

COCONUT CRISPS

1 Tarte Flambée Crust (see page 208)

2 tablespoons melted unsalted butter

$^1/_2$ cup shredded unsweetened coconut

2 tablespoons sugar

1 teaspoon coriander

ESPRESSO SYRUP

4 shots espresso

1 tablespoon light corn syrup

1 teaspoon lemon juice

2 tablespoons brown sugar

SERVES 8

Tarte Flambée with Peaches, Crème Fraîche & Grand Marnier

This is one of the most popular sweet Tarte Flambées at Biró, and we serve it with a flaming shot of Grand Marnier that the server spins over the tarte in a beautiful ribbon of flames. The front-of-house staff was a bit apprehensive about presenting this technique at first, and one of my wine bar servers had a bit of an accident while trying it for the first time under the watchful eye of her guests and our television cameras. She was fine and it made for a humorous television moment, but please be careful if you try this technique yourself.

WINE PAIRING *2001 Chateau Gravas, Sauternes, Bordeaux, France*
NV Egly-Ouriet, Brut Tradition, Champagne, France

1 Tarte Flambée Crust
(see page 208)

$1/4$ cup crème fraîche

$1/2$ cup quark

$1/2$ teaspoon Hungarian paprika

2 peaches, sliced thinly

1 ounce Grand Marnier

MAKES 1 TARTE FLAMBÉE

1. Preheat oven to 450 degrees.

2. Place the tarte dough crust on a sheet pan lined with parchment paper.

3. In a small mixing bowl, combine the crème fraîche, quark, and paprika. Using a rubber spatula or large spoon, spread the crème fraîche mixture over the tarte dough crust.

4. Cover evenly with peach slices and place in the oven.

5. Bake until the edges of the tarte are golden brown, about 5 minutes. Cut and serve immediately.

PRESENTATION

At Biró Wine Bar, we serve this dish traditionally, which is on a wooden board. You could use a cutting board, carefully sliding the tarte from the parchment paper onto the board and then cutting it. At this point you can either drizzle the Grand Marnier over the tarte and quickly light it, or place it in the shot glass, light it on fire, and then spin it out onto the tarte in front of your guests. Either way, allow the flames to extinguish themselves, signaling that the liquor flavor is gone and only the orange essence remains.

QUICK TIP: WHY FLAMBÉ?

You might wonder why chefs flambé, or light dishes on fire with alcohol. Some may do it only to show off, but flambéing is actually an important technique that enables you to cook out the alcohol taste while retaining the flavor profile of the liquor you are using. In this dish, you're using only a small amount of liqueur, but when you're cooking with larger quantities of alcohol, such as when using brandy or cognac in a meat or mushroom dish, you may get a burst of flames while adding it. If unexpected or uncontrolled, this could mean good-bye eyebrows. Make certain you flambé only in an area with high ceilings and proper ventilation, and where nothing, such as curtains, is in the area.

Tarte Flambée with Peaches, Crème Fraîche & Grand Marnier

Pineapple "Ravioli" with Strawberry-Mint Crème

This light and refreshing dessert is simply stunning and is one of the most popular cold desserts featured at Biró. I serve it with fresh strawberries, raspberries, blackberries, blueberries, pomegranate seeds, and whipped cream, but you may wish to pair it with our Vanilla Gelato (see page 212). Use only fresh golden pineapple, which yields the sweetest flavor and most vibrant color, to create our "ravioli" sheets.

WINE PAIRING *1996 Domaine Weinbach Tokay Pinot Gris, "Vendange Tardive," Alsace, France*
Möet & Chandon White Star, Non-Vintage Champagne, Epernay, France

PASTRY-CREAM FILLING AND PINEAPPLE "RAVIOLI"

1 vanilla bean

1/2 cup milk

1/2 cup heavy cream

1/4 cup sugar

3 large egg yolks

2 1/2 tablespoons flour

36 fresh pineapple slices, very thin

Juice of 2 lemons

5 mint leaves, en chiffonade

18 strawberries, julienned

VANILLA SYRUP

1 vanilla bean

1 cup granulated sugar

1/2 cup water

DISH

Berries, for garnish

Pomegranate seeds, for garnish

Mint leaves, for garnish

Pineapple leaves, for garnish

SERVES 6

FOR THE PASTRY CREAM

1. Cut the vanilla bean in half lengthwise and scrape out the seeds with the tip of a sharp knife. Add the vanilla seeds and pods, milk, cream, and 1 teaspoon of the sugar to a saucepan and bring just to a boil over medium-high heat. Whisk periodically to help extract the vanilla seeds from the pods. Remove from heat, cover, and let steep for at least 10 minutes. Pass through a fine-mesh sieve; discard vanilla pods and seeds.

2. In a small bowl, whisk together the egg yolks and remaining sugar until light and fluffy, about 2 minutes. Add the flour and continue whisking until smooth.

3. Slowly pour a bit of the hot milk mixture into the egg mixture to temper the eggs. Whisk in the remaining hot milk mixture until completely smooth. Return the mixture to the saucepan. Over medium heat, bring the mixture to a boil, whisking constantly, and cook for an additional 2 minutes.

4. Remove from heat and place pastry cream in a chilled stainless steel bowl to cool. Place 1 teaspoon pastry cream in the center of 18 of the pineapple slices; top with mint chiffonades and three strawberry slices each. Cover with remaining 18 pineapple slices, pressing down on the edges of the pineapples to create a ravioli shape. Cut the edges off the raviolis with a cookie cutter. If your cutter isn't sharp enough, trim with a sharp knife while using the cookie cutter as a template.

FOR THE VANILLA SYRUP

1. Cut the vanilla bean in half lengthwise and scrape out the seeds with the tip of a sharp knife.

2. Add the seeds and pods, sugar, and water to a small saucepan and bring to a boil over medium heat. Whisk periodically to aid in the extraction of the vanilla seeds from the pods and to dissolve the sugar crystals. Do not allow the syrup to color. Remove from heat and let cool.

3. Pass the syrup through a fine-mesh sieve; discard the vanilla pods and seeds.

PRESENTATION

Place three raviolis on each plate. Garnish with fresh berries, pomegranate seeds, mint leaves, and pineapple leaves. Drizzle vanilla syrup around the plate's perimeter.

QUICK TIP: SELECTING THE PERFECT PINEAPPLE

I'm often asked how to pick the perfect pineapple. The answer is in the color, leaves, and aroma. Ripe pineapples have a golden hue. Their leaves are slightly wilted, and if you pull on them, they come out easily. When ripe, a pineapple will have a pleasant sweet flavor.

Champagne Parfait with Poached Cherries, Whipped Vanilla Crème Fraîche & Black Pepper Cake

Parfait translates to "perfect" in French, and in the case of this dessert, the definition fits. The first layer—cherries poached in port—teases the taste buds with sweet acidity. The middle layer—Champagne bubbles suspended in a silky, slightly tart gelée—cleanses the palate for the parfait's surprising finale: a spicy pepper cake sure to leave your guests wanting more.

It's important to keep the Champagne chilled until used.

WINE PAIRING *2001 Erich Bender, Gold Sylvaner Eiswein, Pfalz, Germany*
2000 Voss Vineyard, Botrytis Sauvignon Blanc, Napa, California

FOR THE CHAMPAGNE PARFAIT WITH POACHED CHERRIES

1. In a medium saucepan, bring the port to a boil. Add cherries and poach for 2 minutes. Remove cherries from the port and set aside. Reduce port by one-half.

2. Bloom the gelatin leaves. Combine water, juice, and sugar in a small saucepan over medium-low heat. Stir until the sugar dissolves and remove from heat. Add the bloomed gelatin leaves and stir until they completely dissolve. Pour the liquid into a large glass measuring cup or bowl and allow to come to room temperature, about 25 to 30 minutes.

3. Meanwhile, place the Poached Cherries in the bottoms of your serving glasses or dishes and place in the refrigerator to chill.

4. Uncork the Champagne and very slowly pour one-half of it into the gelatin liquid. Carefully stir the mixture to incorporate, but do not disturb too many of the bubbles. Add the remaining Champagne. Slowly pour the mixture over the chilled Poached Cherries and chill until solid, about 10 minutes.

FOR THE BLACK PEPPER CAKE

1. Preheat oven to 375 degrees.

2. Place the chocolate, apple juice, and butter in a double boiler and heat until melted. Remove from heat and stir in the condensed milk.

3. In a medium mixing bowl, whisk together the flour, almonds, pepper, and eggs. Fold this mixture into the melted chocolate mixture.

4. Pour the batter into a 5-x-7-inch nonstick baking pan. Bake until the edges of the cake begin to pull away from the pan edges, about 15 to 20 minutes. Allow to cool.

FOR THE WHIPPED VANILLA CRÈME FRAÎCHE

In a stand mixer fitted with a wire whisk attachment, combine the ingredients and whip on high speed until peaks form. Chill.

PRESENTATION

Cut the cake into cubes and place over the layer of Champagne Parfait. Spoon a dollop of Whipped Vanilla Crème Fraîche onto each serving and garnish with a mint leaf. Place the glasses on small serving plates and drizzle Fruit Coulis on the plates.

CHAMPAGNE PARFAIT WITH POACHED CHERRIES

2 cups port

12 bing cherries, pitted

3 leaves gelatin

1/4 cup water

1 teaspoon lemon juice

1/4 cup sugar

1 1/2 cups Champagne or sparkling wine

BLACK PEPPER CAKE

8 ounces white chocolate

1/8 cup apple juice

4 tablespoons unsalted butter

2 ounces sweetened condensed milk

5 tablespoons flour

2 tablespoons ground almonds

1/2 teaspoon freshly ground black pepper

4 large eggs

WHIPPED VANILLA CRÈME FRAÎCHE

1/2 cup crème fraîche

2 tablespoons sugar

1/2 teaspoon vanilla extract

DISH

Mint leaves, for garnish

Fruit Coulis, for garnish (see page 217)

SERVES 6

Heirloom Black Cherries in Port Gelée

Heirloom Black Cherries in Port Gelée

If you're looking for something unique but simple to prepare, this dessert is for you. You can shape the gelée using ice cube trays or mini muffin forms. If you can't find lingonberry jam, substitute raspberry or blackberry jam.

WINE PAIRING *1998 Château des Charmes, Estate Late Harvest Riesling, Ontario, Canada
2001 Robert Sinskey Vineyards, Zinskey Late Harvest Zinfandel, Napa, California*

1. Bloom the gelatin in the port.

2. In a small sauté pan over low heat, warm the lingonberry jam until it liquefies. Add the gelatin and port, sugar, and lemon zest and cook until the gelatin is completely dissolved. Add a few drops Tabasco or to taste.

3. Fill 16 ice cube compartments or mini muffin forms one-third full with the liquid. Place in the refrigerator until set, about 15 to 20 minutes.

4. Place a cherry on top of each gelée cube.

5. Pour the remaining liquid, which should have begun to set, into a food processor or blender and process until foamy. Pour the foam over the cherries and place in the refrigerator an additional 15 minutes.

PRESENTATION

Place four cubes per person onto individual serving plates. Garnish with a dollop of whipped cream topped with almonds and drizzle the plate with Apricot Coulis and a sprinkling of pistachios. Serve immediately.

12 leaves gelatin

$1^2/_3$ cups port

$^1/_2$ cup lingonberry jam

$^1/_3$ cup sugar

$^1/_4$ teaspoon lemon zest

Tabasco sauce

16 heirloom black cherries, pitted and stems removed

Whipped cream, for garnish

Shaved almonds, for garnish

Apricot Coulis, for garnish (see page 216)

Pistachios, for garnish

SERVES 4

Berry-Custard Cake with Fruit Coulis

These delightful cakes are a big hit at Biró. Our staff likes them so much we have to be sure the desserts make it to the tables.

We make our own pound cake for the recipe, but purchased pound cake works just fine. Look for a substantial pound cake rather than a squishy porous one, as you want a toothsome balance to the soft custard.

WINE PAIRING *1997 Niepoort, Vintage Ruby Port, Portugal*
NV Clocktower, Tawny Port, Barossa Valley, Australia

2 tablespoons raspberry or blackberry preserves

1 cup assorted berries

1 cup pound cake, cubed into $1/2$-inch pieces

2 cups half-and-half

$1/2$ cup sugar

2 large eggs

2 large egg yolks

2 teaspoons vanilla

$1/2$ recipe Fruit Coulis (see page 217)

Berries, for garnish

Fresh mint, for garnish

Whipped cream, for garnish

MAKES 6 (4–6 OUNCE) RAMEKINS

1. Preheat oven to 350 degrees.

2. Place one teaspoon of preserves into the bottom of each ramekin. Divide the berries and pound cake between the ramekins and place on the preserves.

3. In a small saucepan, heat the half-and-half to a simmer. Remove from heat.

4. Whisk together the sugar, whole eggs, yolks, and vanilla until pale.

5. Gradually whisk a bit of the half-and-half mixture into the egg mixture to temper. Whisk in the remaining half-and-half mixture. Pour the custard over the berries and preserves. The cake should float to the top.

6. Bake in a bain-marie until set, about 35 to 45 minutes.

PRESENTATION

Invert cakes onto individual serving plates. Drizzle with Fruit Coulis and garnish with fresh berries, mint, and whipped cream. This dessert is great served either warm or chilled.

Berry-Custard Cake with Fruit Coulis

Chocolate Tartlets with Caramelized Raspberries & Lime Gelato

Chocolate Tartlets with Caramelized Raspberries & Lime Gelato

As gorgeous as they are delicious, these tartlets are best served lukewarm or cold—though their delightful aroma will tempt you to eat them the second they come out of the oven.

WINE PAIRING *2000 Voss Vineyards, Botrytis Sauvignon Blanc, Napa, California*
2002 Yalumba, Botrytis Semillon, Eden Valley, Australia

FOR THE CHOCOLATE TARTLET CRUST

1. Place the flour, cornstarch, baking powder, salt, sugar, and zest in the bowl of a food processor and pulse. Add the cold butter and pulse until the dough pieces are the size of peas. While the machine is running, pour in the vanilla and use as much water as necessary, if any, to form a smooth dough. Remove dough from the processor and form into a disk. Chill until firm. Butter the tart forms.

2. Roll dough out onto a lightly floured surface until it is a little less than $1/4$ inch thick. Using a tart form, cut out a piece of pastry and press the pastry into the bottom of the form. Repeat with the remaining forms. Pierce the pastry with a fork and place in the refrigerator to firm for about 15 minutes.

FOR THE CHOCOLATE TARTLET FILLING

1. Preheat oven to 350 degrees.

2. Combine the cream, milk, and liqueur in a medium saucepan and simmer over medium heat until bubbles start to form around the edges of the pan.

3. In a medium bowl, whisk together the cocoa powder, egg yolks, and sugar.

4. Slowly pour the milk mixture into the egg yolk mixture, combining gently. Strain into a large glass measuring cup and then pour into the chilled tart shells. Bake until set, about 30 to 35 minutes.

FOR THE CARAMELIZED RASPBERRIES

1. Combine the sugar, corn syrup, and water in a saucepan and place over low heat until the sugar melts. Increase heat to medium-high and cook until the sugars caramelize to a medium-brown color. Remove from heat and allow to cool slightly.

2. Place the raspberries on the tips of skewers. Dip raspberries into the caramel and pull out while twirling the skewer to create a "cocoon" over the berries. Place on waxed or parchment paper to set.

PRESENTATION

Remove tartlets from their forms and place one on the center of each serving plate. Place a scoop of Lime Gelato on each tartlet and garnish with Caramelized Raspberries. Serve immediately.

CHOCOLATE TARTLET CRUST

1 cup flour

$1/2$ cup cornstarch

$1/4$ teaspoon baking powder

$1/4$ teaspoon salt

$1/3$ cup powdered sugar

1 teaspoon grated lime zest

10 tablespoons cold unsalted butter, cut into pieces, plus more for the tart forms

1 teaspoon vanilla extract

Ice cold water

CHOCOLATE TARTLET FILLING

$1^1/2$ cups heavy cream

$1^1/2$ cups milk

1 tablespoon chocolate liqueur

1 cup cocoa powder

6 large egg yolks

$1/2$ cup sugar

CARAMELIZED RASPBERRIES

6 tablespoons sugar

$1^1/2$ tablespoons corn syrup

2 tablespoons water

$1/3$ pint raspberries

DISH

Lime Gelato (see page 212)

MAKES 8 (4-INCH) TARTLETS

Green Tea Crème Brûlée

Crème brûlée, with its trademark brittle shell and smooth, creamy interior, is always a safe bet for dessert. This one, lightly flavored with green tea, is a refreshing favorite. Use only fresh, high-quality green tea to get a nice strong flavor.

WINE PAIRING *1999 InnisKillin, Icewine, Ontario, Canada*
2003 Nivole Muscato d'Asti, Michele Chiarlo, Piedmont, Italy

6 large egg yolks

7 tablespoons sugar

2½ cups heavy cream

2 green tea bags

2 teaspoons vanilla extract

3 tablespoons light brown sugar

Mint leaves, for garnish

Raspberry Coulis, for garnish
(see page 216)

SERVES 6

1. Preheat oven to 325 degrees.

2. Whisk the yolks and sugar in a medium bowl until thick and pale yellow, about 2 minutes.

3. Bring cream to a simmer in a small saucepan over high heat. Turn off heat and add the tea bags. Allow to infuse for 5 to 7 minutes. Remove the bags, squeezing all the liquid out of them into the cream before discarding. Return the cream to a simmer over medium heat. Gradually whisk the hot cream into the yolk mixture. Whisk in the vanilla.

4. Divide the custard among 6 (6-ounce) ramekins. Bake in a bain-marie until gently set in the center, about 25 minutes. Allow to cool, and then refrigerate until completely cold, at least 3 hours.

5. Sprinkle brown sugar over the custards and carefully melt with a kitchen torch or blow-torch until it bubbles and caramelizes. If you do not have a torch place the custards under the broiler until the sugar colors, about 2 minutes. Chill until the custards are firm and the sugar topping is hard and brittle, at least 1 hour.

PRESENTATION

Place the custards on individual serving plates and garnish the plates with mint and Raspberry Coulis.

Sachertorte

Sachertorte is a dessert as rich in history as it is in flavor. Created in Vienna in 1832 by sixteen-year-old chef's apprentice Franz Sacher for Prince Metternich of Austria, the torte was an instant classic. Cafés throughout Vienna and beyond quickly began trying to duplicate the recipe. Sacher, who went on to own several prosperous hotels, cafés, and restaurants, surprised the culinary world—and Vienna high society—when he sold his original Sachertorte recipe to a competitor café, Demel's, later in his life. Today, Hotel Sacher calls their recipe "Original Sachertorte," while Demel's calls its version "Demel Sachertorte." This is my version.

While it is important to always use high-quality chocolate, in this case you will need couverture, which is an extremely shiny chocolate for coating, containing at least 32 percent cocoa butter. You can find couverture in specialty groceries or online.

WINE PAIRING *1997 Niepoort, Vintage Ruby Port, Portugal*
2001 Robert Sinskey Vineyards, Zinskey Late, Napa, California

FOR THE TORTE

1. Preheat oven to 350 degrees. Line the base of a springform pan with parchment paper.

2. Melt the couverture in a double boiler.

3. In a stand mixer, cream the butter, confectioners' sugar, and melted couverture. Stir in the egg yolks one at a time.

4. In a clean bowl of a stand mixer, whip the egg whites and sugar until stiff. Carefully fold the egg-white mixture into the chocolate mixture. Gradually fold in the flour until combined. Pour the batter into the baking pan and smooth the top. Bake until cooked through, about 55 minutes. Allow to cool completely.

5. Heat the jam in a small saucepan over high heat until syrupy, about 2 minutes.

6. Invert the cooled torte onto a wire rack placed over a sheet pan. Cut the torte in half horizontally. Spread half of the warmed jam evenly over the bottom layer of torte. Place the top layer of torte over the jam and coat with the remaining jam.

FOR THE ICING

Bring the sugar and water to a boil in a large saucepan. Gradually add the couverture, stirring constantly and cleaning the sides of the pan with a spatula often, until it reaches the thick-thread stage, about 4 minutes. Allow to cool slightly.

PRESENTATION

Pour the cooled icing over the cake and gently spread it evenly over the top and sides with a palette knife. Icing that drips through the wire rack onto the sheet pan can be scraped up and reused. Allow the icing to set, and then slice torte into the desired portion sizes. Place the slices on small plates and garnish with whipped cream, berries, and mint.

TORTE

4 ounces couverture

$1/2$ cup unsalted butter, soft

$1/4$ cup plus 2 tablespoons confectioners' sugar

6 eggs, separated

$1/2$ cup plus 2 tablespoons sugar

1 cup flour, sifted

$3/4$ cup apricot jam

ICING

1 cup sugar

6 tablespoons water

$6^1/2$ ounces couverture, chopped

DISH

Whipped cream, for garnish

Berries, for garnish

Mint, for garnish

MAKES 1 (9-INCH) TORTE

basic recipes

Bouquet Garni

2 outer leek leaves

6 sprigs parsley

5 sprigs thyme

12 black peppercorns

1 Turkish bay leaf

MAKES 1 BOUQUET GARNI

Lay out one leek leaf. Place the parsley, thyme, peppercorns, and bay leaf on top of it, and lay the remaining leaf on top of all to form a cigar-shaped bundle. Tie the bundle securely with kitchen twine.

ROSEMARY VARIATION:
Add 5 sprigs rosemary to the bundle.

TARRAGON VARIATION:
Add 5 sprigs tarragon to the bundle.

Clarified Butter

1 pound unsalted butter

MAKES ABOUT 1$^1/_2$ CUPS

1. Place the butter in a sauce pan over medium-low heat. Allow the butter to simmer briskly, without stirring, until the mixture separates into a layer of foamy milk solids and a layer of clear, golden butterfat.

2. Remove the butter from the heat and carefully pass it through a damp cheesecloth-lined chinoise into a resealable, heat-resistant container. Allow the clarified butter to cool completely, and then refrigerate or freeze it.

Duck-Infused Butter with Truffle Oil & Thyme

This is our very popular house butter. We pipe one-ounce rosettes of it onto butter plates, garnish each with tiny leaves of mâche or micro greens, and place a red peppercorn on top. You could also turn the butter out onto a sheet of parchment or plastic wrap and roll it into a log, removing it from the refrigerator or freezer to slice pieces as needed. Allow the butter to come to room temperature before serving.

1 pound unsalted butter, at room temperature

1 tablespoon duck-fat liquid

$^1/_8$ teaspoon white truffle oil

1 teaspoon chopped thyme

Sea salt

Freshly ground white pepper

MAKES ABOUT 1 POUND

1. Place the butter in a stand mixer fitted with a paddle attachment. Mix the butter on low speed until it becomes creamy, about 1 minute. Increase speed to medium and mix until the butter is a pale yellow color. Turn off the machine and switch to the whisk attachment.

2. Turn the mixer to low speed and slowly add the duck-fat liquid, oil, and thyme. Turn off machine and season to taste with salt and pepper. Turn the mixer to medium speed and mix until the butter resembles whipped cream, about 1 minute.

Herb Butter

1. Place the butter, onion, chives, parsley, basil, dill, fennel greens, anchovies, and garlic into a stand mixer fitted with a paddle attachment and cream together on low speed until the ingredients are well blended, about 2 minutes.

2. Switch to the whisk attachment and whip on medium speed for 2 minutes. Season to taste with salt, pepper, and a few drops of Worcestershire sauce. Whip for an additional 30 seconds to incorporate the seasoning.

GARLIC-HERB BUTTER VARIATION:
Add 5 more minced garlic cloves and eliminate the parsley and chives.

2 pounds unsalted butter, at room temperature

1 yellow onion, diced

1 cup finely chopped chives

$1/2$ cup finely chopped parsley

1 ounce fresh basil leaves, en chiffonade

1 sprig dill, finely chopped

2 tablespoons fennel greens

2 anchovies in oil, deboned and chopped (optional)

5 cloves garlic, minced

Sea salt

Freshly ground black pepper

Worcestershire sauce

MAKES ABOUT $2^1/_4$ POUNDS

Aïoli

1. Make a paste of the garlic and salt in a mortar and pestle, working the pestle slowly and always in the same direction. Place the paste in a medium-sized bowl. If you don't have a mortar and pestle, finely mince the garlic and then transfer it to a medium-sized bowl and add the salt. Mash the garlic and salt together with a wooden spoon until it makes a rough paste.

2. Whisk in the mustard and then the yolks until blended with the garlic paste. Slowly pour in $1/4$ cup of the oil in a thin stream, whisking constantly until the mixture becomes thick. Don't add the oil too quickly or the mixture will not emulsify.

3. Add the juice and water, whisking constantly; then add the remaining 1 cup oil very slowly, whisking constantly. The Aïoli will gradually thicken to the consistency of a light mayonnaise. If it becomes too thick for your application, add warm water, 1 teaspoon at a time, until it reaches the consistency you desire. Season with salt and pepper. Use immediately.

HERB AÏOLI VARIATION:
Add $1/2$ teaspoon minced chives, $1/2$ teaspoon minced thyme, and **$1/2$** teaspoon minced rosemary with the mustard and yolks in step 2.

8 cloves garlic

1 teaspoon sea salt

2 tablespoons Dijon mustard

2 large egg yolks

$1^1/_4$ cups extra virgin olive oil, divided

$4^1/_2$ teaspoons lemon juice

1 tablespoon warm water

Sea salt

Freshly ground black pepper

MAKES ABOUT 2 CUPS

Egg Pasta Dough

1³/₄ cups flour, plus more
for dusting

6 large egg yolks

1 large egg

1¹/₂ teaspoons extra virgin olive oil

1 tablespoon whole milk

MAKES ABOUT 14 OUNCES DOUGH

1. Mound the flour on a wooden board or clean countertop. Create a well in the center of the flour that is large enough to completely contain the rest of the ingredients.

2. Pour the yolks, whole egg, oil, and milk into the well; gently whisk together in a circular motion with your fingers, keeping the ingredients contained within the well. Continuing to work in a circular motion, slowly and gently begin incorporating the flour into the whisked egg mixture. Pull only a little flour into the well each time you make a circular pass, as adding too much flour too quickly will result in a clumpy, uneven dough. Retain the well shape by pulling the flour in toward the well with a pastry scraper as needed.

3. When the mixture becomes too thick to work with your fingers, begin incorporating the remaining flour by using the pastry scraper to lift the flour up onto the formed dough. When all the flour has been incorporated, the dough will look jagged. Using your palms, form it into a ball. The dough will not be smooth or elastic at this point.

4. Using the palms and heels of your hands, knead the dough ball by starting at one end of the ball and pushing it forward until you reach the other end. Once the ball has been flattened, re-form the dough into a ball and repeat the process several times. When the dough feels smoother and moist, set it aside and allow it to rest for a few minutes.

5. While the dough rests, use your pastry scraper to scrape the work surface clean. At the culinary school, I often see students make the mistake of adding dried bits of dough they've scraped up to their resting dough. This creates crunchy chunks in your finished dough; discard the leftovers. Lightly dust the cleaned work surface with a bit of flour.

6. Place the dough onto the lightly floured surface and continue to knead, pressing the dough in a forward motion with the heels of your hands. Re-form the ball and repeat the process when the dough becomes flattened. Continue until the dough becomes completely smooth and when you try pulling it apart, it is elastic and slowly snaps back into place. This will take about 15 minutes. Cover the dough with an inverted bowl or plastic wrap and allow to rest for 45 minutes to 1 hour. Wrap and refrigerate for up to 24 hours, or make your pasta immediately.

1 pound baby spinach, stems removed

FOR SPINACH PASTA:

1. Complete step 1 above.

2. Blanch the spinach in boiling water until tender, about 30 seconds. Drain the spinach and place in an ice bath to stop the cooking process.

3. Place the cooled spinach between two pieces of paper towel and press down on it to remove as much water as possible. Repeat this process until the spinach is completely dry.

4. Finely chop the spinach. Place it in a food processor or blender and purée until nearly liquid. We like to see some flecks of spinach in our pasta.

5. Add the spinach to the egg yolks, egg, oil, and milk in step 2 of the Egg Pasta recipe, and continue with the steps.

FOR TOMATO PASTA:

2 tablespoons tomato paste

Add the tomato paste to the egg yolks, egg, oil, and milk in step 2 of the Egg Pasta recipe.

FOR FETTUCCINI:

1. After making the Egg Pasta Dough, divide the dough into four pieces. Keep one piece of it to work with, and place the other three pieces under an inverted bowl or wrapped in plastic so they don't dry out.

2. Set the rollers of your pasta machine at the widest setting. Quickly knead the first amount of dough into a disk shape just a bit narrower than the opening of your pasta machine and lightly dust it with flour. Pass the dough through the machine. Fold the sheet lengthwise into thirds and repeat the process 2 additional times on the same setting to smooth the dough and increase its elasticity.

3. Set the machine down one notch and run the dough through again. Continue to process, folding the dough in thirds lengthwise, working down your machine's settings, and giving the dough one pass on each setting, until you've passed it through your machine's recommended setting for fettuccini. The pasta sheet will become much longer as you work down through the settings. To keep it manageable, gently fold it accordion-style before you pass it through the machine. As the dough emerges, gently support it with your palm and guide it onto the work surface. If it pulls or tears as you pass it through the machine, sprinkle a little flour on the dough just before it's fed into the machine. Once it has passed through, remove excess flour with a dry brush or brush it with the palm of your hand. Repeat the entire process with the remaining pieces of pasta.

4. Attach the fettuccini blade to your pasta machine. Cut the pasta sheets into the length you desire. We cut ours into 12-inch pieces. Feed the sheets through the machine and use the fettuccini right away, or dry it for later use. If you're drying it, it must dry until no moisture remains—several hours—before storing it. You can use a pasta drying rack, or you can use a simple collapsible laundry drying rack as we do at the restaurant. These can be purchased at discount stores for just a few dollars.

FOR 1 RECIPE RAVIOLI: (MAKES SHEETS FOR TWELVE RAVIOLI)

1. Set the rollers of your pasta machine at the widest setting. Take one-third of the finished dough, about 4 to 5 ounces, and cut it in half. Keep one half under an inverted bowl or wrapped in plastic wrap so it doesn't dry out while you're rolling the other half. Quickly knead the first amount of dough into a disk shape just a bit narrower than the opening of your pasta machine and dust lightly with flour. Pass the dough through the machine.

2. Fold the dough in half, end to end, and turn it a quarter turn. Pass it through the same setting and repeat the process to increase the dough's smoothness and elasticity. Fold the pasta sheet in half lengthwise to create a narrower piece of pasta and run it through the machine once more at the same setting.

3. Set the machine down one notch and run the dough through again. Continue to process, working down your machine's settings and giving the dough one pass on each setting, until you've passed it through your machine's recommended setting for ravioli. Repeat with the remaining piece of pasta.

Wild Mushroom Ravioli

We use 2¹/₄-inch to 3-inch cutters for our ravioli. You may use Egg, Spinach, or Tomato Pasta for the filling recipes provided in this book. For our Wild Mushroom Ravioli with Sautéed Baby Spinach & Chive-Garlic Velouté, we use Egg Pasta. For our Lime-Grilled Mahi Mahi with Morel-&-Chanterelle-Stuffed Ravioli, we use Spinach Pasta.

1 tablespoon extra virgin olive oil

3 tablespoons unsalted butter, divided

1 shallot, diced

¹/₂ cup diced morels

¹/₂ cup diced portabella mushrooms

¹/₂ cup diced crimini mushrooms

¹/₂ cup diced chanterelle mushrooms

2 teaspoons finely chopped rosemary

Sea salt

Freshly ground black pepper

2 sheets Ravioli (see pages 206–7)

Eggwash

SERVES 4

1. Melt the oil and 2 tablespoons of the butter over high heat. Add the shallot and sauté until the dices are glossy, about 1 minute. Add the mushrooms and sauté until they have lost all their water and begin caramelizing. Add rosemary. Remove from heat and season to taste with salt and pepper.

2. Place a sheet of pasta dough on a lightly floured surface. Brush the surface of the dough with eggwash. Using the dull side of the ravioli cutter of your choice, create a template for your twelve raviolis by lightly marking the dough, leaving at least ¹/₂ inch between them. Center the mushroom filling on the center of each ravioli bottom.

3. Carefully place a second sheet of pasta dough on top of the first sheet, making certain the long ends match up fairly well. Press down between the mounds of the mushroom filling, pressing out any air bubbles. Using the tip of a paring knife, gently pierce a small hole in each ravioli. Using the fluted end of your ravioli cutter, cut out the twelve raviolis.

4. Bring a lightly salted pot of water to a boil. Place the raviolis in the water and cook until al dente, about 6 to 9 minutes. Remove from the pot and drain.

5. Melt the remaining 1 tablespoon butter in a large sauté pan over medium-high heat. Add the raviolis and sauté, tossing frequently, to coat.

Tarte Flambée Crust Dough

2¹/₄ cups flour

³/₄ cup water

3 tablespoons vegetable oil

1 tablespoon sea salt

MAKES 10 CRUSTS

1. In a stand mixer with the paddle attachment, mix one-half the flour with the water, oil, and salt. Add enough of the remaining flour until the dough comes together in a ball. Switch to the hook attachment and knead for 5 minutes, adding more flour as necessary to make a smooth dough that is not sticky but not too stiff. Cover and let rest for 30 minutes.

2. Divide the dough into ten equal pieces and roll each on a lightly floured surface until the dough is thin enough to read a newspaper through. It should be rectangular in shape.

3. Top with desired ingredients and bake, or freeze sheets between parchment paper until ready to use.

Spätzle

1. In a small mixing bowl, whisk together the yolks, whole egg, and milk.

2. In a medium mixing bowl, combine the flour, salt, pepper, and nutmeg. Pour in the egg-milk mixture and blend by hand until just incorporated. Allow the batter to rest at room temperature for 20 minutes so it becomes thick and elastic.

3. Bring a pot of lightly salted water to a boil. Fill a spätzle press with the batter and press it out into the water in batches. If you do not have a spätzle press, you can pass the batter through a slotted spoon with a rubber spatula. Or you can place batter on a board and cut very thin pieces of it into the water with a knife. When the spätzle rises to the top of the water, it is done. Transfer the cooked spätzle to a bowl of ice water to stop the cooking process. Repeat until all the batter is used. When the spätzle is cool to the touch, it can be drained and used in your recipe or refrigerated for later use for up to 48 hours.

4. Melt the oil and butter in a large sauté pan over high heat. Add the spätzle and sauté until lightly golden, about 2 minutes. Season to taste with salt and pepper.

SAGE SPÄTZLE VARIATION:
Sauté with 2 tablespoons chopped sage.

4 large egg yolks, lightly beaten

1 large egg, lightly beaten

$1^3/_4$ cups whole milk, cold

3 cups flour

1 teaspoon sea salt , plus more to taste

$^1/_4$ teaspoon freshly ground black pepper, plus more to taste

$^1/_4$ teaspoon freshly ground nutmeg

2 tablespoons extra virgin olive oil

2 tablespoons unsalted butter

SERVES 4–6

Lemon-Parsley Glazed Potatoes

1. Place potatoes in a stockpot with lightly salted water to cover and bring to a boil over high heat. Cook until the potatoes are al dente, about 15 to 20 minutes; drain.

2. Melt the butter in a large sauté pan over high heat. Add the potatoes and sauté until lightly golden. Add the parsley and juice and season to taste with salt and pepper.

GARLIC-PARSLEY POTATOES VARIATION:
Sauté 1 clove garlic, minced, with the butter in step 2. You could also use small new potatoes, unpeeled, for this recipe.

1 pound Yukon Gold potatoes, peeled and cut into 1-inch dices

2 tablespoons unsalted butter

2 tablespoons chopped parsley

Juice of $^1/_2$ lemon

Sea salt

Freshly ground black pepper

SERVES 4

Garlic Mashed Potatoes

7 medium-sized Yukon Gold or
Russet potatoes, peeled and cubed

2 to 3 cups heavy cream

1 cup whole milk

10 cloves garlic, peeled and
crushed

Sea salt

Freshly ground white pepper

Freshly ground nutmeg

1/2 cup unsalted butter

SERVES 4

1. Place the potatoes in a large pot and just cover with the cream and milk. Add the garlic, salt, pepper, and nutmeg to taste. Cook, stirring frequently, until the potatoes are tender, about 15 to 20 minutes. Add the butter.

2. Pass the potatoes and cream through a food mill fitted with a fine-gauge disk. Adjust seasoning as necessary. If potatoes are too runny, place back on the stovetop and cook over medium heat until thickened.

GARLIC POTATO ROSETTE VARIATION:
Use only 2 cups cream, adding more cream as needed. It's important that the potatoes are dry enough to pipe but not so dry that they crumble. Place the potatoes in a pastry bag fitted with a star tip and pipe into rosettes.

Montrachet Cheese Medallions

5 eggs, whisked

1/2 cup flour

1/2 cup breadcrumbs

8 ounces Montrachet cheese

1 tablespoon unsalted butter

MAKES 4 MEDALLIONS

1. Heat oven to 400 degrees.

2. Place the eggs, flour, and breadcrumbs in individual bowls.

3. Slice the Montrachet into 4 equal rounds.

4. Dredge the cheese rounds in flour, making certain that they are completely covered. Tap the excess flour from the cheese and dip into eggwash. Completely cover the egg-washed cheese in breadcrumbs and then tap to remove excess. Repeat the process with other cheese rounds.

5. Melt the butter in a small ovenproof sauté pan. Sauté the cheese medallions until they become light golden in color, about 1 minute on each side. Place the pan in the oven and bake until light golden brown, about 2 to 3 minutes.

Crème Fraîche

1 cup whipping cream

2 tablespoons buttermilk

MAKES 1 CUP

Place cream and buttermilk in a glass container. Cover and let stand at room temperature (about 70 degrees F) for 8 to 24 hours. Refrigerate and use on desserts, soups, or savory dishes.

Sautéed Baby Spinach

Melt the oil and butter in a large sauté pan over high heat. Add the garlic and spinach. Using tongs, toss the spinach until it is wilted but still bright green, about 4 to 5 minutes. Drain, season to taste with salt and pepper, and serve immediately.

2 teaspoons extra virgin olive oil

2 teaspoons unsalted butter

2 cloves garlic, minced

1$\frac{1}{2}$ pounds baby spinach, stems removed

Sea salt

Freshly ground black pepper

SERVES 4

Sautéed Vegetables

We use organic baby vegetables for this dish. Feel free to substitute the vegetables of your choice. You may also wish to add your favorite chopped herbs, shallots, and garlic. Depending on the size of your pans, you may need to sauté in 2 batches.

SAUTÉED VEGETABLES

1. Bring a large pot of lightly salted water to a boil. Blanch the vegetables until softened, about 5 minutes. Remove from water and plunge into an ice bath. Drain.

2. Melt the butter in a large sauté pan. Add the vegetables and toss lightly to coat. Season to taste with salt and pepper.

16 baby carrots, stems trimmed

16 pink baby carrots, stems trimmed

16 yellow baby carrots, stems trimmed

16 baby turnips, stems trimmed

16 yellow wax beans, ends trimmed

16 green wax beans, ends trimmed

16 purple wax beans, ends trimmed

16 haricots verts, ends trimmed

16 pattypan squash, stems trimmed

6 tablespoons Clarified Butter (see page 204)

Sea salt

Freshly ground white pepper

SERVES 6–8

Vanilla Gelato

2¹/₂ cups whole milk

1 cup heavy cream

2 whole vanilla beans

9 large egg yolks

³/₄ cup sugar

MAKES ABOUT 1 QUART

1. Prepare the inserts of your ice cream machine as per the manufacturer's instructions.

2. Place the milk and cream in a small saucepan. Cut the vanilla beans in half lengthwise and scrape the seeds out with the tip of a sharp knife. Add the seeds and pods to the milk-cream mixture and bring the mixture to a boil over high heat, whisking constantly to help extract the vanilla seeds from the pods. Turn off heat and allow to infuse for at least 20 minutes.

3. Meanwhile, place the yolks and sugar in a medium mixing bowl and whisk until the mixture is thickened, fluffy, and pale yellow in color. You should be able to cover the back of your spoon with the mixture and form a rose shape when you blow into the mixture. You also may use a stand mixer fitted with a paddle attachment for this step; it will take about 2 minutes on medium speed.

4. Remove the vanilla pods from the milk-cream mixture, pressing any remaining seeds from the pods into the pan. Bring the mixture back to a boil over high heat, whisking constantly. Slowly add about ¹/₂ cup of the hot milk-cream mixture to the egg-sugar mixture and whisk to temper the yolks. Whisking constantly, add the egg-sugar mixture to the milk-cream mixture and whisk until evenly blended.

5. Reduce heat to medium-low. Using a wooden spoon, continually stir the mixture in figure eight patterns, making certain that you are incorporating all the mixture from the bottom and corners of the pan. Cook until the mixture has thickened to a coating consistency, about 8 to 10 minutes.

6. Fill a large bowl half full with ice water. Place a medium-sized stainless steel bowl in the ice water and carefully pass the cream through a fine-mesh strainer into the bowl. Stir the cream occasionally to cool.

7. Pour the cooled cream into the bowl of your ice cream machine and process according to your machine's specifications, usually 30 to 40 minutes. Freeze until ready to serve, for up to 48 hours.

LAVENDER GELATO:

1 tablespoon dried lavender

Stir the lavender into the milk-cream mixture when you turn off the heat in step 2. It's important to use lavender that is not oiled, as oils will break down the milk-cream mixture, resulting in an unpleasant texture. Packages may not indicate whether the flowers contain oil, but you can tell by touch. The flowers should feel dry, not at all greasy, when you press them between your thumb and forefinger.

LIME GELATO:

1 lime, sliced

Add the lime slices to the milk-cream mixture when you turn off the heat in step 2. Remove the lime slices when you remove the vanilla beans in step 4. Transfer the slices to a sieve, and squeeze all the juice out through the sieve to catch the seeds.

BLACK WALNUT GELATO:

¹/₈ cup crushed black walnuts, roasted

Stir in the walnuts into the milk-cream mixture when you turn off the heat in step 2.

STRAWBERRY GELATO:

¹/₂ cup strawberry purée

Add the purée at the end of step 6.

Sautéed Napa Cabbage

1. Melt the butter in a medium saucepan over high heat. Add the bacon and fry until crisp. Add the onion and sauté until glossy, about 1 minute. Deglaze with the stock and reduce by one-half, about 10 minutes.

2. Add the cream and reduce by one-half, about 5 minutes. Add the blanched cabbage and cook, stirring constantly, until creamy. Season to taste with nutmeg, salt, and pepper.

2 tablespoons unsalted butter

4 strips bacon, chopped

1 small yellow onion, diced

$1/2$ cup Vegetable Stock (see page 215)

$1/2$ cup heavy cream

1 large head Napa cabbage, cored, quartered, sliced, and blanched

Freshly ground nutmeg

Sea salt

Freshly ground white pepper

SERVES 4–6

Balsamic Glaze

Place the vinegar in a saucepan and warm over medium heat until steam rises from the liquid. Reduce heat to low and cook until vinegar becomes syrupy, about 45 minutes. Make certain that the glaze does not boil, as it results in a bitter flavor. If using the glaze for garnish, allow it to cool slightly and then pour it into a fine-nozzled squeeze bottle. Store at room temperature. If the glaze becomes too thick, immerse the bottle in hot water.

2 cups balsamic vinegar

MAKES ABOUT $1/4$ CUP

Port Glaze

Place the port in a saucepan and warm over medium heat until steam rises from the liquid. Decrease heat to low and reduce mixture until it becomes syrupy, about 45 minutes. Make certain that the glaze does not boil, as it results in a sharp flavor.

If using the glaze for garnish, allow it to cool slightly and then pour it into a fine-nozzled squeeze bottle. Store at room temperature. If the glaze becomes too thick, immerse the bottle in hot water.

2 cups port

MAKES ABOUT $1/2$ CUP

Beef Stock

6 pounds beef bones

1 tablespoon vegetable oil

2 cups chopped carrots

2 cups chopped celery

4 cups chopped yellow onions

3 cloves garlic

$1/2$ cup chopped vine-ripened tomatoes

2 cups red wine

1 Bouquet Garni (see page 204)

MAKES ABOUT 2 QUARTS

1. Preheat oven to 450 degrees. Place the bones in a roasting pan and roast for 30 minutes. Turn the bones and roast until golden brown, about 30 additional minutes.

2. Place the roasted bones in a large stockpot, reserving the roasting pan and drippings. Place the roasting pan on the stovetop over medium-high heat. Add the oil, carrots, celery, onions, and garlic and cook until the vegetables are caramelized, about 15 minutes. Add the tomatoes and cook for 2 additional minutes. Deglaze the pan with the wine and cook until almost dry.

3. Place the vegetables and any remaining liquid in the stockpot containing the roasted bones. Add the Bouquet Garni and enough cold water to cover. Bring to a boil over high heat.

4. Reduce the heat to low and simmer for 8 hours, periodically skimming the impurities that rise to the surface during the cooking process. Strain through a chinoise or fine-mesh sieve and allow to cool completely. Pour the cool stock into an airtight container and store in the refrigerator for up to 4 days, or freeze for up to 2 months.

Chicken Stock

6 pounds chicken bones

3 cups chopped yellow onions

2 cups chopped carrots

2 cups chopped celery

1 cup chopped leeks

1 Bouquet Garni (see page 204)

MAKES ABOUT 2 QUARTS

1. Rinse the bones under cool running water.

2. Place all the ingredients in a large stockpot and add cold water to cover. Bring to a boil and then reduce heat to low. Simmer for 4 hours, occasionally skimming the impurities that rise to the surface during the cooking process.

3. Strain through a chinoise or fine-mesh sieve into a clean pot, discarding the solids. Simmer over medium heat until reduced to about 2 quarts, 30 to 45 minutes. Allow the stock to cool, then pour it into an airtight container. Store in the refrigerator for up to 4 days, or freeze for up to 2 months.

Fish Stock

4 pounds lean white fish with bones, skin removed

3 tablespoons unsalted butter

1 onion, coarsely chopped

4 shallots, coarsely chopped

2 leeks, white parts only, coarsely chopped

1 cup dry white wine

1 Bouquet Garni (see page 204)

MAKES ABOUT 2 QUARTS

1. Rinse the fish under cool running water. Cut them into 3-to-4-inch pieces.

2. In a stockpot, melt the butter over medium heat. Add the fish, onion, shallots, and leeks. Sauté until the vegetables are softened, about 5 minutes. Pour in enough cold water to cover, then increase heat to high. Add the wine and Bouquet Garni and cook until it reaches a boil. Decrease heat to medium and cook until the liquid is reduced by one-half, about 30 minutes.

3. Strain the stock through a chinoise lined with damp cheesecloth and allow to cool to room temperature. Place in an airtight container and store in the freezer for up to 2 months.

White Veal Stock

1. Rinse the bones under cool running water. Place the bones in a large stockpot and cover with enough cold water so that there is at least twice as much water as bones. Slowly bring to a simmer over medium-low heat, about 1 hour. Occasionally skim the impurities that rise to the surface, but do not stir. Remove from heat; carefully drain the bones in a large colander and discard the cooking liquid.

2. Rinse the bones well under cool running water until the water runs clear and the surface of the bones are no longer slick with film. Clean the stockpot and return the washed bones to it. Add 8 quarts cold water and slowly bring to a simmer over medium-low heat, skimming frequently. Add the leeks, onions, and Bouquet Garni and continue to simmer for 4 hours, skimming frequently to remove impurities. Turn off the heat and allow the stock to rest for 10 to 15 minutes so that any remaining impurities settle to the bottom.

3. Using a ladle, pass the stock through a chinoise into a clean container. Discard the stock toward the bottom, which contains particles that will cloud the finished product. Place the container in an ice bath and stir occasionally to cool. When completely cool, pour the stock into an airtight container and refrigerate for up to 48 hours or freeze for up to 3 months.

8 pounds veal bones

8 quarts water, cold

2 cups chopped leeks, white and light green parts only

2 cups chopped yellow onions

1 Bouquet Garni (see page 204)

MAKES ABOUT 2 QUARTS

Vegetable Stock

1. Place all ingredients in a stockpot and bring to a boil over high heat. Decrease heat to low and simmer for 1 hour. Strain the mixture through a fine-mesh sieve into another pot; discard the solids.

2. Simmer the stock over medium heat until reduced to 2 quarts, about 30 to 45 minutes. Allow to cool completely and then pour into an airtight container and refrigerate for up to 4 days or freeze for up to 3 months.

1 cup chopped yellow onion

2 cups chopped carrots

1 cup chopped celery

1 cup chopped fennel bulb

1 Bouquet Garni (see page 204)

4 quarts water

MAKES ABOUT 2 QUARTS

Glace de Viande

Place stock in a saucepan and cook over medium-high heat until it is reduced to $1/2$ cup and coats the back of a spoon. Skim any impurities that rise to the surface during the cooking process. Allow to cool completely and then pour into an airtight container and refrigerate for up to 4 days or freeze for up to 3 months.

1 quart Beef, Chicken, Fish or White Veal Stock

MAKES ABOUT $1/2$ CUP

Clarification

This clarification recipe is used to clarify, or clear, a consommé. The ingredients it contains attract the particles suspended in the liquid.

1³/₄ pounds lean beef

3 carrots, peeled and chopped

2 leeks, chopped

2 egg whites

1 cup ice cubes

1 recipe consommé, cold

FOR 1 RECIPE

1. Place the beef, carrots, and leeks into a meat grinder or food processor and combine.

2. Place the beef-vegetable mixture into a mixing bowl and blend with the egg whites and ice cubes. Place the mixture into a large stockpot. Add the consommé of your choice (recipes on pages 90 and 97), first removing any impurities that have separated from the liquid during the cooling process, and heat over medium heat, stirring constantly until the liquid comes to a boil. Reduce heat to low and allow to simmer, unstirred, for 45 minutes. It is important that the liquid does not boil or get disturbed through stirring, as it would result in a cloudy consommé.

3. Remove surplus fat and strain the consommé through a cheesecloth-covered chinoise.

Apricot Coulis

4 cups pitted and sliced apricots

1 cup superfine sugar

¹/₂ teaspoon cinnamon

¹/₂ teaspoon vanilla extract

MAKES ABOUT 1 CUP

1. Place all ingredients in a saucepan and cook over low heat, stirring occasionally, until the mixture becomes syrupy, about 15 minutes.

2. Pass through a fine-mesh sieve, discarding the apricot skins, and allow to cool. Place in a fine-nozzled squeeze bottle and store refrigerated for up to 1 week.

Raspberry Coulis

1 pint raspberries

2 to 3 tablespoons superfine sugar

MAKES ¹/₂ CUP

1. Place the raspberries and 2 tablespoons of the sugar in a food processor or blender and purée. Add more sugar if necessary, to taste.

2. Pass the puréed berries through a fine-mesh sieve to remove the seeds. It may be necessary to add a little water to thin the coulis.

3. Place in a fine-nozzled squeeze bottle and store refrigerated for up to 2 days.

Fruit Coulis

1. Place all the ingredients in a food processor or blender and purée. Add more sugar, if necessary, to taste.

2. Pass the puréed fruit through a fine-mesh sieve. It may be necessary to add a little water to thin the coulis.

3. Place in a fine-nozzled squeeze bottle and store refrigerated for up to 3 days. You may substitute the fruits of your choice for this recipe.

$^1/_2$ cup sliced peaches

$^1/_2$ cup sliced apricots

$^1/_2$ cup sliced strawberries

$^1/_3$ cup superfine sugar

MAKES ABOUT $^3/_4$ CUP

Roasted-Red-Pepper Coulis

Purée peppers, garlic, basil, celery, and oil in a food processor or blender until smooth. Season to taste with salt and pepper. Store refrigerated for up to 3 days.

4 red bell peppers, roasted, peeled, seeded, and sliced

1 clove garlic, chopped

1 tablespoon chopped basil

$^1/_2$ stalk celery, chopped

2 tablespoons extra virgin olive oil

Sea salt

Freshly ground black pepper

MAKES ABOUT $^1/_2$ CUP

Pesto

Place the garlic in a food processor and finely chop. Stop the motor and add the nuts, cheese, salt, pepper, and basil; process until finely chopped. With the motor running, add the oil in a thin, steady stream, blending until incorporated. Store refrigerated for up to 1 week.

3 cloves garlic

$^1/_2$ cup pine nuts

$^3/_4$ cup grated Parmesan cheese

1 teaspoon sea salt

$^1/_2$ teaspoon freshly ground black pepper

3 cups loosely packed basil

$^2/_3$ cup extra virgin olive oil

MAKES ABOUT 1 CUP

Tomato Glaze

1/4 cup extra virgin olive oil

2 pounds plum tomatoes, seeded and chopped

1 small yellow onion, finely chopped

3 cloves garlic, crushed

10 fresh basil leaves, en chiffonade

1 teaspoon sea salt

1/2 teaspoon freshly ground black pepper

MAKES ABOUT 1 CUP

1. Heat the oil in a covered saucepan over medium heat. Add the tomatoes and onion and cook, covered, for 5 minutes. Remove the cover and simmer until the liquid has evaporated, about 30 minutes. Add the garlic and basil.

2. Allow the tomato mixture to cool slightly, and then pass it through a food mill fitted with a fine-gauge disk. Season with salt and pepper. If serving the glaze warm, reheat it in a saucepan before serving.

Parsley Oil

1 bunch parsley, stemmed

1 cup grapeseed oil

MAKES ABOUT 1 CUP

Blanch the parsley in boiling water. Drain and pat the parsley dry with paper towels. Place the blanched parsley in a food processor or blender and process until finely chopped. Pour in the oil and process until incorporated, about 1 minute. Pour the oil into a fine-nozzled squeeze bottle and store refrigerated for up to 2 weeks.

Chive Oil

4 ounces chives, chopped

1 cup grapeseed oil

MAKES ABOUT 1 CUP

Place the chives and oil in a food processor or blender and process until well combined. Pour the oil into a fine-nozzled squeeze bottle and store refrigerated for up to 2 weeks.

Fried Herbs and Greens

Fried herbs and greens make a lovely, flavor-packed garnish. Some items, such as sage, stemmed baby spinach, micro herbs, and micro greens work well when left whole. Larger leaves, such as arugula, work best when cut into chiffonades before frying, and leeks work best when cut into juliennes and lightly dusted with flour prior to frying.

To fry your herbs or greens, you will need about four times the amount of oil than the item you're frying. Bring vegetable, canola, or sunflower oil—which have higher burning points and do not impart too much flavor—to 375 degrees in a deep sauté pan or fryer. Fry the herbs or greens until crispy and the edges just begin to brown—less than 10 or 15 seconds, depending on the item you're frying. Carefully remove with a slotted spoon and drain on paper towels. Season to taste with sea salt or even superfine sugar, depending on the application. You can store drained Fried Herbs and Greens in a paper towel–lined resealable container for up to 1 week.

sources

For specialty salts:

Salt Traders
Purveyors of fine salt
www.salttraders.com
800.641.SALT

For high-quality knives:

Wüsthof
www.wusthof.com
Available at fine retailers worldwide

For high-quality cookware:

All-Clad Metalcrafters LLC
www.allclad.com
Available at fine retailers nationwide

For high-quality kitchen appliances:

Dacor
www.dacor.com
Available at fine retailers nationwide

DēLonghi
www.delonghi.com
Available at fine retailers worldwide

Other companies we love:

Vessel
Kitchen and tableware
www.vessel-store.com
Available at fine retailers worldwide

Dornbracht
Plumbing fixtures and accessories
www.dornbracht.com
Available at fine retailers worldwide

Sóko
Sculptured designs for living
www.sokostudios.com
Available at fine retailers nationwide

Teragren
Bamboo flooring, panels, and veneers
www.teragren.com
Available at fine retailers nationwide

Elkay Companies
Plumbing products and cabinetry
www.elkay.com
Available at fine retailers worldwide

Glad Products Company
Storage containers and wraps
www.glad.com
Available at fine retailers worldwide

index

Q

R

T